THE NEW COMPLETE BOOK OF HOME REMODELING, IMPROVEMENT, AND REPAIR

THE NEW COMPLETE BOOK OF HOME REMODELING, IMPROVEMENT, AND REPAIR

A. M. WATKINS

Charles Scribner's Sons

New York

Library of Congress Cataloging in Publication Data
Watkins, Arthur Martin, 1924–
   The new complete book of home remodeling, improvement,
and repair.
   Includes index.
   1. Dwellings–Remodeling.   2. Dwellings–Maintenance and
repair.   I. Title.
TH4816.W38   643'.7   78-21881
ISBN 0-684-15823-X

1 3 5 7 9 11 13 15 17 19 V/C 20 18 16 14 12 10 8 6 4 2

Printed in the United States of America

ACKNOWLEDGMENTS

Some material is excerpted in part or uses basic research from magazine articles I wrote. I wish to thank the following magazines for permission to use such material:

The American Home for material in "How to Avoid the Ten Biggest Home Improvement Rackets" and in "How to Get a Good New Bathroom"; *Better Homes & Gardens* for excerpts in Chapter 25 and "How Much Do Home Improvements Increase the Value of Your House?"; the Building Institute for material in the chapters on kitchens and bathrooms; and *Redbook* for material in "How to Avoid Home Repair Bills."

I am grateful for helpful advice and suggestions from Scribners editors Mort Waters, Jean Koefoed, and Kristine Kalazs.

Contents

INTRODUCTION
WHAT THIS BOOK IS ABOUT

This is the book I needed when my wife and I bought our first house, a charming old Victorian house but one obviously in need of modernization and repairs. The kitchen and bathroom were relics of yesteryear, and not only was the structure sagging seriously, but the old heating and flimsy wiring were on the verge of collapse. We knew about all those things, but we still had a few surprises coming.

Much remodeling and fix-up work were required to haul that house into the twentieth century and make it a charming modern place in which to live. The experience gained earned me a bachelor's degree in home remodeling. Later, when we had sold that house and bought another, younger one that also needed remodeling, some of it also unexpected, I got my master's degree, as well as staked out a claim to write this book. A few other writing credentials are noted in a moment.

While carrying out the many improvements needed by those two houses, I was continually confronted with tough questions that no so-called expert and no available book on home remodeling could answer. The experts who could not help included many home improvement contractors hired to execute the varied work required. Then, as now, practically every book on the subject was basically a do-it-yourself, telling how to nail up 2 x 4s at different angles while standing on one's head, if necessary; how to install wall paneling; how to put down a new floor and put up a new ceiling and all the rest of the usual work done on houses. There was, however, no good book on how to design and plan good home improvements. There was none on basic kitchen and bathroom design, on planning new rooms, or just on adding new windows (a highly important ingredient of a good house, as noted later). And there was very little on the basic facts about the all-important floor plan and room arrangement that influence how well, or not so well, a house will work for you.

I continually needed advice and guidelines about, in a word, the architecture of home remodeling. I could count on little help from professionals because very few kitchen contractors know how to design a good kitchen. Plumbers may be great at hooking up the fixtures and pipes, but rare is the plumber who is also a good designer. And few general home improvement contractors know basic design facts about other parts of a house.

Of course, I could have called on an architect, but finding a good one experienced with home improvements is more easily said than done. Besides, few architects can afford the time and limited fee to give you attention and advice for home improvement work. New house design is more attractive and profitable for architects.

Don't be put off by that big word *architecture*. It means far more than dealing with the style and looks of a house. It also encompasses how well a house functions for you. The great Swiss architect Le Corbusier said it well (if a bit impersonally): "A house should be a machine for living."

The floor plan should work smoothly, the rooms should fit their individual purposes, there should be adequate closet and storage space, and, among other things, the house should be designed and built for low upkeep and easy maintenance. The last includes keeping down monthly energy bills, which, of course, is highly important today.

In short, the primary purpose of this book is to tell you the important planning and design facts that can make all the difference in the world when you remodel or fix up a house. It's the difference between a meat-and-potatoes new kitchen, bathroom, or other improvement (which, alas, most people get) and truly fine remodeling results that is champagne for the soul. That may sound a little high-flown, but excellent new rooms and other features added to a house can transform it into a place where everyday living is sheer pleasure.

A second major purpose of this book is to emphasize the importance of good-quality products and materials. One of the great plagues in home construction is the ocean of cheap, low-quality materials and products that are widely used in houses. The result is shoddy, low-quality performance, with many parts of houses being hard to maintain and keep good looking. They are quick to run down and require excessive service and repairs and often premature replacement.

Yet for only a few extra dollars in first price, nearly every building material and product—from flooring, paneling, and roofing to insulation, appliances, and nearly everything else—can be had in a significantly higher level of quality from which you may expect better performance and greater durability. Yet the labor cost to install good-quality materials and products is no more than the installation cost of the cheap, low-quality version of the same materials and products.

You can also spend still more for the premium, top-of-the-line version of many a product, but this doesn't necessarily pay. It depends on the product.

Two other important basic aspects of home remodeling discussed in this book are the economics of home improvements and home energy. The first involves more than just knowing typical prices for different kinds of remodeling and how to save money. It also involves such things as how much home improvements increase the value of your house (Chapter 3).

As for home energy, it has clearly assumed great importance since the energy crisis broke across the country. Unless you're rich and profligate, many parts of your house should be considered in terms of their energy efficiency. A special section on this important topic is part of this book.

This book, by the way, is a new and revised version of the original edition published in 1963. Reviewing the original, I was surprised at how many fundamental principles of house design and remodeling remain unchanged and will probably remain so well into the future (until someone from outer space comes to us with a new and revolutionary discovery about human shelter).

Other things have indeed changed, and notable new ideas and products have since been introduced, while, on the other hand, some old ideas, long considered sacrosanct, have gone the way of the dodo bird. This new edition attempts to take all those into account.

THE AUTHOR'S CREDENTIALS

"Upon what meat doth this our Caesar feed . . . ?" I am a graduate engineer and professional writer with much experience in the building field. I have been an associate editor of *House & Home* and *Architectural Forum* magazines and am the author of some half a dozen other books on various facets of houses and housing. I have written many articles about housing and houses for such magazines as *American Home, Better Homes & Gardens, Harper's, House & Garden, Popular Science, Redbook,* and others. I am also a homeowner with firsthand experience at fixing up, remodeling, and maintaining houses.

Much of this book therefore reflects what I have learned from personal and professional experience, plus research into many phases of home building, improvement, and remodeling.

This book also reflects my personal opinion for the same reasons given by Somerset Maugham in *The Summing Up:* "It is only because I find it very boring to qualify every phrase with an 'I think' or 'to my mind.' Everything I say is merely an opinion of my own . . . there is only one thing about which I am certain, and this is that there is very little about which one can be certain."

The nature of some of this book is inescapably technical, of course, and requires technical substantiation. There is such substantiation throughout, I assure you, even if every subject is not documented by reams of supporting technical facts.

By necessity, the text of some chapters overlaps material presented in other chapters. Certain facts, for instance, on having a warm new room coincide with essential information in the chapters on heating and insulation. Rather than repeat them, you are therefore referred to the chapter with the background facts. Occasional repetition does occur in some chapters in order to make the chapters self-sufficient and avoid excessive cross-referencing.

THE NEW COMPLETE BOOK OF
HOME REMODELING,
IMPROVEMENT,
AND REPAIR

PART ONE

When is a house
worth remodeling?

The question arises when your house begins pinching or it's no longer adequate or satisfactory. A new kitchen or bathroom, or both, is needed, or the prospect of serious repairs and replacements looms large, such as the imminent need for a new furnace or a new roof and a new paint job (yes, another one).

Will it all be worth it? Or should you sell and buy another, better house?

The answer boils down to more than the cost of it all. Does the house lend itself to remodeling? When all is done, will you have the house you truly wanted? And will you get all that money back when you sell? Not everyone does. The stories are legion of those who have poured small fortunes into repairing and remodeling, yet, when they eventually sold the house didn't get a penny more than they would have if the house had not been reworked.

There are other people, too, who have remodeled wisely and did indeed get at least most of their money back. (Few houses increase in value, dollar for dollar, with the cost of home improvements, for reasons noted in Chapter 3.)

In short, there are basic things to know before you plunge into remodeling any house. There are pitfalls to avoid and also, on the other hand, certain lodes to mine well for first-rate results when you fix up a house. Knowing them can also be exceedingly helpful—and profitable—even for limited remodeling of a house that you like well and don't intend to leave.

The purpose of this first section is to put your remodeling and improvement plans into focus. Basic questions about money and the cost of home remodeling and improvements are also answered here.

CHAPTER 1
THE CASE FOR REMODELING

In the "good old days," when a house was no longer large enough or was otherwise deficient, a family simply sold it and moved on to a new and better house. That's not so true anymore since inflation struck the country with a vengeance as a result of the Vietnam War. House prices rose faster than almost any other consumer cost item. To make matters worse, the interest-rate cost of mortgages also climbed to near-record levels.

Buying another house has become quite expensive especially if one has to give up a low-interest vintage mortgage to take on a new mortgage at a steep increase in the monthly payments. Naturally, more and more people are inclined to stick with their existing houses and correct their limitations by remodeling or expanding. On the whole, the cost can be considerably less than selling out and buying another house.

Other advantages of staying put and remodeling include remaining in your old neighborhood. This can be important, for leaving a community can be a painful loss. Many of us have deep roots in our neighborhoods—friends, children's playmates, ties to schools, churches, and social groups, as well as established relationships with local merchants (and perhaps with a good repairman). Buying another house generally means cutting old ties and starting anew; this can be a severe wrench to people (unless with a stroke of luck you discover the ideal house nearby).

The cost of moving is often overlooked. It can be steep—as much as several thousand dollars. On top of the moving bill, there are costs

The use of wood (Western Pine) gives this remodeled house in the Pacific Northwest warm and handsome looks. *Western Pine Association; Charles R. Pearson, photographer.*

for settling into a new house, including inevitable decorating expenses (new curtains, painting), furniture, and, for a new house, landscaping.

A new house nearly always means additional expenses for extra kitchen cabinets, more storage, and a painful assortment of other bills that easily can add up to $1,000 or more. Your commuting costs may be higher. And of course, there are the closing-cost charges for the mortgage on a new house, as well as the higher cost of the new mortgage. All the costs for a new house can be added with the table on page 6.

Certain other costs not included above can also influence your decision. These include the difference in the cost of commuting to work, not to mention possible differences in commuting time and the cost of upkeep and maintenance in a new house, compared with your present house. By the way, don't minimize the cost of upkeep and maintenance for a new house, particularly during the first year or two

The walls of this contemporary house in Arkansas are made with redwood paneling. Redwood is also used for window frames and trim. Designed by Stephen L. Tucker. *California Redwood Association; Hedrich-Blessing.*

of breaking it in. The initial bills can run high, especially with a stripped-down new house with only a minimum of amenities. Besides, money to be spent for lawn and landscaping outside, new appliances, storage cabinets, and much else inside, mysteriously omitted by the builder, often must be included. According to one telling

COST OF BUYING ANOTHER HOUSE VERSUS REMODELING

1. Cost of buying another house

Cash down payment $_____

Closing costs: title search and insurance, mortgage fees, state and federal taxes, lawyer's fee, appraisal charge, survey, recording deed. Figure from about $500 to $3,000, or 1 to 3 percent of house buying price. A call to a neighborhood bank mortgage officer should get you an accurate figure for your area. _____

Packing and moving expenses _____

New decorating needs (essential lamps, rugs, curtains, special paint, furniture, odds and ends) _____

New appliances, storm windows; anything else _____

Landscaping _____

Other costs related to buying and living in a new house (for example, will you need a second car?) _____

A. Total cost of buying a new house $_____

B. Minus price obtainable for your present house (be realistic—most houses do not bring as much as we would like) −_____

C. Net outlay for a new house $_____

2. Cost of remodeling and improving your present house

Estimated remodeling cost: How many things have to be done? Be realistic. An idea of the cost of the most common remodeling jobs can be obtained from the next chapter.

Total estimated cost of remodeling $_____

Financing and credit charges if remodeling is financed. This varies from about 10 to 18 percent a year, depending on the kind of loan as noted later. _____

Closing costs if you refinance your mortgage to pay for remodeling _____

D. Total cost of remodeling and staying with your present house $_____

E. Difference in cost between buying a new house and remodeling your present house $_____

Cost of new house, Line C above _____

If the cost of remodeling exceeds cost of buying, subtract line C from line D.

Before: This old relic was built in 1840 and, alas, allowed to run down. *After:* Bought for $8,200 in 1959, it is now the Blauhut house in Piermont, N.Y., an impressive example of early nineteenth-century Federal architecture.

survey, new-house owners spend more than twice as much a year for maintenance and repairs for their new houses than is spent by the owners of older houses. Buying a new house does not solve all one's housing problems.

DISADVANTAGES OF REMODELING

Your present neighborhood may be losing appeal; it's no longer desirable. The same for schools, and you seek better schools somewhere else. Your neighborhood, in fact, may be going downhill, and you decide it's time to get out. Lacking strict residential zoning protection, your house may be hemmed in more and more by rooming

This handsome interior was formerly a fifty-year-old four-car garage in Minneapolis. It was remodeled by architect Hugh G. S. Peacock. How its outside looked before remodeling and now is also shown. *Warren Reynolds.*

houses, stores, gas stations, and factories. Or creeping urban decay nearby is getting closer.

Large-scale remodeling is no picnic. It often involves delays and much concern. You will live amid a stream of workmen for what seems like years. It takes patience and endurance. If temperamentally unsuited for it, you may do better to sell out and get another house. Or your house may be so old and structurally run-down that it is unsuitable for remodeling. The structure should be sound to begin with.

HOW MUCH REMODELING IS PRACTICAL? THE OVERIMPROVEMENT DANGER

There's a limit to the amount of money you should pour into a house if you want your money back when you later sell. For years real estate brokers have found that many a perfectly good, if not excellent, old house will not sell when it's overpriced for its neighborhood. The owners may have turned it into a restored masterpiece, but in doing so, they broke through the ceiling of neighborhood house values.

In other words, they overimproved for their area and hit a wall of resistance from buyers. People will not spend $90,000 where the top value of other houses in the neighborhood is $75,000. Buyers tend to shop for a house where most of the houses in an area are in their price range, just as water seeks its own level. No matter how much money was spent on improving a house in an area of $75,000 houses, that's generally the top price that any buyer will spend for a house there. That's buyer behavior; you fight it at your own peril.

Some experts offer a flat and arbitrary ceiling rule: Don't improve a house by more than 30 percent of its current value. Otherwise, you pass the point of diminishing returns. You will not get your money back if you decide later to sell.

EXCEPTIONS TO THE RULE

Many of us like our house and neighborhood, and we would like to stay put. But there's no need to resign ourselves to the shortcomings of the house just to remain in the same place. If we can change the house, if we can gain the extra room we want or otherwise improve its comfort and convenience, the house's value to us will increase. That has to be weighed against the possibility that we may not retrieve our entire investment if we sell the house someday. And that will not bar us from enjoying a good house up to the hilt while we're in it. Besides, depreciation is to be expected every year.

The rule of diminishing returns applies mainly to uniform neighborhoods. It does not hold firm in all parts of a town and in many housing developments built since the end of World War II. Many people have remodeled, and most houses around are worth considerably more money than their original cost.

A notable example is the original Levittown that was built after World War II on bleak Long Island potato fields. More than 16,000 houses were built there at sale prices starting at $8,000 to $10,000. It was the first large postwar housing development. Social critics, shooting from the hip, blithely condemned it to the slums of the future.

They were wrong, to put it mildly. Levittown has blossomed over the years. It is surprisingly attractive (partly because of thousands of trees planted by the builder then with its houses) and has made fools of the critics. Some thirty years later many of the houses, greatly expanded and improved, have been resold at prices of $50,000 to $60,000, or up to a nearly 800 percent increase in value! Inflation accounts for less than half. The rest comes largely from the improvements made to the houses.

A house located in an area that is on the rebound may also qualify as an exception for breaking the overimprovement rule. Downtown areas in a growing number of cities are reviving. More and more people are buying up and restoring old, often run-down relics. This takes work, to be sure, but it can pay off. You can see blocks of these rehabilitated houses in West Greenwich Village and parts of Brooklyn in New York; in Hoboken, New Jersey, a classic small-town example, we think; in Nyack, New York; and in a growing number of cities elsewhere. Because this trend has been increasing, the value of *all* houses in such areas has risen, often by more than the cost of the improvements. Later the houses have often yielded fat profits when sold.

WHAT SHOULD YOU DO?

If you choose the road of restoring an old house in an old neighborhood, be sure to pick an area that has basic appeal and desirability. You will have much going in your favor if it's a neighborhood where a trend is already under way, where others have started to fix up and improve their houses.

If in doubt, no matter where the house is located, get suggestions from a banker or two and from real estate brokers. Estimate the total

Remodeling a townhouse can be difficult because of its narrow width and no place for windows except front or back. New York architect Peter Samton solved this common difficulty for his own townhouse by letting oceans of light and air in with a wide glass wall–skylight in the rear, and with an open kitchen. The rest of the house isn't bad, either. *David L. Hirsch.*

cost of the improvements desired. This behooves you to make a complete list of all improvements and repairs desired, not only for new living space but also for modernizing a kitchen or bath and bringing up to date such essentials as the wiring and heating plant.

The decision may hinge on practical considerations and emotional reasons. If you expect to be transferred within a few years, extensive remodeling is obviously unwise. On the other hand, if you plan to stay where you are because you really like your house and the neighborhood, remodeling is your best bet (even if you must put more money into it than a real estate conservative would recommend).

Cut through the surface to your bedrock desires. If you really want a new house and a fresh start or perhaps a step up to a bigger, more impressive house, don't waste money on remodeling.

Or do you really like and enjoy your present house? Are you so strongly attached to your neighborhood that moving would be a severe wrench you will regret? With only a little more room or a few extra facilities, would your present house be perfectly satisfactory? Then remodeling can be a richly rewarding experience.

After all the hard pro-and-con facts are weighed one against the other, how do you feel about moving versus remodeling? This is largely an emotional decision, tempered by realities, to be sure. But it is usually the best indication of what to do.

CHAPTER 2
HOW MUCH DO
HOME IMPROVEMENTS COST?

How long is a piece of string?

The cost depends, first, on the kind of improvement and, secondly, on the people doing it. As an example, consider two families living in similar houses in the same neighborhood. One spent $4,000 for a new kitchen, the other $6,200, even though both started with basically the same space and much the same old kitchen.

The first family kept down their cost by planning a no-frills kitchen with no structural changes and a minimum of new appliances. The second family wanted and paid for extra countertop space and storage cabinets. They also made a few structural changes, including the installation of a large new window for extra light and air. Naturally, their kitchen cost more.

The cost of a home improvement will, however, generally fall within a given range of prices for that particular work. It will depend on such variables as the size of the job, optional extras, quality, and the care with which you plan. Don't underestimate the latter. Good planning can save much money and result in a better job.

Here is the range of prices charged by contractors for the most common home improvements. If you do it yourself, providing your own labor but buying the materials, the cost will generally run about 50 percent less, with variations according to the kind of remodeling. As a rule, construction costs for new houses break down to a materials–labor ratio of about 60–40. The ratio of labor in remodeling works is often more because of its rebuilding aspect.

A new, remodeled kitchen: $3,500 up to $10,000. Most people spend

This "Carpenter Gothic" house was built in 1893 but later neglected. It was bought by the author in 1959 for $18,000. The cost of improvements (described in the text) came to $10,000. The house sold nine years later for $38,000. In 1978 it was worth $75,000.

about $5,000, give or take $1,000. Since a sizable portion of the cost of even a basic remodeling will be the sum spent on cabinets, shop hard for good prices, but be aware of quality differences as well. The cheapest cabinet can be quite tempting because the cost may be half the expenditure for the best kind. But if you want a kitchen to last for many years and retain its good looks, expect to pay more for the cabinets. If you're redoing a big kitchen, replacing appliances, and want a gold-medal kitchen in all ways, prepare to spend from $7,500 to $10,000, sometimes more. The only ways to cut that cost are to have a skilled do-it-yourself kitchen craftsman in your family or to be a kitchen contractor yourself.

As a rule, kitchen prices break down to about $200 to $300 per linear foot of new installed countertop and cabinets. A good contractor can give you the local price per foot in your area. The cost can jump sharply if structural work, such as tearing down a wall or adding new windows, as cited earlier, is to be done.

Remodeled bathrooms: Contractors' prices to remodel a full bathroom will range from about $2,500 to $4,000 for the conventional kind, and far more if you go along for a super-deluxe Roman bath model. A full remodeling would include replacing the three main fixtures (tub, toilet, and lavatory); new faucets, lighting, and floor and wall tile; and odd accessories, such as medicine cabinet and exhaust fan. If the fixtures are to be relocated, the cost will go higher, so try to stay with the present fixture locations.

For a complete new full bath, built where there was none before, you can expect to spend about $1,000 or more in addition to the prices given above. This amount can vary widely, depending on the structural work required and the degree of difficulty in running new water, drain, and vent lines.

A new half-bath (toilet and lavatory only) generally can be done for from $750 to $2,500, if major structural changes are unnecessary. The low price is for a half-bath installed in an existing enclosed space, needing little or no new construction and located close to existing plumbing lines. Costs obviously go up when structural work and long-distance plumbing extensions are required.

A new addition to your house: The range is $25 to $35 per square foot of new enclosed floor space. This is approximately the same as the cost of new-house construction. A local builder can tell you what it is where you live. A two-story addition generally will cost less per square foot than a one-story addition of equal living area because it requires less foundation and roofing work.

New interior living space: $10 to $20 per square foot of finished floor area. This means converting raw interior space such as a porch or garage into finished new rooms. Again, the price varies according to how much structural work is required.

New attic room: $15 to $20 per square foot. The cost is highest if a dormer is required to provide sufficient ceiling height in the new room. At least one new wall or partition and new windows are generally required, as well as heat and plenty of insulation.

New basement room: $1,500 or more. How much more depends partly on whether the basement is dry to start with or how much waterproofing is necessary. Beware of a basement cluttered with pipes and ducts, which may have to be relocated. The cost may be staggering. (See also Chapter 13).

Enclosing an existing porch: $10 to $20 a square foot, or roughly $1,500 to $3,000 total. The largest cost item is generally for new windows. If the existing structure is not sound to start with, be prepared for a substantial expense to shore it up.

New insulation for an existing house: Roughly 20 cents a square foot for at least 6-inch-thick insulation to be put down at the attic floor of a house by do-it-yourself labor. An attic with 1,500 square feet of area therefore will require $300 worth of insulation. That's based on the rule-of-thumb price of 1 cent per square foot for each unit of R value (see Chapter 17), and 6-inch insulation generally carries an R value of about 20. Contractors install the same insulation in an attic for 50 to 100 percent more to cover labor costs.

Wall insulation runs from 50 to 90 cents per square foot of interior wall when done by a contractor. The price is on the low side when rock wool, fiberglass, or cellulose insulation is used; it's higher for urea-formaldehyde foam insulation.

New aluminum or vinyl wall siding: $100 to $175 per "square" (100 square feet of wall siding installed). A typical house requires about 18 squares for a total installed cost of from $1,800 to $3,150. The price varies according to the number of windows, wall breaks, and corners, which complicate the work and therefore increase the cost, and according to the type of siding used.

Insulated siding costs about 10 percent more and almost always should be specified, unless you don't want to save energy. If your walls are not insulated, expecting insulated siding to be an effective insulator by itself is like asking a baby to do a man's job. A siding contractor who claims wall insulation is unnecessary with new insulated siding either is ignorant of the facts or is trying to fleece you. You *can* save money on wall insulation by having it installed when the walls are being re-sided because both jobs can be done at once.

Storm doors and windows: $25 to $50 per window; $75 to $100 each for storm door installed. The price varies greatly according to size and quality.

New roofing: $30 to $60 per square (100 square feet) for good, though not the best, asphalt roofing shingles. That's $750 to $1,500 to reroof the average house. To have a simple pitched roof with no breaks done will cost the least. The extra labor for a roof with a lot of ridges and valleys will cost more. Costs also go up if the old roofing must be removed first or if top-grade roofing is used.

New wiring: $10 to $15 for each new outlet; $20 to $35 for each new regular wiring circuit installed. The price of new heavy-duty circuits for new appliances can run twice the cost.

Cost figures and prices for other kinds of remodeling and home improvements are given later; see the chapters on specific subjects.

CHAPTER 3

HOW MUCH DO
HOME IMPROVEMENTS INCREASE
THE VALUE OF YOUR HOUSE?

You will get the largest return in increased house value with a new kitchen, new bath, new family room, or a third or fourth bedroom. Those are the Big Four, the most popular and desirable features sought by home buyers, and what they will pay the most for.

Don't, however, expect the value of your house to increase dollar for dollar of the money spent for such improvements or for any other improvement on a house. A 100 percent return is asking too much. The nature of remodeling and home improvements makes them more expensive than providing the same feature in a new house at lower new-house construction costs. And few home buyers will pay more for them in an existing house than for the same feature in a new house.

Put another way, new houses tend to exert a leveling effect on the prices of used houses and each of the individual components in used houses. And by and large, prices for used houses tend to be lower than for new houses.

No matter how desirable the new improvement may seem to you, no one can tell for sure how much it will add to the value of a house. If it is a new kitchen, bath, family room, or third or fourth bedroom, you can generally count on the value of your house going up by about 60 to 75 percent of the money spent. Occasionally there are exceptions and it will be more—or less. But that's about the best return you can count on for the reasons noted above.

A new kitchen is likely to increase the value of a house more than any other remodeling. A storage wall separates this kitchen from the family room at right. Details of the dining area are shown above. Designed by architect John Milnes Baker, Katonah, N.Y. *Tom Crane*.

But the value of your house will go up that much only if the work is well done, only if the finished product conforms with the style and feeling of your house, and only if it is appropriate for your neighborhood. A big $20,000 luxury bathroom is no more appropriate for a $40,000 house than a skating rink inside an igloo. People continually scorn such advice and end up losers. There also seems to be a great compulsion among some homeowners to remodel mainly to add value to their houses. This is usually a mistake, with a few exceptions noted below.

The main reason for remodeling a house should be to make it a better place for you and your family, not for an unknown buyer. Luckily, improvements that are most desirable for the family living in a house (you) generally tend to be the ones that do pay off the most in increased value when the house is sold.

Also remember that no matter how desirable the improvement, recovery of much of your money is unlikely if it overimproves the house right out of the class of the neighborhood. This is virtually an ironclad real estate principle, as described in the preceding chapter.

HOW MUCH OTHER IMPROVEMENTS ADD
TO HOUSE VALUE

Of all things, central air conditioning ranks high up there in value added. It increases the value of a house by about 50 percent of its cost. Besides, air conditioning is virtually essential for selling a house in much of the hot South, and it can help considerably in many parts of the North. It adds the most value when it is added at minimal cost by use of the existing ducts already in place for central heating. If you must spend more for new air ducts, as in a house with hot-water heat, this extra cost is not likely to come back to you in a higher resale value.

The value of air conditioning in a resale may be less in the future, however, because of the rising cost of the electricity needed to run it. This is hard to predict. Those who desire air conditioning are likely to continue finding it desirable, thus valuable, in the hot South, but because of increased operating costs, it may have less impact on a prospective buyer in marginal summer climates in the North. As for individual room air conditioners, these have never added much to house value because they are halfway measures and often unsightly.

Other home improvements that have increased in value because of the energy crunch include fireplaces, which have become popular and desirable even in places with southern climates like Georgia, Florida, and southern Texas. In such areas, a fireplace can take the chill out of the air on many a winter day without the need to turn on the house heating system (if there is one). That's nice, and it saves money.

Adding a full-fledged fireplace and masonry chimney, however, can cost a bundle of money, as much as $2,000 to $4,000. It's unlikely that anyone will get this sum back in increased value for a house. If you already have a masonry fireplace in your house, you can be smug because it has probably increased the value of your house (unless you live in the tropics). A freestanding fireplace can be added for as little as $500.

Energy-saving features like wall and ceiling insulation and storm windows and doors have also assumed new importance and are a decided asset when you sell a house. Before the energy crunch most home buyers couldn't care less about such things. But now a growing number of alert home shoppers insist on these features when they shop for a house. The lack of insulation and storm windows will impede the sale of a house or mean a reduced price for it.

A new furnace, new wiring, new roof, and other such maintenance repairs fit a special category. They generally add little or nothing directly to the value of a house, but they are nevertheless important because they can keep your house from sliding downhill in value owing to obsolescence. Without needed repairs and refurbishing, a house begins to look the worse for wear, and its value starts sagging fast.

Besides, even if the disrepair is not particularly obvious, like a roof that looks all right but leaks underneath like a sieve or a furnace that can't keep you warm, the house will still suffer reduced value. Most buyers will deduct the cost of making the corrective improvements from the price offered to buy the house. To detect such invisible defects, a growing number of home buyers are hiring inspection experts to find such flaws. Spending money to maintain a house in good condition not only helps hold its market value but also gives you the benefit of the renewed house while you're still living in it.

THE ALL-IMPORTANT GARAGE

Adding a garage can add good value to a house—50 percent or more of its cost—because a garage is valued highly for protecting a car from cold, snow, and rain. In mild and warm climates, a carport may be all that's needed, and it, too, is desired and therefore valued. Conversely, a house without a garage is like an egg without salt. It's just not good. There are cases when the lack of a garage may have lost the sale of a house.

This brings up a common mistake. Avoid a garage conversion that adds a needed room but leaves the car out in the cold. People often do this because it's an easy way to add a low-cost new room, but it can boomerang. In Pennsylvania, for example, a three-bedroom house in an attractive residential area went unsold for a long time because its garage had been converted to a family room, and there was no place left on the property to build one. Only after the family room was reconverted into a garage did the owner succeed in selling. This is not a local phenomenon. One large national real estate firm found it too had to do a number of such reconversions before it could sell houses in many parts of the country.

Think twice before you convert a garage to a new room. Be sure that the room will fit into your floor plan. Because of the usual garage location on the other side of the kitchen, it is generally an awkward spot for a new room. One exception is turning it, of all things, into a new master bedroom. This can provide privacy as a result of its being isolated from kids' rooms on the other side of a house.

Also be sure that you have a place on your property for another garage. Before going ahead, you can avoid still another common problem encountered with garage conversion that detracts sharply from the value of a house: poor workmanship. This seems to plague garage conversions, with new rooms born out of old garages frequently cursed with the telltale signs of amateur do-it-yourself labor. Six thumbprints are seen all over the room. If you tackle a garage conversion yourself, be sure to do it right, or hire an expert at least to finish up and smooth out all the joints and edges (as well as remove the excess thumbprints).

Incidentally, no matter what kind of improvement you make, be sure that it fits well into the floor plan and design of your house. Avoid common errors such as a new upstairs bedroom that can be reached only by travel through another bedroom. A house in Oklahoma was not sold because two rooms had been combined to make one large but unattractive room that stood out like a sore nose. The house was sold only after the price had been reduced.

In a California area where most houses had three or four bedrooms, two bedrooms were added to a $75,000 house that already had four. Later, when the owners put the house up for sale, they soon found out that six bedrooms were more than people in that area wanted. The house remained unsold for two years. Then the seller reduced the price to $75,000, its value before the two bedrooms were added. Only then did a buyer appear.

BIG IMPROVEMENTS THAT ADD SMALL VALUE TO A HOUSE

The common denominator is a new room or other improvement that does not add *essential* living space to a house, such as a new study, no matter how handsome its fine paneling, or a new patio, porch, or basement recreation room, or elaborate outdoor landscaping, no matter how beautiful. That's because home buyers are in no mood to spend extra for such luxury items when they're house shopping and are pressed to get as much basic house for their money as possible.

The basement recreation room was, to be sure, a popular feature at one time, but today it adds no more value to a house than the tail fins of yesteryear add to today's car prices. People don't pay extra for this feature when they can buy another house without it for less money. (But then the same buyers after moving in proceed to put in their own new basement rec rooms!) Impressive landscaping also turns people off because of the extra maintenance and labor that flash into mind when they see it. It may perhaps increase the value of a house if you're lucky to find the unusual buyer who is indeed turned on by lush landscaping in bloom and who is also rich enough to pay your price.

A SWIMMING POOL

A new pool is the chanciest investment of all because of its mixed notices from home buyers. When one famous comedian moved to Hollywood and bought a high-priced house there, the first thing his wife did was fill in the pool because of fear for the life of their small child. Many couples with children pass up houses with pools for the same reason, and they constitute a significant portion of all home buyers. Still, a pool can add excellent value to a house, particularly in a fashionable neighborhood in a warm climate, like Florida's Gold Coast and much of southern California. In other places, where there is less summer heat, the need for a pool is offset by people's fear of them as a hazard for kids and also because it's often a pain in the neck to maintain.

As much as any other home improvement, a swimming pool

should be considered mainly for its satisfaction of your own desire for one and very little for its added value to the house. If you put in a pool and later decide to sell your house, try to put it on the market in hot weather, when the pool will exert its greatest appeal.

In recent years, tennis courts have been added to houses, but like pools, a tennis court can be a double-edged improvement, depending on where you live and the kinds of home buyers who are likely to want your house. If your crowd includes tennis-playing families, your new court could well carry extra clout for selling your house. On the other hand, a tennis court is viewed by some people as just another unwanted home maintenance chore; thus no extra value is added to the house.

IMPROVEMENTS MADE TO SELL A HOUSE

It seldom makes sense to spend money to remodel or improve a house just to sell it at a higher price, but there are several exceptions, notably a new paint job on the outside of a house when it is obviously needed. This can transform a house into a Cinderella and win the day for you. A house that looks run-down—and nothing creates that impression faster than worn, faded, peeling, or flaking paint—turns off home buyers faster than termites. First impressions are crucial.

Painting the inside is usually less important. It depends on whether the interior is truly shabby and run-down or suffers merely from ordinary wear and tear. New carpeting, however, can be worth its cost because old, worn, and frayed carpeting can pull down the appearance of the whole inside. If you paint the interior and redecorate with new carpeting, be discreet. Too much color, for example, may hurt more than help. Use neutral tones, like resale white, when you paint and soft gold or beige for carpeting. These are more likely to go with the furniture a new buyer will bring to the house.

In short, avoid gaudy colors and questionable taste. I know of a house in Massachusetts that was not sold for two years because it had been redecorated in strong colors, including fire engine red carpeting. It finally sold at a reduced price, the carrot offered to the buyer to make up for the questionable interior colors.

A FINAL CHECK

Suppose you are still in doubt about the financial wisdom of making a specific home improvement. Will it pay when you sell? Is it desirable in your area?

"Look at the competition," says a spokesman for Home Equity/ Homerica, a national employee relocation and real estate firm. In other words, look at the nearby houses with and without a particular improvement. Do houses with it sell well? Is it really an improvement that is desirable in your area? A handsome new kitchen is accepted nearly everywhere, but a steeple on the roof is clearly not. Steeples are for churches, not houses.

To repeat, a home improvement adds the greatest value to a house when it is chiefly to make the house better and more suitable for you and your family. If it's genuinely good for you, it generally will be good for the house and therefore is likely to be good for another family. Then it will usually add value to your house.

CHAPTER 4

HOW TO FIND AND REMODEL A GOOD OLD HOUSE
(INCLUDING THE TEN MOST COMMON FLAWS FOUND IN OLD HOUSES)

The house and shelter magazines publish home remodeling stories all the time on the subject of how John and Betty Smitheroo turned a sow's ear into a silk purse. It's a dream of many a couple, especially people looking for an old house at a bargain price. Major remodeling is also increasingly common among homeowners who decide to stay put rather than buy an expensive new house.

Major remodeling can pay off well, though it takes stamina and, of course, the proper mental attitude. It will be a personal triumph only if the house is basically sound to start with. You must face up to reality and have a good idea of all to be done, as well as what the total cost will be.

OLD HOUSE ADVANTAGES
These include the same advantages in favor of remodeling, instead of moving, given in Chapter 1. Going a step farther, this chapter tells how to find and buy a good old house and how to deal with the design and structural aspects of remodeling it.

Usually the older the house, the lower its price, but there are other benefits—an abundance of space, large rooms, tall ceilings, and other amenities of yesteryear seldom found in recent construction. You may find such a treasure in your present neighborhood perched on expensive land that would cost you dearly if bought as a vacant lot.

Before: An old wreck like this can be worth remodeling if its foundation and basic bones are sound, assuming it can be bought at a reasonable price. Remodeling turned this old farmhouse in Virginia into the attractive house shown.

There is also, of course, the growing number of old houses in cities and downtown areas that are coming back in value, also noted in Chapter 1. Finding this kind of old house can be worth double its cost in terms of living close to work.

If necessary, the cost of remodeling can be financed along with the house itself under one mortgage. Suppose an old house is priced at $40,000 and $25,000 worth of improvements are needed. Your total cost could be financed with one mortgage as if it were a $65,000 house.

The dirty work of modernizing can be done before you move in, an inestimable advantage. Workmen will not be underfoot, and they can work faster and more efficiently when not coping with people living in the house.

But first get firm price bids for the necessary improvements and an appraisal of the house value after remodeling. Naturally, the mortgage lender wants assurance that the improvements will make the house worth $65,000. This involves planning and talking with bankers.

An old house is, of course, a bargain only if its price plus the cost of necessary improvements does not exceed the price of a new house of comparable size. This will tell you if you have really sniffed out a bargain. A rough estimate can be made from the cost figures in Chapter 2, but firm bids for essential improvements should be obtained before you buy the house.

CHECKING AN OLD HOUSE YOU MAY BUY

The trick, of course, is to avoid a house with serious defects, like termites that have burrowed deep into the underpinnings, or plumbing pipes with atherosclerosis that will soon choke and stop working (though not till after you've bought the place).

If you're not a construction expert, the best way to discover such internal ailments is by hiring a professional consultant who inspects houses for a living. The fee ranges from $100 to $200, depending on the house, and you may have to pay additional for travel if the house is distant. These inspectors are increasingly numerous and can be located under "Home Inspection Services" in the classified pages of your telephone book. If none is available where you live, your next best bet is to hire a good builder, contractor, or architect who specializes in renovating old houses. Beware of the friend or relative who will do it free, for the report you get is often worth nothing, too.

A primary test of any house you expect to live in is the quality of its floor plan, room layout, and suitability for your family—in other words, its basic design. Is it good? Rules for judging the floor plan and other aspects of house design are the same as those for judging the remodeling potential of an existing house (see the following chapter).

Does the house appeal to you? Do you really like the house and have no doubts about it? As when you married, you should have few doubts about your affection for the house you live in or you won't be happy. But don't go overboard in the other direction, falling headlong in love at first sight with the deceptively "charming" old house. It loses its charm quickly when the prices come in for rebuilding it.

Here are the ten most common flaws and inadequacies to watch for in an old house. The list is based on interviews with home improvement contractors, repairmen, and others familiar with old houses, such as Arthur Tauscher, president of Home Inspection Consultants, the first such firm of its kind in the United States. Tauscher recorded the flaws he found in a random sampling of 1,000 houses over ten years old that his firm had inspected for prospective buyers. The two most frequent defects were overloaded wiring (in 84 percent of the houses) and termites or wood rot (in 58 percent).

Knowing these most likely defects in a house can help you avoid being soaked a high price for an old house. But don't necessarily turn down such a house because of a few major defects. You might get the house at a truly low, bargain price once you've pointed out its deficiencies to the seller. In addition, don't be overwhelmed or depressed by all the things that can go wrong. No more than a few of them are likely to be found in old houses in reasonably good condition and especially in houses less than twenty years old.

1. *Obsolete, old-fashioned kitchen.* You can spot this at a glance, especially with a good look at the floor near the kitchen sink. If the floor is worn, if it is rotting there, the whole kitchen needs to be modernized. Even if the floor is comparatively good and new, the rest of the kitchen can still be a nightmare of poor and inadequate design, no matter how pleasant it may seem. Be hardheaded, and judge it realistically. The cost of modernizing an old kitchen and cost figures for modernizing most other parts of a house that follow are given in Chapter 2.

2. *Run-down bathrooms.* Or not enough bathrooms. There's seldom any secret about the condition of a bathroom in an old house. The fixtures are small antiques, the floor and walls are old, and the only remaining question is how long you may be able to tolerate it before you toss in the towel (no pun intended) and absolutely must have a new bathroom or two.

3. *Little or no thermal insulation.* This was formerly a casual omission in old houses, but it has leaped up near the top of the list of serious drawbacks in houses because of the energy crisis. You should check for storm windows and doors and for weatherstripping around windows and doors (to keep out cold air jets), as well as for walls and ceilings well padded with insulation. Biggest cost items here are for insulating noninsulated walls ($750 to $1,000 and up) and buying new storm windows ($500 and up).

Nearly all houses built before 1950 were built with no insulation. Many houses built after about 1955 were built with attic insulation but little or no wall insulation. Most houses built since the 1960s got both wall and ceiling insulation, though not necessarily enough.

Nonetheless, insulation has been added to some houses built without it. Attic insulation often can be seen between the attic floor joists. (Insulation under the roof between the sloping roof rafters of the attic does little good. It should be at the attic floor unless there are finished rooms where the attic formerly was.) To be sure that the walls are insulated, ask to see the seller's paid bill for having the walls insulated. Or look inside them by removing a few electric switch or outlet plates and peering in with a flashlight, as noted in Chapter 18. During cold weather you can get an indication of the insulation inside by holding your hand against the inside surface of an exterior wall. Then hold your hand against an interior partition. The exterior walls should not feel much colder than the inside wall. If they do, much heat is leaking out; there is little or no insulation.

4a. *Poor heating.* This subject has also assumed high-priority importance because of the energy crisis, and it should be viewed in two ways in a house you might buy: the condition of the heating plant and its annual operating cost. The condition depends on the house age or, in a very old house, on the age of its present heating system. Many houses built before 1940 were built with a coal heating plant which often has been converted to oil or gas. If the original hot-water or steam heat is still in a house, how much longer it will last is questionable. Look at the boiler nameplate to see if it is cast iron or steel. (No nameplate is an indication of a low-quality heater.) The cast-iron kind will usually last longer. Look for signs of cracking and around the exterior base for rust and general deterioration. If the heater is a large, old, hot-air gravity furnace with no fan, it too is likely to expire at any time.

A heating plant in a house only ten or fifteen years old also can be troublesome. Sometimes the unit is too small for the house, a common flaw in post-World War II development houses. The best way to check this is to visit the house on a cold day. Have the system turned on, and raise the thermostat up to 80 degrees. How long does it take for heat to reach each room after starting? A warm-air system should provide heat within ten or fifteen minutes; a hot-water or steam system within a half hour. Also listen for noisy operation.

Does the heater burn gas, oil, or coal? Gas burners last the longest and are generally best of all. If in doubt about an oil burner, a serviceman should give it a combustion test. (He checks the exhaust gases leaving the heater. They should not exceed 600 degrees F after twenty to thirty minutes, and the CO_2 content of the flue gas should be between 8½ and 14 percent. The burner flame should be bright yellow with orange tips and no smoke.) Look and sniff around the bottom of the oil tank and on the floor below the tank for signs of oil. If there are signs, the tank probably leaks and should be replaced.

Though infrequently found in houses, radiant heat in a house should be approached like a pig in a poke. You can't tell what you're getting. It's a system with the heat distributed through pipes laid in the concrete slab floor. Defects in it are difficult to correct. Though a good system when properly installed, many of them were not put in as well as they should have been, particularly in development houses. It should have indoor-outdoor temperature controls (a small temperature-sensing device on an outside wall wired to the inside controls).

Coal heat, even rarer, can be a real problem. If the unit is more than fifteen years old, converting to automatic gas or oil heat can be risky. If it is older and you prefer automatic heat, expect to replace the entire heating plant.

Take the name and phone number of the heating dealer who services the system. This is usually noted on a card near the heating unit. Ask him about the system. What kinds of repairs are needed? How long will the system last? He may or may not come clean with you, but whatever you may learn is worth the effort.

4b. *Expensive heating.* The most expensive of all heating is electric heat, which can cost twice as much as oil heat, up to five times more than gas heat, as explained in Chapter 20. Gas heat is still the preferred, low-cost central heat even though its cost has risen since the bitter cold winter of 1976–77. The cost of gas was so low in relation to oil and electricity that despite its having risen faster than oil or electricity, it has a long way to go before it costs as much as oil and much longer before it approaches the cost of electric heat.

Because converting to gas heat is now not allowed in many parts of the country, a house with gas heat can be worth several thousand dollars more than a house with oil or high-cost electric heat. That's because the annual heating bill for gas can run from several hundred dollars to $1,000 *less* each year than oil or electric heat for the same house. The exact savings vary according to the house and the price paid locally for each heat energy. You must determine this separately for each house. Check past heating bills, if possible, and find out from the local utility companies what other people nearby pay for heating with each type of energy. This may take time and effort, to be sure, but the annual heating bill that is at stake can mean a difference of thousands of dollars to you in the next five to ten years.

5. *Worn-out wiring.* The older the house, the more likely the wiring is inadequate. The wiring problem arose because most houses built before World War II needed only enough wiring capacity for lights and a few small appliances. Then came the wave of large appliances and other electric equipment in houses that today call for far heavier wiring.

Look for the main electric board, also called the service entrance, usually in the basement near the electric meter. Read the rating marked on it. (There is also an ampere number on the meter, which is something else again and has nothing to do with the board.) Its rating should be *at least* 100 amperes and 240 volts; with a large family and many appliances, you'll generally need a 150- to 200-ampere service rating.

The size of the main electric board in your present house may tell you what's needed in your next house. If it's inadequate, make an appropriate adjustment upward. You will also want what's called a three-wire electric service to a house. If it's not present—in other words, if there is only two-wire service—you will probably have to pay to have a new, three-wire service installed, assuming that you want all your major appliances to work. Look for three overhead wires in tandem running from the electric pole to the house. If only two are visible, it is an obsolete 120-volt service. Be sure you're looking at the overhead electric wires to the meter, not the telephone wires.

Look also for plenty of electric outlets, switches, and lighting fixtures throughout the house. There should be one electric outlet in each wall of every room, two or more in long walls, at least two or three outlets concentrated above the kitchen countertop work space for appliances; a wall switch for every ceiling light fixture; and (for ideal wiring but seldom seen) a light switch at each door in rooms with two or more doors.

6. *Termite damage and wood rot.* These occur mostly in houses more than five to ten years old, but they are hard to detect unless you are an expert. Have a termite expert check the house before you buy. FHA and VA officials generally require this before they will approve a mortgage on an old house. Its importance cannot be overemphasized. Wood rot can be searched out at the same time.

7. *Sagging structure.* The foundation settles and wrenches the house out of joint, or beams sag as a result of wood rot. Look carefully at the squareness of the exterior walls, for level windows and doors and a level first floor. Stand about 2 feet back from each corner of the house, and sight laterally straight down the walls for trueness. A major bulge with bent or broken wall siding spells trouble. A few inches out of plumb is usually of small importance. Inside the house, the condition of basement beams and supporting columns is particularly important. Notice also if all doors line up squarely with their frames.

Nearly all houses settle a little, so don't panic if the structure is not perfectly true. On the other hand, severely cracked walls, windows and doors out of joint, and sloping floors should be carefully investigated. Sometimes an old house may need only one or two new supporting posts and beams underneath at a cost of a few hundred dollars. But a major structural failing can mean extensive rebuilding at a much higher cost. Get bids beforehand on the cost of shoring up the house.

8. *Poor plumbing.* Common troubles are weak water pressure, owing to clogged or corroded pipes, and a bad septic-tank system. Bad plumbing is mostly a problem in houses with iron or steel pipes that are older than twenty-five years. Copper, brass, and bronze pipes will last much longer than steel or iron but were not introduced until about 1940. A magnet can tell you if the pipes are iron or steel. They will attract the magnet, but copper, brass, or bronze will not. Test for water pressure by turning on the top-floor bathroom faucets. Turn on the bathtub and sink faucets, and flush the toilet at the same time. If the water slows down to a trickle, you can expect plumbing woes. The pressure in the street mains, however, may be low, and then a booster pump will be needed. A call to the water company should tell you if the street pressure is adequate.

Is there a septic tank, a cesspool, or a city sewer? If there is no street sewer, be wary even if the house is comparatively new. Overloaded septic tanks and cesspools are major problems in many areas. Septic-tank problems are also more likely in a house with an automatic washing machine and several children. When was the septic tank or cesspool last cleaned? Cleaning is normally needed every three or four years. Who did the cleaning? Call him and ask about the condition of the tank. A good source of information on septic-tank problems is the public health department. It can tell you if such problems are prevalent locally. Septic-tank repairs may run from $100 to several thousand.

9. *Roof and gutters.* What kind of roof and how old is it? An asphalt shingle or built-up roof on a flat or low slope more than fifteen years old will soon need repairs or replacement. Walk around the house and stand back to inspect the roof and gutters. A good roof will be even and uniform. A worn roof will contain broken, warped, or bent shingles, giving a ragged appearance.

To inspect a flat or nearly flat asphalt roof, go up on the roof. Look for bare spots in the mineral surfacing, separations, breaks in the felt, and rusty flashing around the roof edges and around the chimney. Note the condition of the horizontal gutters, especially if they are wood. Are they clogged with leaves or clean and well maintained? The best time to check for roof leaks and bad gutters is during a heavy rain (even if you get a little wet). Check inside the attic for water stains and discolorations, the ceilings below for stains and cracks.

10. *The faucet water heater.* Is there a separate water heater and tank or an indirect coil water heater that is inside the hot-water heating boiler? If it is a separate tank heater, check the nameplate for capacity and type, and judge it according to the standards in Chapter 23. Open the little door at the base of the tank where the pilot light and burner mechanism are. Look in with a flashlight for signs of rust or leaks. These are the first signs of trouble.

The condition of a coil water heater (built inside the regular hot-water house-heating boiler) is hard to ascertain except by an expert. The common complaint about such a heater is insufficient hot water. If possible, see if its heating capacity is given in gallons of hot water supplied per minute (gpm) and rate it according to the standards in Chapter 23.

FLAWS THAT VARY ACCORDING TO YOUR LOCATION

The location of a house, its climate zone, or a special condition peculiar to the area can be the tip-off to certain flaws.

Wet basements are widespread in areas with damp soil, such as Long Island and much of New Jersey. Cracked or settled foundations are a special problem in marshy places, as around New Orleans in houses close to the levees. They are also a problem in houses built on filled or reclaimed land that was once marshy.

Septic-tank and cesspool troubles are prevalent with damp, low-lying ground or hard clay soil, as along the Atlantic seaboard from Long Island south to Florida. Rusty water pipes are troublesome in cities like Philadelphia with hard and corrosive water.

Roofs in hotter climates such as the South and Southwest are most likely to need frequent repair or replacement. The intense sun of Texas, New Mexico, and Arizona is savagely hard on a roof. Poor air-conditioning units are more likely to be found in the hot South, where they labor hardest and longest, just as run-down heating is more likely to be found in the cold North. To check on local problems when you're moving into a new part of the country, call on a few local contractors, repairmen, banks specializing in short-term home improvement loans, or the local FHA or VA office.

OTHER OLD-HOUSE DEFECTS

If you're out of breath from all the things that can go wrong in an old house, don't give up. Remember that I said that many houses are not likely to have all of them. A fairly complete listing, across the board, is presented here to give you an overall picture of what is commonly found in many old houses, but not in every single one. Besides, checking an old house should be done for you by a professional house inspector. Anyone ignoring this advice does so at his or her own peril. I have also gone into specific detail in this chapter for readers who wish to know much on the subject. To continue:

Outside. Is the exterior paint in good condition? Most houses require new paint every three to five years. If the paint is failing, the kind of failure is highly important. Paint normally chalks as it ages, leaving a dull, powdery surface. It should not blister or peel (flaking). This is a sign of more serious trouble, especially if it shows on a recently painted house.

If there is an outside chimney, is it snug against the house wall? Or is a crack developing between the chimney and house? Chimney separation, like a marital breakup, can require serious and expensive work to heal. If the damage is serious enough, repair is not always possible; a complete rebuilding of the chimney may be called for.

A crawl space under the house should be inspected. Crawl in with a flashlight. Is it dry? Is the wood substructure free of rot and condensation? Any evidence of termites? There should be insulation under the house floor or around the inside walls of a closed-off crawl space, plus a vapor-barrier material over the crawl-space earth. The underside of approaches and outside stairs should be inspected in the same way.

Inside the living quarters. Does the kitchen conform to the work-triangle principle? (See Chapter 8.) Is there adequate space for modernizing, if necessary? For adding new equipment such as a dishwasher? Inspect metal cabinets for rust and corrosion; wood ones for warping; both kinds for ease of operation. Check the sink for chipped enamel, rust stains, and scratches. Try the faucets for quick hot water and good pressure. Look under the sink, a crucial place, for signs of water leaks, rust, and rot. Is there a kitchen exhaust fan, and is it properly located (in the ceiling or high on the wall over the range)?

Open and close all windows and doors. Look for ease of opening and closing.

Small wall cracks are inevitable, especially in plaster walls. Serious cracks are deep ones that start at the corner of a room or are deep gashes at the joint where the ceiling and wall meet.

You should see light when you look up the chimney from the fireplace (with the damper open, of course). Every fireplace should have a workable damper. Every chimney should be lined with flue tile; i.e., you should not see the bricks. Absence of chimney lining can be serious but is correctable. How well the fireplace works usually can be judged merely by burning paper in it. If smoke pours back into the room, the fireplace may be defective.

Are the bathroom fixtures of adequate design and in good condition? Is the bathtub under a window? It's best when it isn't. Check the joining of the tub with the floor and wall for a good waterproof seam. Are wall and floor tiles in good condition? An interior bathroom without windows should have an exhaust fan connected to a convenient (but safe) switch. An old-fashioned bathtub with legs (no matter how quaint), no tile floor, and no wall tile around the bathtub and shower are drawbacks. (Okay, a quaint, leggy old bathtub can be quite nice.)

Is the attic easily accessible? If you can reach it only by setting up a ladder, this will be a nuisance, particularly if the attic is used for storage. Are there large attic air vents? Check for attic insulation while you're there. In winter, check the insulation for dryness. If it feels moist to the touch, attic ventilation is inadequate or there's no vapor barrier under the insulation.

Look for moisture condensation and wood rot. If present, they usually can be corrected with good attic ventilation, but make sure that the condition has not advanced so far that the beams are seriously weakened. Are there signs of roof leaks, such as stains or discoloration? A clue to good, overall construction quality, incidentally, is a chimney that is totally self-supporting and independent of house framing. A chimney may be framed into the house, but attic floor joists and beams should not be tied directly into the brickwork.

Miscellaneous. Is redecorating or new paint needed? Are there screens and storm windows and doors, or will you have to buy them? Do appliances come with the house? How old are they? Are they in good condition? Will your car fit in the garage? What about the condition of the driveway and sidewalks?

Before starting out to judge an old house, arm yourself with a few tools: a clipboard, paper, and a pencil for taking notes; a 50-foot tape; a flashlight to look into dark corners; a knife or ice pick to detect termites and wood rot; a magnet to determine whether pipes are iron or not; a level to check structural trueness; a screwdriver and pliers; a 4-foot ladder; and coveralls for crawling under porches and into crawl spaces. Too much? Embarrassing? Not for the largest single purchase most of us ever make.

REMODELING AND REPAIRS THAT ARE MOST LIKELY

Nobody knows for sure about the most common repairs and remodeling jobs needed in houses. Accurate national statistics do not exist. FHA records from its home improvement program are, however, an indication of repairs and improvements an old house may need, as well as the most common repairs to expect in your present house. Here is what they are from a recent year:

Type of improvement	Percentage of families that did it
Additions and alterations (new rooms, garages, carports, etc.)	20.7
Insulation	17.5
Exterior paint, siding	12.5

Heating	11.0
Interior paint, other finishing	9.5
Plumbing	8.3
Roofing	5.3
Miscellaneous	15.2

The above percentages are in terms of the number of families that did the above work with FHA loans. They are not in terms of the amount of money, all told, spent for the kinds of work done, which is a different matter. The figures are for single-family houses, which account for about 90 percent of all FHA improvement loans.

PART TWO
Basic things to know before you remodel or alter a house

The first apartment I lived in as a youth when I came to work in the big city (New York) was a drab trio of rooms in the rear of an old apartment house. The sun and natural light hardly ever were allowed in. It was on a cross-street canyon downtown on the West Side. Inside the apartment it was perpetual dusk.

Later I moved a few blocks south to a bright, cheerful place in Greenwich Village. It had big windows front and back and no tall buildings around to keep out the sun and light. On the first morning there I awoke in a blaze of bright sunshine and light that flooded in as in a Van Gogh painting. What a transformation! Compared with the canyon I had just left, it was Shangri-la.

I was dramatically introduced to an essential ingredient of good design in any house or apartment. The rooms should be bright and cheerful, though this doesn't necessarily happen by accident. It's part of the architect's job.

Good design is good architecture. You start with a good floor plan and good room arrangement, and then come a series of other requirements that must fit into place. Is each room large enough for its purpose? What about traffic routes, in other words, allowance for circulation of people inside, not only for quick and convenient access to one room from another but also for easy travel in and out of the house. And of course, a house should be inexpensive to heat in winter and cool in summer.

Those are just a few of the basic things to know about house design and construction when you remodel. An understanding of what makes a house tick—its basic layout and design—is essential first of all. Its architecture has to do with far more than mere appearance and style. There are also such things to know as when and where it pays to add new space, when not to, which walls can be easily removed, and what problems may be raised by zoning ordinances and building codes.

CHAPTER 5

HOW TO AVOID
THE MOST COMMON
REMODELING TRAPS

Do you really have a good plan? Will the new space *work* for you and work well? How can you tell beforehand?

Consider, for example, a highly common flaw in many old houses and also surprisingly in many comparatively new ones. The whole house is laid out so that it faces the front street, and as a result, the tail ends up wagging the dog. There is a front porch, living room, dining room, and kitchen, in that order, from front to rear. Nationally known architect Peter Blake has said that the front porch was fine "when the street was a kind of communal meeting place, but today our streets are gasoline alleys." With the new appeal of outdoor living and rear gardens, the same house has ceased to be satisfactory.

Interior remodeling can turn the entire house toward the rear to face a private outdoor patio or garden. You turn your back to street traffic and noise. A picture window could be installed in the rear to let in the outdoors. Sliding glass doors for easy access to a rear patio are another good idea.

Another common and deceptively irritating drawback is a kitchen isolated at the rear of the house. A rear kitchen no longer makes sense for several reasons. It was relegated to the back of the house when we had cooks and servants. Today we are our own servants, yet are often stuck with an obsolete, remote kitchen location. A woman trapped in a rear kitchen has to traipse from one end of the house to the other every time the doorbell rings and make the same long walk the other way on returning from a shopping trip laden with groceries. These are good reasons for a kitchen near the family entrance. They also emphasize that a house is for living.

An understanding of the following principles can help you diagnose the drawbacks of a house and also help you avoid errors when new space is added to the house. Space should be added in the proper place for your family's living habits, not just where it is convenient to add for a remodeling contractor.

WILL YOU HAVE GOOD ZONING?

Zoning is a big word used by architects that boils down to making a house private and quiet where it should be quiet, pleasant for company, as well as for the family, where it should be pleasant, and easy to work in when there are things to be done.

Houses have three main zones: living, sleeping, and working. Each zone should be separate from others yet properly related to the others, the street, the sun, and the outdoors.

Are the bedrooms separated from the noise of work and play? Can you entertain guests without waking the children? A buffer zone, not just a mere partition, should shield bedrooms from the rest of the house. This can be a hall, a bathroom, or adroitly placed closets. Can unfinished laundry be left as is without being in view of a chance visitor? It depends on the zoning.

The two-story house is an example of natural zoning between the second-floor bedrooms and the rest of the house on the first floor (but it has disadvantages, too, such as the time and energy expended going up and down the stairs). Even better, if not an ideal example of good zoning, is a house laid out like an H or a U, the living and sleeping zones at opposite ends of the house, neatly connected across the middle by the kitchen and utility work zone—and all on one level. Though theoretically ideal, this is expensive to build because of the large wall and roof area. Careful design can give much the same results in a more compact plan. Good zoning also goes hand in hand with room arrangement and good circulation, which refers to the movement of the people within the house.

FIVE TESTS FOR GOOD CIRCULATION

What is a good floor plan? The few main routes in a house used over again are the key. You can spot them by these tests:

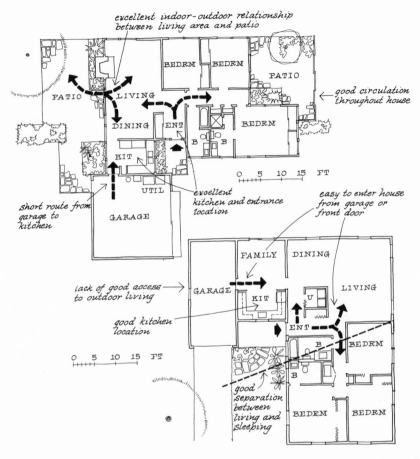

The floor plans here and on page 44 emphasize the importance of circulation and zoning within a house. The principles apply to all houses.

1. *Does the family entrance lead directly from the garage or driveway to the kitchen?* This is all-important. The main entrance for a family is usually through the kitchen. Hence the garage and driveway should be near the kitchen for quick entry and swift grocery unloading. The garage to kitchen route should be sheltered from rain. Travel through the kitchen plainly should not run smack through the kitchen work area (where food is prepared).

2. *Is the kitchen centrally located?* The kitchen should be a command post, not a foxhole. From the kitchen a woman should have

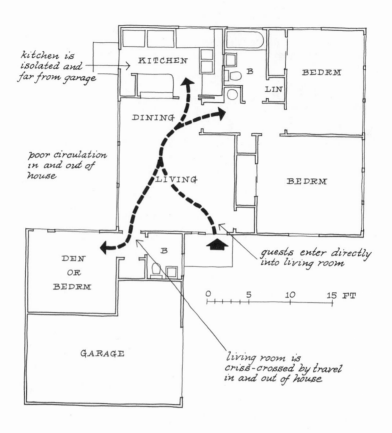

control over the entire house. She should be near the front door and family entrance. She should be able to watch children playing outside and also be near the dining room, living room, and outside patio. The remote, isolated kitchen is a widespread curse. It probably leads to more wear and tear on people, particularly mothers of small children, than any other planning defect.

3. *Does the front door (main entrance) lead directly to the center of the house?* Guests enter here. A center hall or foyer will help greatly. It will shield people inside from casual visitors, as well as from the inrush of wind, snow, and rain. The main entrance should be close to the driveway and street. A coat closet near the front door is essential.

4. *Is the living room shielded from cross-traffic?* It should not be a main highway for people going in and out of the house. It should be a

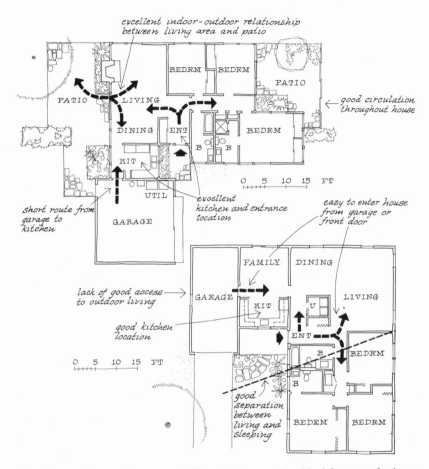

The diagrams here and on page 46 illustrate how good and bad features of a house plan can help or hinder life in a house.

dead end so you can read, talk, watch TV, or entertain guests in peace without kids running through every few minutes.

5. *Is there good room-to-room circulation?* Can you go from any room to any other room without passing through a third room (except the dining room)? From any entrance to any room without walking through a second room? The main bathroom in particular should be accessible from any room and not require passage through another room. (Flouting this rule has blackballed houses from FHA mortgage approval.) And beware of bedrooms in series which require passing through one to reach another.

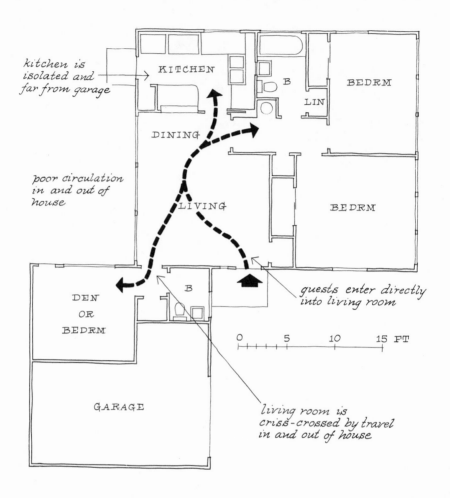

kitchen is isolated and far from garage

KITCHEN

B

BEDRM

LIN

DINING

poor circulation in and out of house

LIVING

BEDRM

DEN

OR

BEDRM

B

guests enter directly into living room

0   5   10   15 FT

GARAGE

living room is criss-crossed by travel in and out of house

IN WHICH DIRECTION SHOULD YOU EXPAND?

A review of your lot's characteristics can throw new light on remodeling plans. For example, merely moving the front-door location from the front to side can sometimes open up new opportunities for revitalizing the whole front of a house with a minimum of new construction.

Divide the land around your house into three zones: public, service, and private. The public zone is the front lawn in public view. The service zone includes sidewalks, driveways, a clothes-drying area, and trash storage. The private zone is for patio, play, and garden. Sheer logic calls for giving over as little of your land as possible for public and service use and retaining a maximum for private use.

Ideally, a house should be set forward on its lot toward the street, with small public and service areas in front and on the side. The back of the house is opened up for maximum private use. This means a minimum of front lawn to be mowed, a short approach driveway and walks, and reduced snow shoveling, and if new utility pipes and wires are needed from the street to the house, they will be short and economical.

Sometimes the same happy results can be achieved by turning the house only halfway and orienting it to one side or the other, not necessarily to the rear. It may be a solution if you have a wide lot with little depth. In all cases, of course, work for privacy between you and your closest neighbors.

ORIENTATION IN RELATION TO THE SUN AND WIND

Does bright sunshine pour delightfully into your bedroom when you awaken in the morning? Does cheerful sunlight flood the kitchen and dining room at breakfast time? Or does it seem that you always have to turn on lights during the day?

The orientation of a house and the rooms within—their exposure to the sun—makes the difference. You may be unable to do much about the whole house, short of turning it around on a giant turntable. Nevertheless, new living space can be greatly enhanced with proper orientation. Simply replacing a few windows or adding one can swiftly transform a small gloomy room into an incredibly pleasant and "large" space. (See Chapter 29.)

If rooms are properly oriented in relation to the sun, they will be warmer and easier to heat in winter, fuel bills will drop substantially, and there will be a minimum of window condensation. In summer the same rooms will be 5 to 10 degrees cooler. Regardless of where you live in any part of the Northern Hemisphere, the winter sun is in the south almost all day long. It rises in the southeast and sets in the southwest. But in summer the sun rises in the northeast, travels a much higher arc across the sky, being almost directly overhead at noon, and sets in the northwest. Specific ways of properly orienting a house in relation to the sun are given in Chapter 28.

Actually, the house itself can face any direction. The important thing to remember is that the big windows of your daytime living areas (kitchen, dining, and family room) should face south for sunshine and natural light to flood in. A southern exposure is not so important for the living room, unless you use it a good deal during the day; many people use it only at night.

New bedrooms obviously have less need for sun and are best on the north or east. On the east, you may welcome that bright sun flooding in first thing in the morning. Bedrooms on the west can get awfully hot in summer by the time you are ready for bed. Thus, it is a good idea to put a new carport or garage on the west as a sun shield in summer or on the north as a wind shield in winter.

SUN VERSUS A COOL BREEZE

A new patio or porch that faces west can get much too hot for comfort on a summer afternoon and evening. It usually goes better on the south, east, or north, provided, of course, it is conveniently near your main living area. A southern or southwestern exposure can be good for a terrace or patio only if it is protected from the western sun in summer and northwestern winds in winter. A few protective trees or a simple fence on the west side can do this.

The prevailing breezes also bear on the best location for patio or porch. A call to the nearest airport will tell you their usual direction. Of course, the requirements for catching the breeze may clash with the need for good protection from the sun; then a compromise is in order. The sun is usually your bigger foe, and protection from it ranks first.

Large windows facing south also mean less glass exposed to cold north winds in winter. Additional winter protection can be had with a windbreak of evergreen trees on the north, as is frequently seen shielding farmhouses in the wind-scourged Great Plains. (The evergreen windbreaks planted throughout the Great Plains—one of Franklin D. Roosevelt's little-publicized New Deal conservation projects—turned out far more successfully than its most ardent advocates expected.) If you live in the South, a southern orientation may be less desirable. You may do better if a house faces north with the patio on the north or northeast. Try to avoid a southwestern or western orientation.

Every room need not face south. The principles of good orientation are what to remember. You may be confronted by a clash between the needs of good orientation and remodeling a house in relation to the street. To make matters worse, you may be torn between these considerations and a third one—locating new rooms so that they take advantage of a splendid outside view. It's a dilemma. Something must give.

Unfortunately, the best solution may require a compromise depending on the house and the needs you consider foremost. Not everybody can look out on a distant mountaintop. It's fine if you can swing it. If not, or if you live on flat land, a nearby flower garden or lawn can be quite satisfactory. Every house need not face Mecca.

WHAT ABOUT STORAGE SPACE?
This means avoiding jam-packed closets and not enough shelves and other places to hold clothes and everything else that families have. Having ample storage space for all things may not rank up there in the life-can-be-beautiful department, but it's not far below.

Many nooks and crannies exist for storage in even the smallest house. Break down your requirements into two parts: live storage for the things used from day to day and dead storage for such things as trunks, screens, sleds, and garden equipment which are used only part of the time.

Live storage requires chests, drawers, closets, and shelves, sized and planned for a particular need and located at the point of use. Dead storage may call for special facilities; a basement or attic helps here. For easy access, an attic, however, should have a drop-down staircase at least.

Each person in a family needs a closet *at least* 24 inches deep and 48 inches wide, or 8 square feet. For a family of three or four, a house should provide 40 square feet of total closet space; 60 is even better. Full-width and ceiling-high closet doors are best, since you can see everything inside at a glance. There should be an interior light and adjustable shelves, and the closet floor should be raised about 2 inches to keep out dust (from the floor of the room outside).

Storage needs obviously vary from room to room: in the living room for books, magazines, records, card tables, and fireplace wood; in the dining room for linen, silver, and dishes; in the family room or playroom to hide the clutter of toys; and in or near the garage for garden tools and bikes.

Bedroom storage

Space under beds can be reclaimed with sliding drawers (but use good rollers). They are best for semidead storage (items not required every day)—e.g., for blankets, out-of-season clothing, and even linens. If you currently use bedside tables, consider replacing them with a headboard over the bed for books and magazines, or shelves on each side of the bed. The old pull-down Murphy bed may be a good idea for new additions or guest rooms where space is at a premium and the bed isn't needed every night.

Built-in storage

Here's where you can have your cake and eat it, too. Built-in storage is often cheaper than furniture and can serve a double purpose, especially in new rooms added to your house. Famed architect Frank Lloyd Wright was a master in this area. He would line walls with built-in seats and cushioned couches, and the space underneath was used for drawers and cabinets, which also cut down on housecleaning problems.

In addition, the space under a built-in window seat can double as a chest for children's toys. The dead space inside interior walls can be reclaimed by built-in shelves and small cabinets. Simply break open the wall, and install them. Storage walls are superb for this. There are special ceiling-high wall cabinets with shelves and drawers that also serve as a partition between two rooms. They are available from good furniture stores, though you have to shop for them, or you could have them built.

A host of factory-made storage units are now available for a variety of uses. You don't have to call in a carpenter every time. They can be chosen and grouped in different combinations, not only for storage walls, but also for dividers, headboard arrangements, and handsome living- and dining-room cabinets with tabletop counters. Plastic drawers are also becoming popular because of their light weight, versatility, and rugged construction. They don't expand and contract with weather changes.

Storage standards

These recommendations are from the Southwest Research Institute:

1. A coat closet near the main entrance.

2. Storage in the living room for books, records, card tables, fireplace wood.

3. Adequate kitchen cabinets (specified in Chapter 8).

4. Storage near the dining room for linen, silver, and dishes.

5. A place for ironing board, soap, and laundry necessities in the utility area.

6. Built-in bathroom storage for towels, soap, and toilet paper, as well as a medicine cabinet and laundry hamper.

7. A big enough closet in each bedroom (minimum sizes noted earlier).

8. A convenient place for trunks, boxes, sleds, screens, and similar things.

9. A place near the outdoors for lawn mower, garden tools, and summer furniture.

10. Total floor area of all general storage, excluding closets already noted: Under 40 square feet is poor; over 50 is good.

CHAPTER 6

WHEN SHOULD YOU USE AN ARCHITECT?

The cost of an architect often scares people when the use of one is suggested, but hold on. His fee will be less than you may think if he's used only for initial guidance and consultation or merely to edit your plan. The small price paid him can be worth many times over. Even a full consultation fee for an architect can be money well spent.

When you see glamorous home remodeling stories in magazines, remember that a good architect or designer planned nearly every one. It wasn't just chance that the results are handsome and well done. It therefore makes plenty of sense to consider calling in a good architect, especially for a major alteration or addition.

An architect knows how to add the most usable space at the least cost, how to redo the house to give maximum livability, which walls can be safely torn down, and what solutions offer handsome results. He or she also knows how to juggle the various ingredients for good orientation, site planning, and efficient room layout.

An architect also knows the local codes and zoning ordinances. He can steer you to good contractors, advise you about the contract, and help you avoid legal snarls and potential pitfalls. All this is in addition, of course, to the heart of his work drawing up plans for you. Without an architect you may have to pay a contractor for the plans needed for major work, so you might as well have it done by an expert.

An architect can do well for you when you are adding—not just altering—living space. Even when you are remodeling existing space, such as modernizing an old kitchen or bathroom, as noted below, an

A good architect can make all the difference in the world. This and the following photographs are remodeled houses designed by architect John Milnes Baker of Katonah, New York. The new addition for this two-story house blends perfectly with the basic house (at far left, next to the garage). *Photographs by Tom Crane.*

architect can help greatly. His touch can help you avoid a remodeled look by balancing improvements in the house so that they are integrated into one coherent design, instead of looking like separate structures, painfully stuck onto one another.

On the other hand, an architect is generally unnecessary when you make maintenance repairs, such as installing new heating or cooling, new wiring, a new roof, new wall siding, and so on. Then you are

A waterfront location and the shape of the site for this house virtually demanded that a portion of the new living space required be added with a second-story tower solution.

safe with a good contractor. A simple remodeled kitchen or bathroom also should not require an architect. That's when you're merely redoing the old kitchen or bathroom, in other words, replacing the old with new fixtures and other equipment without a major change in the basic plan.

If, however, you plan a whole new kitchen or bathroom, an architect's plan could help considerably. Sometimes a really good kitchen contractor can do well, but no one can equal the handsome, top-design results of a really good architect.

ARCHITECT'S FEES

The fee will obviously vary according to the scope of the work. To keep the cost down, blueprints may be all you need. Rough drawings and consultation can be done for as little as $250, on the basis of $25

The new addition (at right) fits the original design like a glove. The interior (page 56) is also shown.

to $40 an hour and depending on the amount of planning detail desired. The price goes up another step if you want complete specifications for all materials to be used. It is highest—from 15 to 20 percent of overall cost—if the architect provides day-to-day supervision. That's more than the 12 to 15 percent usually charged for a new house because remodeling is tougher work.

Use an architect who is experienced with remodeling work and likes it. A young architect associated with an architectural firm is often glad to take on remodeling jobs on his own time, for additional experience perhaps or for the love of the work until he can branch out on his own.

The names of architects who do remodeling can be obtained from the nearest chapter of the American Institute of Architects (AIA). Contractors and builders should also be able to recommend a few (though some builders and some contractors, not knowing the difference between good and bad design, will pooh-pooh the idea).

There are also architects to avoid. Some have a reputation for extravagance. Thus, the same care should be exercised in choosing an architect as in choosing a contractor or repairman. Ask for the names

of other people he has done work for, see them, and find out how well they fared. It's as simple as that.

When you hire an architect, sit down with him and say in detail what you want. Prepare a list in advance of everything you wish. If possible, get out the original blueprints of your house. This can save him much time and trouble, thus will save you money, too, as well as help avoid reconstruction problems.

The architect prepares preliminary sketches and plans for your approval, followed by finished plans and specifications. Minor corrections are made, if necessary. Then the plans and specs are given to contractors for bids. If a certain specification is unduly expensive, a good contractor may recommend an alternative.

Suppose you think the total bid is too high. Don't automatically blame the architect, since every square foot of space you want costs more money. A three-way conference with architect, contractor, and you can usually thrash out compromises. Then you are in the clear and the job should roll smoothly.

Caution: Avoid midstream changes during construction, as these can cost you dearly. Try to think of everything you need while the job is still in the planning stage. Changing your mind after the work has started can throw a monkey wrench into the schedule, regardless of how slight the change may seem to you.

Sometimes the contractor can accommodate you at little or no extra expense. But more often than not he has no alternative but to charge you accordingly. Thorough advance planning is highly important.

CHAPTER 7
TEN FUNDAMENTAL TIPS THAT SAVE YOU TIME AND MONEY

No matter what part of your house you plan to remodel or change, keeping in mind the following facts about how a house is designed and built—and rebuilt—can pay off handsomely.

1. *Use the existing space.* The quickest, easiest, and least expensive addition of new living space to a house obviously is by finishing off an existing but unused area such as an attic. It is economical because much of the necessary structure—the floor, walls, and roof—is already there.

Use your imagination. If the attic is too shallow to provide enough headroom, perhaps the entire roof can be lifted. This can be easier than it sounds. Of if you have a one-story house that's too small, adding a second story can often be done for less than the cost of adding ground level rooms.

The same principle applies when new space is added horizontally to a house. If you can enclose a corner of the existing structure, for example, only two new walls may be required rather than three. Or add to the existing house where little-used existing space can be given full-time use in the new addition. Simply add space adjacent to a large foyer, hall, or an oversized room where the existing space could be better utilized as part of your new rooms and thereby reduce the amount of new construction required. You may change the character or function of the old space, but so what? The test is whether it will serve you better.

Good design shows up in the entries of these two houses. Note how the windows and doors all line up with each other.

2. *Don't start work without a plan.* One of the most grievous disappointments with remodeling occurs after a new addition is attached to a house. A happy family treks outside to savor the grand new addition for the first time, but what they see may be a heartbreaking calamity—the new addition appears stuck out from the house like a third ear. Its style, architecture, and roof lines clash with the original structure.

This sad view is much less likely if a complete plan of the work is prepared in advance. This is essential not only for additions but also for many other remodeling jobs. If you do not use an architect, a good contractor will automatically prepare professional drawings before he starts work. You can see at a glance if the new extension blends with the house and particularly if the new roof will conform with the old. If things look awry, that is the time to make design changes. Some contractors build a sound structure but have little sense of style.

Here's a suggestion. Take pictures of your house, have them blown up, and sketch in changes you plan. Use a grease pencil, which is easily erased, and experiment as much as you wish. How do the changes look? Ideas will come to you simply by doing this. The cost is small, and it can be well worth the effort.

3. *New roofs, windows, and doors should conform with the old ones.* The style and architecture of an addition should be compatible with your existing house. A new roof that is a straight-line extension of the old is best for unity and cohesion and makes the house look larger than when the new roof is at a different level.

New windows and doors should line up with the tops and bottoms of the old ones. If smaller new windows are used, they should line up with either the top or the bottom of old windows.

One problem, generally unsolvable, is the achievement of a perfect match between the new and old roof shingles and siding. A good contractor will probably promise you no more than "the closest possible match."

Old roof shingles and walls fade and bleach with time. Even if the identical products and colors are used, their newness will make them look different. Furthermore, roof shingles and wall materials undergo small changes from year to year. The manufacturer's dye may differ slightly from one batch to another; a perfect match with his former product is literally impossible. Unfortunately, little can be done about this. When it happens, brace yourself, and don't be inconsolable. The new materials will gradually start to blend with the old as fading and bleaching take place.

4. *Determine the location of buried utility lines.* Before work is started on a new addition, find out where the water and gas pipes and wires are buried outside. It can be an expensive surprise if, say, the septic tank is later discovered under a new room. It will have to be relocated at no small cost. These things are usually shown on the original plans of a house. Sometimes, however, they were buried at a different location from that originally shown without the plans having been changed. If possible, locate all utilities.

5. *Don't freeze the bedroom location.* Every new bedroom does not have to be automatically added to the bedroom wing of a house. Another location may be better and less expensive. Don't blind yourself to such a possibility, especially for a new master bedroom. This may be better located on the side of the house away from children's bedrooms, particularly when children are beyond the infant stage. Architects do this in custom houses to assure privacy for parents and children alike. If you have infants, you can put in an intercom system to hear them at night.

A new family room or other room may be your chief need, and an existing bedroom may be the ideal location for it. Take advantage of its location, and add a new master bedroom instead, perhaps with its own study and bath; it can be attached to the bedroom wing or on the other side of the kitchen.

6. *Be sure that new work is permitted by local zoning rules.* Zoning rules generally call for a minimum of space left clear on all sides of a house. Setback requirements limit how close to the street you may build. Off-street parking for at least one car may be required, in addition to a garage or carport. Or carports may be barred altogether.

Some towns will not allow one-story or split-level construction. Some may dictate the architectural style. Others are zoned strictly for one-family houses, and an inspector will scrutinize any alteration that may look as if it could become part of a rented apartment. This generally bars a second kitchen, for example, and casts suspicion on any new room with a sink, running water, and gas or electricity service adequate for a range.

New work, therefore, should not be started until you are sure it is permitted. Consult local officials. Obtain a copy of zoning rules and building codes from your municipality. If your plan is rejected, you can appeal to the local zoning board for a variance. Reasonable requests are often granted. You are allowed to depart from the rules. You will have to appear at a hearing, and it can help to enlist the support of neighbors in advance or at least to sound them out for potential opposition.

7. *Obtain a building permit.* A building permit is required for most major alteration jobs and nearly all new construction. It requires filing an application accompanied by a construction plan. The contractor normally handles this for you unless you serve as your own contractor, and then you must do it. Allow at least a week for processing.

Not all remodeling, however, requires a permit. Finishing off a basement, redoing a kitchen or bath, new roofing, and a new heating plant are examples of work that usually do not require a permit. In general, work that entails a change or addition to the basic structure of a house requires a permit.

While a permit may not be required for new plumbing, wiring, and heating, they must nonetheless conform with local building codes, and often the work must be done by licensed contractors. The purpose of a building code is to assure safe, sanitary, and fireproof construction (although some old codes are obsolete and restrictive).

8. *Refer to the original plans of your house.* The original plans can be invaluable. If you don't have a set try to get them from the builder of the house if he is still around. Another source is your local building department. It may have plans on file for all but the most ancient houses.

The original plans can provide information on the construction details, the thickness of walls, and the size and location of the main beams, as well as show walls which should not be tampered with because they contain pipes or ducts that would cost big money to change (as noted below). This knowledge can help a contractor immensely. He isn't forced to bid in the dark on new work and therefore need not hike his price as a safeguard against unforeseen problems.

9. *Know which old walls can be altered or moved.* Some walls can be easily torn down or moved; others not. It depends primarily on whether a wall is load-bearing or not and what utilities may or may not be hidden inside it.

A load-bearing wall helps support the house above. Sometimes called a structural wall, it can't be moved without the risk of collapse. It can be eliminated, however, when it is replaced at the ceiling by a supporting beam of the proper size and strength. It is less expensive to move, alter, or eliminate a non-load-bearing wall unless, as mentioned earlier, it is one with ducts or pipes.

One way to identify a load-bearing wall is that it generally runs parallel to the longest outside walls at right angles to the floor and ceiling joists. A look in the attic or at the floor joists at the basement ceiling will tell you which way they run. Any wall in the house that runs at right angles to these joists is nearly always a load-bearing wall. This applies to interior partition walls as well as to exterior walls. Conversely, an interior wall that runs parallel to the joists is generally a non-load-bearing wall; it can be altered or removed.

The kind of house you have will also indicate the kinds of walls. In a rectangular house with a gabled roof, the long exterior walls support the roof, and the interior load-bearing walls run parallel to them and support the ceiling. Remodeling costs will be lower when these walls are left alone. The shorter exterior walls at the ends of the house together with the interior partitions parallel to them are usually non-load-bearing walls. They generally can be altered or removed at the least expense. This means that the most economical expansion of a gabled-roof house is adding to one or the other gable ends—i.e., extending the length of the house.

All four exterior walls of a house with a hip roof are load-bearing; they support the roof. Any interior wall parallel to the longer exterior walls is load-bearing. Any wall parallel to the two short outside walls is non-load-bearing. Adding a wing to any side of a hipped-roof house will therefore require some reframing of the existing house.

A wall that harbors pipes or ducts inside—a carpenter's nightmare—may be so expensive to alter that it's best to leave it alone. You can sometimes locate the apparatus without a Geiger counter by a look at the basement ceiling to see where pipes and ducts start upstairs. They are found in walls close to radiators and warm-air heating vents. Electric wires in a wall, on the other hand, ordinarily can be rerouted at small expense.

When exterior walls are torn down, salvage the doors and windows and as much of the rest as possible for the new addition.

10. *Save money by subcontracting work yourself.* Hundreds of dollars can be saved by doing your own subcontracting. A magazine editor I know who did this saved $500 on a bathroom remodeling job. He had a $2,400 overall bid from a "one-stop" contractor to handle the whole job; i.e., provide new fixtures, plumbing, glass shower stall, and ceramic wall tile, plus other such things as new electric fixtures, painting, and the necessary carpentry work. To save money, the editor decided to subcontract each part of the job by himself. In other words, he hired the plumber, tile man, electrician, and carpenter and scheduled the work of each. The bills for each added up to $1,900.

You also take over the chief contractor's responsibilities. You will expend much time and effort scheduling the various workmen. But you save what he would otherwise charge you for his time, office overhead, and other related expenses. This may run from 20 to 30 percent of the total cost. You can also save on other kinds of work, not just bathroom remodeling.

But be forewarned. You should be temperamentally suited to making many phone calls and to riding herd on a parade of workmen. You should be familiar with the work of each trade involved. This is where the knowledge and experience of a good overall contractor can be well worth what you pay him to handle the complete job.

It may be best, in fact, not to do your own subcontracting on a major remodeling job unless you are a contractor. Remodeling is a tough business that takes special knowledge and experience. It is, after all, akin to custom building. Even the most knowledgeable layman is not always equipped to do it. Moreover, when you deal directly with certain subcontractors, they are likely to quote you higher prices than they would otherwise quote a regular contractor.

Although sometimes it may pay to subcontract the work for a kitchen or bathroom, finishing off an attic or basement, or any other job that requires no more than three or four trades, extending a house or adding a new wing is a different matter. As many as ten to fifteen different trades will be involved, and you can easily overlook an essential one, or bring them on the job in the wrong sequence, or pick dumb workers.

PART THREE
Kitchens and bathrooms

There is much more to a good kitchen than shiny appliances and roomy cabinets. Is it planned for efficient and convenient food preparation? Are there adequate countertop areas and ample, well-designed storage areas? What about the quality of the cabinets, sink, faucets, countertop material, and appliances? Is the room pleasant and cheerful with plenty of air and light?

Even the most glamorous kitchens pictured in advertisements are often deceptive and poorly planned (because many are lavish but fake arrangements set up in a photographer's studio). The ingredients for a good kitchen break down into several major elements.

Knowing the basic guidelines is also important to get a good bathroom. The quality of fixtures, for example, varies immensely from the low side of poor to excellent. They are the heart of a good bathroom, though many people never realize how far short they fall here. This and other key points about bathrooms are included in this section.

CHAPTER 8

REMODELING
THE KITCHEN

The three main ingredients for a good kitchen are proper appliance location, adequate and well-placed countertop space, and plenty of storage for necessities near the point of use. It is not quite as simple as that, however, because of the expense involved and because limited size and awkward shape of the space you start with can make things difficult.

A couple I knew had such a problem. They ended up with a near-perfect new kitchen, later featured in a national magazine. But this was only after they had called in an architect and discarded five trial plans in a row before they hit on the sixth and final layout.

You need not hire an architect, but you should know the essential points of a good kitchen. But before we get into them and the layout of the kitchen components, an appraisal of kitchen location and size is in order.

A CENTRAL LOCATION

The importance of a central location has been noted earlier and should be repeated. The ideal location is one that is near the garage, near the family entrance to the house, near an outdoor patio or living area, and not far from the front door. That may sound like a tall order but isn't. The kitchen is a hub around which most family activities revolve. If your present kitchen is isolated at a rear corner of the house, say, perhaps it is worthwhile to move it to a better location. New plumbing will be the chief expense but need not be prohibitive, compared with the cost of changing pipes around at the present location. Wiring and lighting are another expense, but these costs will not vary much with location.

GOOD KITCHEN EXPOSURE

Is your present kitchen and dining room bright, pleasant, and flooded with sunlight during the day, especially in the morning? Or is it cast in shadows much of the day and perhaps later cursed with heat and glare? It depends on the exposure.

Southeast is generally best for kitchens and dining rooms. This will give you bright morning sunshine the year round. A kitchen facing the south gets less morning sun, especially in summer, but more in the afternoon. An east-facing kitchen gets only morning sun. A kitchen on the north gets little morning sun except in summer (which may be fine if you live in the South) and is exposed to cold winter winds.

A kitchen on the west or southwest is probably worst of all; it gets the most sun heat in the late afternoon, which can make it insufferably hot. Turning a poor exposure into a good one may be managed merely by moving a window, adding a new window, perhaps adding a ceiling skylight, or shading a big window exposed to hot sun.

IS YOUR KITCHEN LARGE ENOUGH FOR REMODELING?

According to a pioneering study at Cornell University, the minimum kitchen work area should be 96 square feet (12 x 8 feet or the equivalent). This is the minimum area needed to start with, excluding dining space. According to the Small Homes Council of the University of Illinois, the smallest work area for a U-kitchen arrangement is 8 x 10 feet. With a separate oven and dishwasher, the minimum should be 112 square feet (8 x 14 feet, for example.) These are minimums; try for more. An ideal size for most families is 175 to 250 square feet, or a room 12 x 15 to 20 feet.

THE ALL-IMPORTANT WORK TRIANGLE

Even the most glamorous kitchen can be a disaster because of shameful appliance scrambling (usually by men). They ignore a fundamental design principle—locating the refrigerator, sink, and range in that order in the form of the much-publicized "work triangle." It saves steps and conforms to the natural sequence of food preparation—from

Open planning and an overhead skylight bubble make this kitchen bright and cheerful. The ledge behind the kitchen counter shields the clutter of dishes at mealtime from people in the dining room. *Ernest Braun.*

refrigerator to sink center to range. It is the starting point, as well as the bedrock, of a good kitchen plan.

According to the Cornell study, the refrigerator-to-sink-to-range should form a triangle of between 12 and 22 feet all the way around. The ideal for most women is 16 to 20 feet—about 5 feet from the

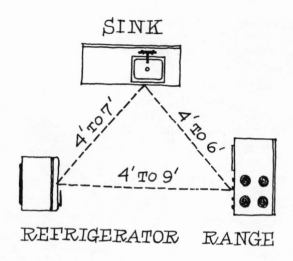

SINK

REFRIGERATOR RANGE

An efficient work triangle, formed by refrigerator–sink–stove, in that order, is essential for convenient cooking. The shortest to longest dimensions recommended are given.

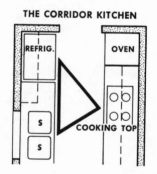

THE CORRIDOR KITCHEN

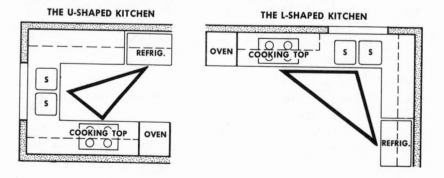

THE U-SHAPED KITCHEN

THE L-SHAPED KITCHEN

center front of the refrigerator (or refrigerator-freezer) to the center front of the sink; about 5 feet from the sink to the center front of the range; and about 7 feet from the range back to the refrigerator.

The space near the refrigerator is often called the mix center. The refrigerator door clearly should open toward the sink, and a handy countertop space at least 18 inches wide is needed for unloading food taken from the refrigerator.

The sink center, both a preparation and cleanup area, is the core of the kitchen. The dishwasher, the garbage disposer, and the main supply cabinets go here. Counter space at both sides of the sink is essential. The range or cooking center also requires counter space on both sides, as well as cabinets. Some experts say the sink should be placed under a window, but this is not essential, especially if this location disrupts the kitchen plan. A separate oven can be located in a less important area. It too should have counter space for hot dishes on at least one side.

WHAT IS THE BEST KITCHEN SHAPE?

The work triangle can form one of four basic shapes: the U kitchen, the L, the corridor or pullman kind on two parallel walls, and the one-continuous-wall arrangement, which is in effect a flattened-out triangle. There is also a fifth, the island kitchen, which has increased in popularity in recent years.

The U shape permits the best traffic and work triangles. It is compact and efficient. Every appliance is within a few steps of any other. The U adapts well to an open-plan kitchen. The L-shape kitchen is efficient and adapts itself to almost any space. The corridor kitchen can be good if it is not a passageway for people walking from one part of the house to the other; it is also inhospitable by its nature, not good for a family that likes to sit and talk in the kitchen. The one-wall plan should be your last choice because it is difficult to achieve an efficient work pattern and ample counter space with it. The island kitchen, not shown, is a compact plan that locates the range and its own adjacent counter on an island inside the room so that it forms a convenient triangle with the refrigerator and sink areas, each on a nearby wall.

THREE MOST COMMON KITCHEN FLAWS

A Small Homes Council study of the kitchens in more than 100 housing developments revealed the three most widespread flaws to be too

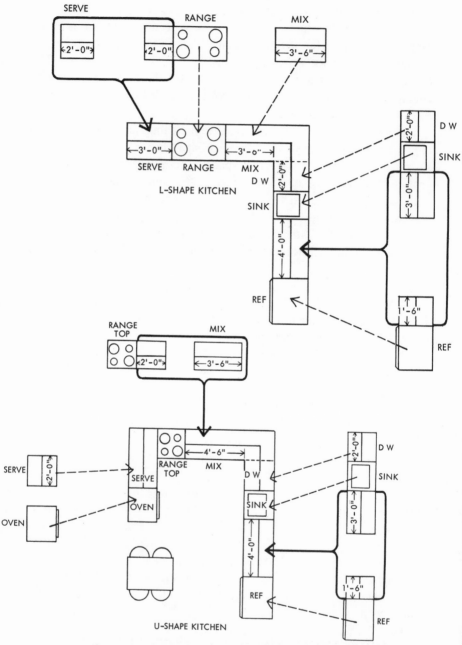

These diagrams show how the University of Illinois's design method is applied when a new kitchen is planned. When two or more separate counters are combined, the total counter length for the combination is the sum of the widest one plus one foot.

little cabinet storage, insufficient countertop space, and no counter at all next to the range. Here are the SHC's minimum standards:

• At least 8½ lineal feet of base-cabinet storage; 11 to 13½ feet is ideal. This includes the cabinets under the sink and the storage portion of the range.

• At least 5 to 8½ lineal feet of wall cabinets.

• At least 1½ feet of counter space on each side of the sink, on at least one side of the range, and on the open side of the refrigerator. The refrigerator door should open toward the sink.

NEW WAY TO PLAN A KITCHEN

With a new concept, developed by Professors William H. Kapple and Helen E. McCullough of the University of Illinois's Small Homes Council, anyone can lay out a good kitchen. It employs the work-triangle principle in terms of the five essential work centers and their required countertop space. It puts great emphasis on adequate countertop space, which is essential, and also emphasizes countertops because adequate storage space follows almost automatically in the space above and below adequate counters. You begin by knowing the minimum recommendations for the five work centers, as follows:

1. Refrigerator with 18 inches of countertop space on the open-door side.

Special note: At this point you must decide on a kitchen that flows either from right to left (thus, from refrigerator to sink to range, going counterclockwise) or from left to right. The right-to-left kitchen is generally favored simply because most people are right-handed. But don't be frozen with that flow if your refrigerator door opens the other way or if a clockwise left-to-right plan works better for you. The following steps illustrate planning a right-to-left kitchen. If you decide the other way is better, merely reverse the flow.

2. Mixing center, which consists of a 3½-foot counter next to the refrigerator, sink, or range.

3. Sink with 3 feet of countertop on one side, 2½ feet on the other (for dishwashing, food preparation involving water).

4. Range with 2 feet of heat-resistant surface at least on one side, preferably the left.

5. Serving center, which consists of at least 2 feet of countertop, preferably next to the range or, second best, next to the refrigerator.

Each of the above work-center recommendations is based on each center standing alone. In many cases two of them will be next to each other against the same wall. Then the adjacent surfaces are combined, and less total countertop space is needed.

A rule to remember when two or more adjacent work centers are combined is that shared countertop surface should be 1 foot more than the requirement of the larger.

For example, suppose your refrigerator center and mixing center are next to each other. The refrigerator center by itself requires 18 inches of countertop, the mixing center 3½ feet. When combined, the total required is 4½ feet (the larger, 3½ feet—plus 1 foot).

If the same two work centers are also combined with the sink center, a total of 4½ feet of shared countertop surface is still all you need between the refrigerator and sink. The same rule applies, this figure being obtained from the 3½-foot mixing center (largest among the three grouped together), plus 1 foot.

In similar fashion, all five work centers would be combined if grouped together against one long continuous wall (one-wall kitchen). Then the total countertop surface would amount to 10 linear feet for all five combined work centers. This is considered the minimum countertop space for an efficient kitchen. More is better. If you can, be generous. You will earn a rewarding bonus in an important room.

PLANNING A NEW KITCHEN STEP BY STEP

A process which may seem complicated at first soon becomes clear; the logic and simplicity are astounding. Start with the refrigerator, and go around the walls, adding each appliance and work center in sequence. If a door or any other nonusable wall space interferes, jump across it. Add the next required component on the other side. Remember that snags are inevitable, adjustments and juggling are to be expected. It's a trial-and-error process that depends on wall space, kitchen size, and shape. Here is how it's done step by step:

1. Draw a diagram of your kitchen to scale. Either ½ or ¾ inch to the foot works well. (Special pads of graph paper to simplify the work can be had at stationery stores.) Try for a U-shape or L-shape arrangement, though this, of course, depends on your kitchen shape.

2. Make scale cutouts of the five work centers, using the minimum counter dimensions given above. Typical appliance dimensions should be used, but these should be double-checked later against the appliance you get. A variation of even an inch or two can disrupt the plan.

3. Locate the refrigerator work center (refrigerator plus 18-inch counter) at the extreme right, the starting point. (Remember that this assumes the right-to-left sequence; reverse if you prefer left-to-right.)

4. Continue from right to left, adding each of the required work centers in sequence. Remember that total length of a shared counter when two or more work centers are combined is less than otherwise needed.

Thus, add the mixing center (3½-foot counter) to the left of the refrigerator (as you face it). If it is to be combined with the refrigerator counter, it will be a 4½-feet-long counter.

Add the sink center. If the right-hand counter is next to the mixing counter, a combination 4½-foot-long counter will serve for both. If your walls permit a continuous counter from the refrigerator to the sink, a 4½-foot counter is enough; more could help if you have space. If a dishwasher is included, it should be on the left side of the sink.

Add the range center: cooking range plus 2-foot counter preferably on the left side.

Add the serving center: a 2-foot counter after the range. If it is combined with the range counter, the total space needed for both is only 3 feet. If it cannot be placed here, put it next to the refrigerator, the second-best location.

Add a separate wall oven, if desired. It can go almost anywhere, since once loaded, it can be turned on and not demand much attention until the bell rings. A location near the range is best. It should not be next to the refrigerator because of its heat unless insulation is put between the two. Some counter space should be put on one side of a wall oven.

5. Consolidate your plan. If your kitchen lacks enough continuous wall surface to accommodate all the necessary centers, obviously something must give. It is best, however, not to trim a little here and a little there. Instead, group the work centers together with fewer separate units.

In addition, sometimes a door can be eliminated or moved. Perhaps a wall can be removed. Or a few feet may have to be added onto the kitchen by new construction. This should be your last alternative because of the expense. If no other out is possible, consider adding on new space to the kitchen by cantilever construction,—i.e., building out with no undersupport. The floor is extended out past the present exterior wall without a new foundation wall required below.

A new large window, facing south, makes this kitchen particularly cheerful. Open shelves (far left) put dishes within easy reach. The refrigerator end of the kitchen and the storage and serving counter are shown in the second photo. Cabinets are made with a rugged Formica skin, which wipes clean with one swipe.

Does the overall countertop length equal or exceed the required minimum of 10 feet? Check the size of the work triangle from refrigerator to sink to range to see that it falls between the recommended 12- to 22-foot overall perimeter.

6. The best location for storage cabinets is under the counter and on the walls. Use the minimum standards given. Obviously, cabinets should be located to store particular equipment and utensils near where they are used. Cabinets for dishes and tableware are best at the serving center, nearest the dining room. Storage at the mixing center should provide for such things as bowls, sifters, grinders, and mixers, plus flour, sugar, and spices. Sink storage should allow for dishwashing supplies, strainers, brushes, knives, and vegetables that don't need refrigeration. Pots and pans are most conveniently stored in the range.

SPECIAL NOTES

The standard countertop height is 36 inches above the floor. If you are short, a little lower, such as 34 inches, may be more convenient. Standard depth is 24 inches. Although most appliances conform to these dimensions, you need not be frozen to them. Some appliances also come in 30- to 34-inch heights. A baking and mixing center is often lowered to 32 inches for convenience. You could install a pull-out shelf or tabletop at this height. Sometimes to conserve space, counter depth can be reduced to 22 or even 20 inches. This shortest depth is squeezing it a little but may be unavoidable.

There should be at least 10 linear feet of base cabinets and 10 linear feet of wall cabinets. This counts "full-use" cabinets such as cabinets under the counter. It does not include part-use cabinet space, such as below a sink, drawers in a freestanding range, blind corner cabinets, or wall cabinets above the range or refrigerator.

Corners are often a problem. Base cabinets should be added around a corner (giving a continuous countertop around the corner) only if you gain cabinet space by turning the corner.

Peninsula and island cabinets are a good way to add base cabinets and extra countertop space. A peninsula cabinet sticks out at right angles from a wall cabinet toward the middle of the kitchen. It is worthwhile only if it can project at least 3 feet. An island counter-and-cabinet stands by itself in the middle of the kitchen. It should be at least 3 feet from the range and at least 3 feet from the nearest base cabinet. A serving table or counter on wheels often can be just as good, particularly if you don't have the space for a permanent island.

Other suggestions: shallow cupboards 8 to 12 inches deep built in the unused wall space around doors and windows (good for hanging pots and pans); the unused space above and below a built-in oven (but insulate it from the oven heat); high shelves to the ceiling above existing cabinets for infrequently used things; a long-shallow cabinet of perhaps 6 inches depth at the back of a deep counter.

Cabinets that face each other should be at least 3 feet apart. A dining table or snack bar should be at least 3½ feet from the nearest appliance or cabinet. Neither the refrigerator nor the wall oven should be put in the middle of a continuous countertop run.

CHOOSING A GOOD SINK

Specify a sink of stainless steel or enameled cast iron. Stainless steel does not chip easily; both are easy to keep clean and will last indefinitely. Steel will show water spots in hard-water areas, and you shouldn't take the word *stainless* literally; careless use can stain it.

Enameled cast iron requires scouring to kill black marks, its most annoying drawback. It looks fine but is often confused with the porcelain-on-steel sink, the cheapest, poorest kind. Porcelain on steel requires constant scrubbing, chips easily, and quickly loses its gloss. Avoid this kind. Try for a double-basin sink if you have the space, a boon for such things as draining dishes, though you may not want to sacrifice valuable counter work surface for it.

A good faucet

That means one that is easy to keep clean, keeps its luster and glitter, and doesn't drip like a head cold, always requiring a new washer or two. The single-lever ("one-armed") faucet has become standard. Its operating convenience and efficiency make the conventional double-control faucet as old-fashioned as a washboard. With a single-lever control, the right temperature and quantity of water are had with the touch of a finger. (You adjust the volume of water by pushing the handle back and forth. Moving the handle to one side or the other at the same time gives hotter or colder water. Scalding hot water is avoided by pushing the handle to the right setting before the water is turned on.)

Nearly all single-lever faucet brands are of good quality; some are top quality. But if you get the usual double-control conventional faucet, be careful to get a good one; nearly every manufacturer makes cheap, shoddy kinds as well as better-quality sets. See the section on bathroom faucets in Chapter 10 on how to tell the difference.

Regardless of the kind of faucet you get, almost all manufacturers offer special optional features: a spray hose attachment for rinsing (but look for a thumb lever that turns it on and off); a soap dispenser that will cough up soap on demand; and of all things, a separate dispenser for hand lotion or whatever else you might want dispensed at your fingertips. These features must be requested in advance so they will fit the other parts you are getting.

COUNTERTOP SURFACES

New countertop surfaces may gleam handsomely, but how long will they stay that way? Are they easy to clean, stainproof, and rotproof? It depends on the materials used. Here is a rundown of countertop materials in order of desirability.

A plastic laminate (Formica, Micarta, Panelite, for example) wipes clean with one swipe, will not stain or rot, and has good heat resistance to spilled boiling water. But hot pans can mar it, and knives may cut it. It should last at least twenty years if it is the high-pressure kind.

Sheet vinyl, lower in cost than a laminate, is easy to clean and quiet with dishes. Its chief limitation is poor resistance to heat. Hot pans will stick to it or melt it, and boiling water can damage it.

Linoleum is colorful, attractive, and heat-resistant but shows stains, scratches, and knife cuts. Because water can rot it, don't use linoleum near the sink.

Stainless steel is highly durable, stainproof, heatproof, easy to clean, and surprisingly resilient. But it is hard on knives (naturally), will show scratches, is noisy, and shows water spots.

There are also ceramic tile, marble, and wood. Chief features of the first two are good heat resistance and durability, but both are hard on dishes. Tile will not stain, but marble will. Both are easy to clean. Wood is best for a chopping center; it does not chip, crack, or dent, but it does stain easily. It will show heat-burn rings and should be kept rubbed down with a good sealing agent (hot mineral oil).

The ideal kitchen, therefore, would have a combination of materials: tile, marble, or stainless steel where hot pans are put down (range center); wood for chopping and food preparation (mix center); plastic laminate or vinyl for good looks and easy cleaning elsewhere and particularly around the sink. This combination is expensive but is best of all if you can afford it. The proper surface in the right place not only means low upkeep expense, less work, and longer satisfaction but is also a decided plus feature if you put the house up for sale after a few years. Then the kitchen will still look new.

STORAGE CABINETS

Choosing between wood and steel cabinets comes down to a matter of personal preference. Both are made in a variety of colors, styles, and quality. A few dollars more will give you a lustrous, easy-to-clean surface in either wood or steel.

Wood cabinets should have a hard, sprayed-on finish. Insist on cabinets made of kiln-dried treated wood, or warping may be a problem. The best finish on steel for low upkeep and long life is baked enamel. Steel cabinets should be "bonderized," a special treatment that increases durability; ask for it. A good cabinet will be made of cold-rolled steel at least 22 gauge in thickness (the lower the gauge number, the thicker). The drawers of both kinds should move in and out smoothly; they require metal slides and nylon rollers. A slight push zips the drawer closed with no hassle; this is a small feature perhaps but one that gives great pleasure every day. Drawers should not sag or stick when opened all the way. Magnetic latches and adjustable shelves are the desirable features.

LIGHTING AND WIRING

Good kitchen lighting is more than just a single bright, centrally located ceiling fixture. To work at the sink of a kitchen so equipped is to stand in one's own shadow. Illumination must spread to wherever it is needed: over the sink, above the main work surfaces, and under kitchen cabinets. Fluorescent light tubes are especially useful in the latter case, their shape, size, and even light distribution being advantages. Warm-toned tubes are preferred. The harsher cold tones are often hard on the eyes and have the unfortunate side effect of causing some foods to look unappetizing. There also should be at least two or three well-placed electric outlets along the wall behind the countertop for plugging in small appliances.

Visualize where your small appliances—mixer, toaster, knife sharpener, and others—will be used. Electric outlets should be located in the wall nearby, above the countertop level. New wiring normally will be required, along with new outlets, particularly because some appliances require heavier wiring than ordinary lighting outlets.

Good design will hold up for years. These cabinets were introduced in the 1950s by Mutschler Brothers of Nappanee, Indiana. They're still as modern as tomorrow.

Many building codes require special wiring for kitchen outlets. The wiring and lighting alone for a kitchen may cost from $150 to $400, more if it is an elaborate job. See Chapter 32 for other wiring tips.

REMOVING COOKING HEAT AND FUMES

A good exhaust hood located directly over the range, ducted to the outdoors, is the best way to keep the kitchen well ventilated. The hood should cover all or most of the burners. This normally calls for a hood about 20 inches deep from front to back and 3 feet wide. Locate it no more than 24 inches above the range, if possible. A higher location means diminishing ability to catch rising fumes.

The larger the air-blowing capacity of the fan inside the hood, the better. The minimum requirement is at least 40 cubic feet per minute (cfm) of capacity for each linear foot of hood length. Thus, a 4-foot-long hood should have a fan with a capacity of at least 160 cfm (4 times 40). Minimum air capacity for a peninsula or island hood is 50 cfm per foot of length. The fan should come with an HVI (Home Ventilating Institute) certification tag. It's best not to accept a hood without this tag.

The larger and thicker the grease filter inside the hood, the better. Compare the size and thickness of one brand with another when you shop. Be sure that the filter can be removed easily for cleaning.

A noisy fan can be quite bothersome. The amount of noise varies according to the brand and even the model. Gauge the noise by listening to the hoods run in a showroom before you buy. Better hoods come with variable-speed fans, a good feature to have. This permits you to cut down the speed (and noise) during light cooking.

Exhaust fans (no hood)
An exhaust hood can get rid of as much as 85 percent of cooking vapors. An exhaust fan by itself is only about 50 percent efficient at best, even less if it is too small or improperly located.

The fan must be located in the wall directly over the range, from 1 to 2 feet above the range surface, or in the ceiling directly overhead. Any other location is practically useless. A fan only a few feet to one side of the range or the other will catch no more than about 10 percent of what it should; the rest is ordinary kitchen air.

The fan should have minimum air-handling capacity of at least 300 cfm. The goal is a fan that can change the air in the kitchen every three to four minutes; 15 air changes an hour is an acceptable minimum. Figure the total air volume of your kitchen in cubic feet, and divide by 4 to determine the fan size required. A kitchen 12 x 15 feet with an 8-foot ceiling height therefore has 1,440 cubic feet (12 x 15 x 8). This, divided by 4, gives 380, the minimum fan size in cfm. A kitchen with 1,200 cubic feet of volume or less should have a minimum 300 cfm fan.

Exhaust fans and exhaust hoods create noise. The quietest are those with a low turning speed, which is measured in rpm (revolutions per minute) and is usually noted on the fan nameplate. Ratings between 1,400 and 1,750 rpm may be thought of as normal. The noisiest ones turn faster—as high as 3,000 rpm—and should be avoided.

To get a fan that is good as well as quiet, check for the HVI rating on the fan or in the manufacturer's literature. Also check its sones rating, a measure of its operating noise similar to decibel ratings (see Chapter 30).

A good trick for reducing fan noise is to locate the fan at the far end of its duct, as far from the range as possible. The grease filter, however, should be located at the inlet.

The problem of venting a hood above a range located against an interior wall can be difficult but not unsolvable. The fan could still be installed overhead with its exhaust duct inside the ceiling running between beams to the nearest exterior wall. This need not cost a lot, especially when carpenters are on the job for other work. There are also ranges that have built-in exhaust systems. At least one pulls your cooking heat and fumes *down* into an exhaust duct and filter.

Ventless hoods

Another alternative is the use of a ventless hood. Though they are less efficient than direct exhaust to outdoors, many people find them satisfactory. A ventless hood is basically a big filter that removes only smoke and grease from the air it processes. It does not get rid of heat and moisture, which are discharged back into the kitchen. Don't expect a ventless hood to cool the kitchen during hot weather.

The quality of a ventless hood depends most on its grease-filter efficiency and its fan air-handling cfm. The larger and thicker the filter, the better. Since there are no industry standards available for judging filters, you have to compare the size by thickness and density of one brand with another. Also compare cfm ratings; the more air handled, the better; but consider the noise factor, too. The hood size, of course, is also important. It should be large enough to cover all or most of your burner surface.

Odor removal

Some ventless hoods filter cooking odors. The only really good one is the kind that contains from 2 to 3 pounds of activated charcoal. The charcoal normally lasts about a year or two and then must be replaced. There are other kinds of odor-removal filters, such as an ozone generator, which is not as effective as the charcoal kind. In addition, authorities say too much ozone can be a health hazard.

Considering cost, the price of a duct built into the ceiling with a conventional exhaust hood could well make the duct a better choice (especially since heat, smoke, and odors are pushed outside). In addition, noise can be reduced by locating the fan at the end of the duct, as mentioned above. Unfortunately, there are no other solutions to the heat and smoke problem, short of putting the stove outside or eliminating cooking.

Operating tips

If you install a hood (exhaust or ventless) or an exhaust fan and it doesn't perform well, investigate the movement of the air being drawn into the fan. The air should sweep across the range before being drawn up into the hood or fan. There should be no open windows or open doors close to the range. Then the fan will draw air in from this easy source, bypassing the range and leaving cooking fumes untouched.

APPLIANCES

A bewildering number of new models and new features for old appliances are continually being introduced. Do shop and do keep your eyes open for special features you will like. But also be on guard for the eye-catching "sales" feature designed chiefly to sell an appliance and actually of little or no real worth.

Carefully visualize how a special appliance feature may or may not help. Why pay extra for a questionable gadget that has no real worth in your kitchen, even if it is ballyhooed in television advertising?

Quality and serviceability also vary greatly and may be hard to judge at first glance. Not only are certain brands better than others, but the quality and usefulness of one manufacturer's different models can vary greatly. As mentioned elsewhere in this book, just about the best guides to quality are *Consumer Reports* and *Consumer's Research* Magazine (but not even they are infallible).

Built-in appliances give a neat, unified appearance to a kitchen but may require more space and generally cost more than freestanding ones. With a limited budget, consider the use of refrigerators and ranges that are freestanding but have a built-in look. Of course, some of your present appliances can be incorporated in a new plan, with the layout adjusted to accommodate them.

The range

Choosing between a gas or electric range, assuming gas is available, is largely a personal decision, depending on which you like better, with one exception: Gas is much cheaper than electricity. Even though gas costs have risen and may continue to rise faster than electric costs, electric cooking will still cost considerably more than gas cooking for a long time. The reasons are given later in the energy section of this book.

In 1978, cooking with gas cost about $5 a month for a typical family, but an electric range cost about $20 a month, more or less. The exact cost figures for each kind of cooking vary according to your local cost for each energy, and this can fluctuate from one area of the country to another.

The cost of gas would therefore have to rise by some 400 percent before it costs as much as electricity for cooking. Since price rises that steep for gas are unlikely in the foreseeable future, cooking with gas should remain cheaper than electricity for a long time.

Cooking with gas is cheapest of all if gas is also used for home heating and water heating. Then your gas rate drops to a low category as a result of high use. That also applies for electricity; the more used each month, the lower your unit cost. With an all-electric house, your cost for an electric range can be lowest of all. Again, the exact cost figures for your family vary according to local utility rates. Making an accurate cost comparison between gas and electricity requires knowing your local rates. If you need help, call your friendly (I hope) local utility people.

Both gas and electric ranges are available in modern models that are convenient, fast, good-looking, accurate, easily cleaned, and automatic. Both offer built-in ranges and freestanding ranges. The built-in kind usually looks and fits in better. Built-ins with separate cooking tops and ovens are particularly popular for remodeling. The oven unit can be a single oven and broiler, a double oven, or an oven and independent broiler. The unit comes without top or side panels and is installed in a custom cabinet or right into the wall.

One kind of built-in is called a drop-in range. It is a one-piece range with counter-high surface burners and an oven below. It drops into a counter and fits over a base cabinet about as high as a conventional range storage drawer.

There is also a freestanding range called a slide-in. It looks like a built-in but is inexpensively installed. It is squared to fit neatly between adjacent cabinets, or at the end of a line of cabinets, or backed up to a cabinet of the same size. Optional side panels are available. Chrome trim on the sides can overlap the adjacent counters to give you a continuous countertop and keep spilled crumbs from falling between the range and cabinets.

The high-oven range is still another kind with a neat contemporary look. It can be hung on a wall or set on a special base cabinet. An eye-level oven and broiler are above the surface burners, which usually slide out. Panels for the top and side are optional.

Refrigerators and freezers

Refrigerators and freezers are in use all day every day, and that's why their cost of operation is among the highest of any appliance. A high-efficiency refrigerator and freezer can cut operating costs considerably.

High-efficiency means better insulation; the interior keeps cool longer. Less electricity is consumed. Its main electrical components are also better. That means the initial purchase price is higher, compared with regular models, but operating savings repay it within two or three years. All the savings every year afterward are your reward for initially having bought wisely.

A combination box, in other words, a refrigerator with a freezer compartment, requires less space than individual units. It's recommended when the freezer of a combination model is large enough for your frozen food needs.

If not, obviously a separate freezer would be better. Choosing between a combination model or a separate unit clearly requires evaluating your need for fresh food-storage space versus freezer space. Combinations are available with the freezer compartments at the top or bottom, and there are also new wide, vertically divided models with separate full-height refrigerator and freezer sections, each with its own door, side by side.

When there is a separate freezer in the kitchen, the refrigerator needs freezing space only for ice cubes, and perhaps not even for that. If the freezer is not located in the kitchen, you will probably want a freezer compartment in the refrigerator big enough for day-to-day needs such as frozen juices and vegetables.

Freezers generally require defrosting only a few times a year. Thus, a combination model may have an automatic defrost system only for the refrigerator portion and manual defrost for the freezer. The most advanced frost-free combinations and freezers have fans inside that circulate the air. This may mean an increased need to cover or wrap the foods in the refrigerator (foods in the freezer obviously should be well wrapped in any case). But no freezer space is lost to frost buildup, packages stay dry and easy to remove, and their labels stay legible.

When buying a refrigerator, be sure to specify which way the door should open. It should open toward a counter in the direction of the sink. Most units have a right-hand door, which means the hinges are at the right and the door opens on the left. You will want a left-hand door if your refrigerator-to-sink-to-range triangle is left to right (going clockwise). The same principle applies to combinations, of course, and also to a separate freezer, depending on where you locate it.

Dishwashers

The newest full-size dishwashers do an excellent job, providing automatic washing and drying, with hotter water than your hands can stand. They can be loaded in any order, at any time, thus keeping the kitchen free of clutter, and the machine is turned on when it has a full load. Other facts to know about dishwashers that follow may be old stuff to some readers, but they're included here for the benefit of those who are new to the kitchen and dishwasher scene.

You can eliminate hand rinsing of dishes before loading by getting a unit with an automatic prerinse cycle. All you do before loading is discard food waste. Many models contain booster heating coils to assure hot enough water. This is important because washing efficiency depends greatly on the use of hot—160- to 180-degree—water, which you may not have from your water heater or, for that matter, don't want that hot for the rest of the house. (See Chapter 23.)

Many models offer a choice of features. "Rinse only" is handy when you wish to hold a few dishes only for later washing. A "pots and pans" setting omits the drying phase so that sticky food particles stay soft and easy to remove with a scouring pad. A dishwasher with this setting gives you a head start on tough baking dishes, broiler racks, and so on, which you clean up later by hand. Dishes made of heat-sensitive materials such as plastics are safe in a machine with a "wash only" setting that does not go through the high heat of the drying cycle. "Fine-china" cuts the water force to protect good glassware as well as delicate china. (But it's still not advisable to put platinum- and gold-trimmed china or platters with overglaze decoration through a dishwasher.) Newer models have an air-drying setting, which washes but does not force heated air over the dishes, thus saving electricity.

There are built-in dishwashers, portables, and convertible models. The built-in kind is permanently installed in a 24-inch counter space with attached plumbing. The portable is rolled to its place of use. Its pipe is attached to the kitchen faucet, its drain pipe hooked over the sink, and its cord plugged into an electrical outlet. The convertible is the in-between model chiefly for those who want a dishwasher now but later want to build it into a remodeled or new-house kitchen. It is a full-size unit that will fit into a 24-inch cabinet space.

Food-waste disposers

A disposer grinds up waste and flushes the small pieces down the drain. It is usually installed directly under the sink. It lets you peel vegetables and fruits in the sink and push the peelings down the drain. It can also take such other waste as fat trimmed from meat, fruit pits, and any bones that will fit. Probably its biggest appeal is saving time by letting you scrape and rinse plates directly into the sink.

A disposer will not, however, handle such trash as paper, bottles and bottle caps, cans, and other such nonfood items. You still need a trash basket for wastes of this kind.

There are two basic kinds of disposers: the batch-feed model and the continuous-feed model. Garbage is loaded into the batch-feed kind, and a lid is put over the sink opening and turned to start the unit. A wall switch usually starts the continuous-feed kind, and waste is fed in steadily during operation. The continuous-feed kind is more convenient, though the batch-feed type may be desirable in a family with small children (as it cannot operate without its cover in place). Whichever you get, check the quality; it can vary considerably from brand to brand.

In other words, don't buy the cheapest one and expect it to work well, never act up, and last a long time. Because quality can also vary from year to year with model changes, it's difficult to provide specific buying recommendations here. Look into the latest recommendations in *Consumer Reports,* and as with other kitchen equipment, ask kitchen contractors which brands they have found to work best and give the least trouble.

There are also trash compactors which compress your garbage to roughly one-fourth its unmashed volume and are periodically emptied. They sell for about the same price as dishwashers, or from $250 to $400, plus installation. Though a handy gadget for fighting back at the growing mountain of trash to get rid of, a compactor is probably the least essential regular appliance required or desired in a kitchen. Besides, some manufacturers say not to toss food waste into theirs; others say no wet garbage; and certain other limitations should be known, depending on the brand you buy. Familiarize yourself with these beforehand. A compactor can be freestanding in the kitchen, or it can be built into a 15-inch-wide base-cabinet space under the kitchen counter. It's up to you.

Appliance design and looks

When shopping for appliances (and cabinets), seek out designs that are classically simple rather than elaborate. The simpler they are, the longer they retain appeal. Many elaborate kitchen styles tend to be fads that are fashionable for a few years, then quickly fade. They may look exceedingly new and different when you first see them in a showroom, but that's why they are there. Like tail fins on cars, they may have a few moments of great popularity, but you soon find that you could well do without curlicues, overdone hardware, and so on. If you truly like such things and know exactly what you want, fine. If in doubt, simplicity is the best rule.

DECORATING THE KITCHEN; PAINT
AND WALLPAPER

Obviously, the color, cabinet style, and overall decor you wish depend on personal taste. Light colors, even white, will make a kitchen look and feel bigger than it is. Conversely, dark colors make the room look smaller—quite small if you started with a small kitchen. In such a room, try off-white and, say, a speckled, light-colored floor, which camouflages dirt. Of course, light colors will also show dirt more quickly, so you may want a compromise.

Light, warm colors, such as yellow, are good for your kitchen if it receives limited sunshine. Avoid cool colors, such as blue, unless there is plenty of warm sunshine to compensate.

Paint or wallpaper in kitchens should be grease- and moisture-resistant and nonabsorbent to avoid picking up odors. It should have easy-cleaning properties so that grease and food spatters can be wiped off. Semigloss paint is a good compromise between enamel, which is easiest to wash but glary, and flat paint, which is pleasant but sometimes hard to clean. Any wallpaper can be treated to make it resistant to grease and moisture and easy to clean. But some allegedly scrubbable papers are merely treated, not vinyl-coated, and generally won't stand much scrubbing.

Some wallpapers come already treated. Better still, you can choose any paper you wish and have it given a treatment for resistance to grease and any other kind of dirt encountered (not only for the kitchen but for any other rooms).

COST OF A NEW KITCHEN
Don't launch a complete new kitchen unless you're prepared to spend at least $3,500 to $5,000, if not more. Unhappily, it costs this much, despite advertisements to the contrary.

For one thing, the prices you generally see in ads are for equipment only, a disposer, say, at $89.50, but it costs another $60 to install it. The cost of all equipment and cabinets, in other words, accounts for only about 50 percent of the total kitchen cost; the balance goes for installation, labor, and new wiring and piping, plus a variety of other installation necessities most of us do not think of.

For another thing, there are the notorious bait ads seen regularly in newspapers—for example, "Complete New 10-Foot Kitchen for $695!" Fall for this, and a slick dealer will unload a small pile of cheap kitchen cabinets on your doorstep, then demand another $1,500 to install them. The price goes even higher if new appliances are needed. Many of us feel that we would never be taken in by such larceny. Nevertheless, having seen such ads, we get a deceptively low idea of kitchen costs. We are later shocked when a reputable dealer quotes upwards of $3,500, which is actually a low figure for a complete kitchen.

Sometimes money can be saved if you buy the appliances yourself. You may be able to obtain them from an appliance dealer who will give you a special deal. But not always. A kitchen remodeler gets his appliances at a low wholesale cost and may add only a nominal markup. You could ask for a price breakdown of the work to be done with and without appliances, then compare it with the cost of appliances if you furnish them yourself.

The kitchen cabinets generally account for the biggest portion of the total price. By and large, a low bid for them generally indicates inferior quality. You'll be cursed with infuriating doors and drawers, plus poor finish and paint. This means that cabinet specifications should be carefully checked against the standards in this chapter.

Plumbing and wiring also cost money. The amount depends on how much of each is required for your kitchen. Plumbing costs are lowest when your existing water supply and drainpipes can be utilized with a minimum of alteration. Wiring cost is unpredictable. If much new electrical equipment is installed, it may be too much of a load for the capacity of your present house-wiring system; then a whole new and larger electrical service may be required. And then, of course, structural alterations, if required, are not done for nothing.

First get bids on the whole job installed in the ideal way you want it. If the cost is higher than you can pay, as is often the case, then begin shaving here and there. Ask contractors how they can best come down in price. What is expendable? What can be omitted at the greatest savings and then perhaps installed at a later time when you're back on your feet financially? Sometimes a minor change in the plan can affect a major price reduction by eliminating a knotty installation chore. But don't save pennies by compromising on quality products and easy-maintenance materials. What you save initially you lose several times over in increased service and upkeep costs.

When work starts on a new kitchen, your household will be disrupted, to put it mildly. Allow at least a week or two for completion, regardless of what the contractor may say. Your kitchen may be out of business even longer. Hook up a temporary stove in the dining room or at least have a few electric hot plates to fall back on. You could also arrange to leave children with nearby relatives or friends (and you can reciprocate when they redo their kitchens).

FINDING A GOOD KITCHEN CONTRACTOR

Some of the best kitchen designers and contractors are the members of the American Institute of Kitchen Dealers (AIKD), which includes a Council of Certified Kitchen Designers. Ask kitchen people you may deal with if they are members of one or the other. Or write to the

AIKD for its free directory of members. Its address is 114 Main Street, Hackettstown, New Jersey 07840. Send a stamped, return-addressed number 10 envelope. Another way to find a good kitchen contractor is via the old stock advice which is still valid: Ask everybody you know for the names of those who may have done a good kitchen for him or her. Before signing with a firm, call the Better Business Bureau about it.

CHAPTER 9

HOW TO REMODEL A KITCHEN AT LOW COST

Since the lion's share of a kitchen's cost goes for the cabinets, this is obviously where to start to save money. The trick, of course, is to cut costs without cutting essential storage. Anyone can save by knocking out cabinets here and there or by skimping on cabinet quality, the second false saving. "There's a tremendous difference in quality among cabinets," a veteran contractor told me, and his words rang in our ears when my wife and I planned the new kitchen that's the subject of this chapter.

Nearly everyone knows that good storage at the right places is essential, but not everyone realizes that it can also cut your food bills. It lets you buy large economy-size items and store them easily. In addition, ample storage and well-arranged shelves and cupboards, as well as refrigerator and freezer space, all make it easier to store food items in a logical way. Then a half-used can of filetmourette won't turn up rancid six months later behind the macaroni or the dried beans.

When we remodeled the old kitchen of our second house, our biggest savings were made by providing considerable storage capacity with a minimum of conventional full-fledged cabinets. We provided essential storage at certain locations in three other big ways. First, we installed sheets of pegboard on the walls, with plenty of hooks chiefly above the countertop, for frequently used items that we need within arm's reach. These include our black iron frying pans, which hang above the range, and little things like the colander, can openers, corkscrews, and lemon squeezer. Clearly, the more kitchen

Open shelves and pegboard hangers over the range put dishes and pots within handy reach and cut remodeling costs. More open shelves are on the opposite wall, though not shown.

items you can hang on the wall (and by the windows), the less you need spend for conventional storage space. Besides, these visible implements are often attractive displayed this way.

Secondly, we saved by keeping expensive cabinets to a minimum and providing a large amount of storage capacity with open shelves. Open shelves worked well in our first kitchen for many dishes in daily use, and we exploited this idea even more the second time around. The shelves, shown in the accompanying photographs, accounted for one of the biggest savings.

The third economy was a tall, roomy pantry cupboard, freestand-

The other half of the kitchen shows how the refrigerator begins the work-triangle sequence. A drawback of this kitchen is the chopped-up windows with 12 glass panels each. They cut down light entry and are a big, time-consuming cleaning bore.

ing against the wall opposite the sink. It is 20 inches deep and 30 inches wide and contains adjustable shelves behind two swing-open doors. Attached at one side and accessible from the side are open shelves 10 inches deep and 12 inches high. This open cabinet is as tall as its pantry cupboard mate in front. The cost per cubic foot of this piece is lower than that of standard cabinets, and it gives absolutely maximum storage space per square foot of floor space.

Now back to the basics. Top priority for efficient storage is locating the right kind needed in the right place. For example, our pots and pans are stored in the range area; plates, trays, and table silver are stored where they are needed for final assembly of a meal preparatory to serving. You don't compromise on these basics without compromising kitchen efficiency. You can, however, include adequate storage and countertop without going overboard. By necessity our kitchen planning took that tack.

Good cabinet design and construction were requirements on which we also refused to compromise. We paid roughly 20 percent extra to have all the cabinets (including the freestanding piece) finished with a rugged plastic laminate surface (same material as tough countertop plastic), and we specified topflight hardware, such as nylon rollers that slide in and out freely. Such features had paid off handsomely in our first kitchen in thoroughbred performance. The plastic laminate cabinets, for example, are easy to keep clean and retain their good looks virtually forever (which is why I laud them, as well as other things like nylon rollers).

COST BREAKDOWN

Here is the cost of the different parts of the new kitchen in 1974 when it was installed:

Eight kitchen cabinets and countertop (13 feet), including installation	$2,332
Dishwasher and electric range (existing refrigerator kept)	$ 602
Plumbing and wiring for sink, dishwasher, range, new electric outlets, and overhead light	$ 675
New vinyl flooring, installation	$ 225
Carpentry and installation of freestanding cabinets	$ 91
Miscellaneous: new sink, faucet set, light fixture, perforated hardboard	$ 150
Total cost	$4,091

As you will note, the kitchen cabinets and related countertop surfaces account for nearly 60 percent of the total cost. If you order cabinets but install them yourself, you can save about 15 to 20 percent of the total cost. If you build the cabinets yourself, in addition to installing them, then, of course, you save a much larger chunk of the total cost. Virtually your only expense is for materials, including hardware.

The plumbing and wiring costs were disproportionately high partly because new wiring had to be installed for the electric range. In addition, new plumbing was needed for the sink because the new sink was relocated to give more table space. Lesson: Whenever possible, locate a new sink at or near the position of the old one and you will save considerably on hook-up cost.

I am no six-thumbed slouch at pitching in with do-it-yourself savings. I installed the pegboard, various pieces of wood trim, and miscellaneous items, and my wife did the painting, all of which nearly any homeowner can do. That knocked several hundred dollars off the remodeling bill. You will also feel good as a result of having provided part of the actual labor for your kitchen.

I also served as my own contractor for the plumbing and wiring hookups. I found and hired an electrician and plumber and made the necessary plans and arrangements for each to do his work. That took pressure off the kitchen contractor, leaving him free to concentrate on what was the main part of the job. Self-contracting saved roughly 25 percent of the cost of the wiring and plumbing. If the responsibility had stayed with the kitchen contractor, he would have charged that much more.

CHAPTER 10

HOW TO GET A GOOD NEW BATHROOM

The old adage about getting only what you pay for applies to the bathroom more than to any other room or nook of a house—if you know when to stop.

Three main fixtures are all you need for a bathroom, but like kitchen cabinets, great differences in quality exist in each. This requires attention if you want a bathroom that will perform long and well. The nice thing is that the extra price of good-quality fixtures need not be large.

I discovered the big difference between good and not-so-good bathroom fixtures when a new bathroom was put in my first house. To cut costs, I got the lowest-priced products—and later paid the piper. The faucets and fixtures in that bathroom soon began to tarnish, to show obvious wear, and to balk in operation. They were impossible. That was especially true for the noisy, low-cost john, an example of primitive design that has not changed since the Spanish-American War.

Later I remodeled another bath, but forewarned by experience, I concentrated on getting topnotch, though not necessarily top-price, products. Shopping knowingly paid off. To this day, long after their installation, all the parts of that bathroom continue to glitter and perform like champions.

Like many other building products, most bathroom parts are made and sold in three grades of quality. Advertising copywriters call them good, better, and best. That translates into a bottom-of-the-line (lowest quality), middle-of-the-line, and top-of-the-line versions of each product. Avoid the stripped-down bottom-of-the-line product like the plague. It is generally identified by being called a builder, economy, or competitive line. The few extra dollars required to step up to middle-of-the-line quality can mean a surprising improvement in durability and performance. The next step to the top-quality, premium line may not be worth it, however.

Many times, but not always, buying well-known national-brand bathroom products offers some protection. It depends on the product. Competition sometimes compels big-name manufacturers to add low-priced, stripped-down models at the bottom of their lines. Unfortunately, stripping out some desirable quality is often the only way to do it.

It is unwise to leave the choice of fixtures to a plumber. For one thing, most plumbers tend to stick with all the standard product lines of one manufacturer even though new products of other manufacturers excel for a particular job. For another, many plumbers, like manufacturers, are compelled by long experience and past losses to keep their prices down by providing low-priced products. It's occupational conditioning. It falls on each of us to learn a bit about bathrooms before we remodel, the purpose of this chapter. It will help you decide exactly what you want. But first, you should know a few facts about bathroom planning.

A NEW HALF-BATH

It's euphemistically called a powder room and is considered almost a necessity, particularly on the first floor of two-story houses. But finding a good location for it can be a problem.

A good location might be right before your eyes. An area as small as 24 x 42 inches will provide minimum space for a toilet and washbasin. A friend of mine proved it by converting a small closet into a half-bath.

Look around your house, and don't limit your examination to the outside walls. There are still a few places where obsolete building codes may require a window, but most codes now permit an interior location with forced ventilation by means of an exhaust fan or ceiling skylight.

When looking for a location, don't be blinded by existing walls. Determine whether enough of the wall can be moved or altered easily to permit a small half-bath. If not, and appropriate unused space is not apparent to the eye, consider building it into the corner of a large foyer, say, or an expendable corner of a nearby room. Space for a full new bathroom should be at least 5 x 7 feet, inside dimensions, as an absolute minimum.

HOW TO KEEP THE COST DOWN

Locate the new bath close to existing plumbing lines as previously mentioned, to reduce installation costs. Best location is above or below another bathroom or close to the kitchen pipes. It is particularly important to try to use the existing bathroom-pipe vent, if possible. A new vent is expensive.

The vent is usually a 3- or 4-inch diameter pipe for exhausting waste gases and can be seen coming out of the roof above an existing bathroom. Some plumbing codes let you use the same vent for a new bathroom, saving the cost of a second one. Managing such economy will depend on the new bathroom location and fixture arrangement. Discuss it with your plumber. Can he save you money by connecting to the existing vent?

LOCATION VERSUS CONVENIENCE

A new bathroom obviously should be accessible to the rooms around it. Several points about bathroom location, noted earlier, should be emphasized again. Access to a bathroom decidedly should not require passage through a bedroom unless the new bathroom is designed as a master bath. This is a major blunder.

Even worse is a location that requires passage through the bathroom, of all things, to reach another room, thus effectively locking up the occupants of the shut-off room. This was done to a house I know. After it was remodeled, access to one of three bedrooms was possible only through the main bathroom. It is a glaring defect that kept the house from being sold later, until its price was lowered.

The same rule generally applies to the location of a master bathroom. We like to think of the master bathroom as a luxury for privacy, so it is often isolated next to the master bedroom, where guests cannot use it. Guests end up in the children's bath, which is often a mess. Locating the master bath off the center hall, instead, and making it off limits for kids avoids conflict. It also obviates the hectic last-minute cleanup of the children's bath when guests are expected or, unhappily, arrive unannounced. You may not have children to contend with, but if you decide to sell someday, a prospective buyer might well have half a dozen kids. So make the master bathroom accessible.

INTERIOR PLANNING

A full bathroom should be large enough to accommodate two people at once. Though a 5 x 7 bath will do if planned well, this is generally the smallest space you can get away with (and is the usual size of the small bathroom in many builder houses).

Remodeling an old bath does not mean that you are restricted to the same fixture location as before. Many bathtubs are thoughtlessly put under windows, causing exposure to chilly drafts, as well as the need to be an acrobat to open or close the window when not in the tub. Keep a tub or shower stall away from the window. It is best, in fact, when no fixture is located directly under a window.

The position of the washbowls should not interfere with traffic through the room. They need plenty of light, and the more space you give them, the greater the countertop area possible on each side. The two washbowls in tandem is a good way to solve the morning rush-hour problem; sometimes it can also be a low-cost alternative to adding another bathroom. As for the toilet location, it may be objectionable if it can be seen when the door is open. Put it out of sight if possible.

CHOOSING GOOD FIXTURES

The big three are the bathroom sink, or lavatory, the bathtub, and the toilet. Each comes in three basic grades of quality. Knowing this can help you avoid a peck of trouble later owing to chipping, leaking, noisiness, and balky operation.

The bathroom sink

Good, better, and best here boils down to a sink made of enameled steel, the bottom of the line; enameled cast iron, the middle; or vitreous china, the top. A steel bowl is least desirable because it is difficult, if not impossible, to fuse a durable enamel finish onto steel. It's only a matter of time before the finish begins to pop off.

Porcelain enamel, a form of melted glass, is the finish on both steel and cast-iron bowls. It adheres to cast iron much better than to steel, so a cast-iron lavatory bowl has a far more chip-resistant and hence permanent finish. Cast iron is especially recommended in a child's

Left: A spacious countertop is much appreciated in a bathroom. Large sliding mirrors enhance the size of the room and cover a built-in medicine cabinet. *Tile Council of America.*

Right: Rough vinyl plastic skin provides an excellent waterproof countertop for this custom-made lavatory. A cabinet like this can be designed to fit any space and can be inexpensively made. The opening is put in the middle to receive whatever bowl you choose. *The Building Institute.*

bathroom, for its ability to shrug off a lot of tough knocks without showing them (this is why it's often specified for schools and hospitals).

The vitreous-china bowl, the top of the line, is not necessarily as chip-resistant as enameled cast iron, but it's still very tough indeed. It is a premium item chiefly because of its gleaming finish and handsome looks. It's also more versatile than cast iron because it can be formed into a greater variety of shapes and sizes and costs only a few dollars more than cast iron.

A china bowl is generally your best choice, and enameled iron is next best. Whichever you choose, don't be cursed with a mini-size bowl. Some are so small that merely washing your hands can bruise your knuckles, as well as being too small for washing your hair or bathing a new baby. Once it's hooked up you're stuck with it. Yet the price difference between a luxuriously large 20-x-24-inch bowl and the smaller but commonly sold 17-x-19-inch model is as little as $10.

First choose the particular shape and size you want. Availability may dictate the kind you choose. Many of the appealing new round and oval bowls, for example, are available only in vitreous china.

A washbowl can be bought separately and then mounted in your own countertop or lavatory cabinet. Most manufacturers offer lavatory cabinets (vanities) complete with countertops and drawers. Or you can draw up your own plans and have a complete cabinet or wall-hung lavatory made to order. This need not be expensive. The cost of my custom-made 32-inch-wide cabinet was less than $100. It includes a large center hamper drawer, plus a gleaming sprayed-on paint job; the cost of the bowl and faucet set was extra.

There are also pedestal lavatories. These are simply the commonly used sink-plus-floor-pedestal support. Some kinds are mounted on the wall and also may have a pair of vertical leg supports. The pedestal lavatory requires the least space.

The bathtub

Bathtubs are traditionally made of enameled steel or enameled cast iron. Tubs are not made of vitreous china. The material doesn't lend itself to such large size moldings except at prohibitive cost. Enameled steel tubs are lowest in price and ought to be adequate, provided they are not subjected to rough use. They can be manhandled into place and installed by one person, an advantage in do-it-yourself installation. Cast-iron tubs require two men for installation. List price of the typical enameled steel tub is about $100 to $125. The cast-iron tub is usually a better buy because of its durability and superior resistance to chipping. It costs about $100 to $150 more than a steel tub. There are also tough plastic tubs and sinks, described later.

Often, when a spanking new tub is installed, people unhappily discover that it's too small, too shallow, or both. That's because the typical tub is 30 inches wide, 14 inches deep, and 4½ or 5 feet long. Consider stepping up to a larger size—at least 32 inches wide, 16 inches deep, and 5 feet long. The increase may seem small, but it can make a big difference in bathing comfort, including the bathing of

This tile bath and shower was located in limited space, as shown. A rectangular tub with a seat works out very well. *The Building Institute.*

children, and it can also mean less water splashed on the floor. An optional feature worth having is a slip-resistant tub bottom.

To cut costs, many manufacturers have cut the depth of their tubs down to 14 inches and even 12 inches, which is low; it hardly comes off the floor. Shallow depth is usually what you will get unless you specify a standard 16-inch depth. This is practically mandatory if you like tub baths and want to avoid wild splashing over the floor, especially with children. A square tub can be satisfying, especially if it is large enough and has a seat at one or both ends. Most families need one at least 4 feet square but end up with a smaller thing hardly larger than a washbowl.

Bathtubs come in as many different colors as a rainbow. A colored

A luxury bath with an adjoining atrium requires money and taste. *Tile Council of America.*

tub will generally cost 5 to 10 percent more than the same tub in white. Tubs are also available in a variety of models designed especially for the person who believes in luxury bathing. There are tubs with body-contoured shapes, reclining back designs, and beveled headrests, and if you're really a Roman bather at heart, there are large ultra-deluxe tub "pools" of up to 4 x 6 feet in size. The deluxe tubs range in price from about $300 to $750, depending on size and special features.

The toilet

There are three basic kinds of toilets, according to government standards for plumbing fixtures:

The wash-down toilet: This is the aboriginal toilet, unchanged since the Spanish-American War. It's the bottom-of-the-line model. Its small water surface (56 square inches minimum) and shallow water seal (2½ inches from water surface down to drain) mean it needs frequent cleaning and leaves much to be desired for sanitary reasons. It's also prone to clog because of its small (1½-inch) water outlet.

The small-diameter outlet and primitive overall design mean it is noisy, too. Toilet noise is chiefly caused by water rushing through narrow passages. So the smaller and narrower the inlet and outlet paths, the louder the noise. A wash-down toilet is easy to spot: The water drains out the front of the bowl. Some building codes now prohibit the wash-down, and fortunately, it's being phased out by many manufacturers. But there are still many of them available in the supply channels, so take care to avoid them.

The reverse trap: The middle-of-the-line model flushes water out through a rear trap—thus, its name. It is cleaner, more sanitary, and more efficient than the wash-down because of the greater water surface, deeper water seal, and large-diameter drain passage. Larger passages also make it quieter.

There are, however, marked differences among brands. Some have a greater-than-minimum water surface, larger-than-minimum drains, and a better flush mechanism.

Prices range from about $60 to $150, depending on the brand, the quality of flush mechanism (a look inside the tank will tell you this), and the degree to which a model exceeds the minimum government standards.

Siphon jet: This is the quietest and most efficient toilet. Flush action is excellent, because water from the tank is discharged through jets located around the top rim of the bowl. Also called a quiet-flush unit, it is identified by its one-piece construction and its low-slung shape. Prices start at about $150 and go up to about $400 for the super-deluxe models.

Incidentally, no matter which toilet you may like, checking on its operating noise may be difficult because you seldom can hear one work in a showroom—it is not hooked up. You have to take someone's word. But what may seem quiet to a plumber may be noisy for you. Keep your eyes out for a good one. Make a special note when you see a quiet model in the home of a friend or relative so that you can get the same kind. Also note those that are particularly noisy so you won't get that kind. If you can afford the best, the quietest as well as most efficient, no question about it, get a low-slung, one-piece, top-of-the-line siphon jet.

There is also a handsome wall-mounted toilet which hangs entirely above the floor. It eliminates the big floor-cleaning problem encountered around a conventional toilet. This kind can also be comparatively quiet if you get the right brand; some wall-hung brands, on the other hand, are noisy. The quieter kinds are identified by their low-slung tank and one-piece construction. A conventional high tank, separate from the bowl, is the tip-off to noisy operation, sometimes as loud and noisy as the cheapest wash-down toilet. Check this in advance. Incidentally, a wall-hung job can be installed in new or old houses. The wall may require some beefing up (with 2 x 6 framing), but this is seldom a problem.

Left: Low-slung, one-piece construction is a characteristic of this premium toilet that flushes with virtually no noise. This model also includes self-ventilation action that flushes odors, too. *American-Standard.*

Right: Lightweight fiberglass-reinforced bathroom fixtures like this tub are easy to install and also provide rugged service. *Universal-Rundle.*

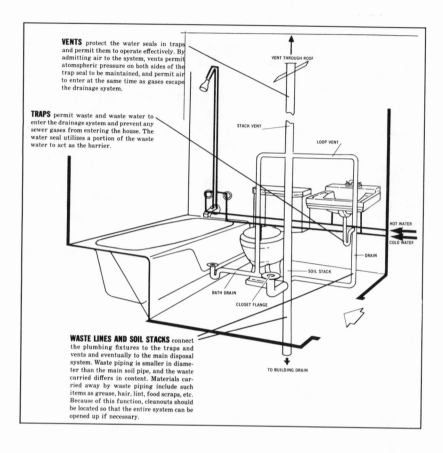

VENTS protect the water seals in traps and permit them to operate effectively. By admitting air to the system, vents permit atomspheric pressure on both sides of the trap seal to be maintained, and permit air to enter at the same time as gases escape the drainage system.

TRAPS permit waste and waste water to enter the drainage system and prevent any sewer gases from entering the house. The water seal utilizes a portion of the waste water to act as the barrier.

VENT THROUGH ROOF

STACK VENT

LOOP VENT

HOT WATER

COLD WATER

DRAIN

SOIL STACK

BATH DRAIN

CLOSET FLANGE

WASTE LINES AND SOIL STACKS connect the plumbing fixtures to the traps and vents and eventually to the main disposal system. Waste piping is smaller in diameter than the main soil pipe, and the waste carried differs in content. Materials carried away by waste piping include such items as grease, hair, lint, food scraps, etc. Because of this function, cleanouts should be located so that the entire system can be opened up if necessary.

TO BUILDING DRAIN

Like the floor-mounted quiet-flush toilet, the wall-hung toilet is also more expensive than standard models. But nearly every delighted owner of one or the other says it is well worth the expense.

Like cars, toilets come with optional features that can be worth having. These include an elongated bowl shape that is generally better and more sanitary than a round bowl, so specify it. Self-ventilating bowls are also available; they're especially good for an interior bath. And there is the water saver, the toilet which uses roughly one-third less water per flush than regular models. If you have high-cost water, this can make quite a dent downward in your water bills, since toilet flushes account for the major portion of most families' water use.

Water spigots, faucets, and shower heads
These are called the fittings or bathroom trim by the trade. They are
taken for granted by nearly everybody else, and we are then cursed
with trim that quickly tarnishes or rusts, bathroom drip, and the constant need to replace washers. Getting faucets that will operate long
and well is important because they are subject to harder and more
frequent use than almost any other part of a house (except a swinging
door in a house full of kids).

But you can't count on getting good faucets and other trim simply
by ordering a good bathroom sink and tub. Fittings are ordered and
shipped separately and are not always made by the manufacturer of
the fixture to which they will be attached. Like other parts of a
bathroom, faucets also are made and sold in three quality grades,
low, high, and luxury.

Avoid the bottom-of-the-line, cheapest faucets and trim for two
reasons. First, they are usually made with quick-to-wear-out rubber
washers and valves, so they soon drip like a head cold. They always
seem to need new washers, not to mention frequent regrinding of the
valve seat.

Secondly, these bottom-line faucets and trim (meaning water
spouts, hand bars, and other metal appurtenances) are made of a relatively soft alloy—usually zinc—and then given a thin coat of chrome.
They may shine in the showroom, but once put to use, they begin to
tarnish as quickly as they drip. There are exceptions, but you can
generally spot the cheapie faucets by their handles, which have two
or more spokes radiating out from the center, like a wheel. With a
few exceptions, the better kinds have solid handles, with a ridged cir-
cumference for gripping.

Good faucets and trim, the middle-line kind, cost only a little more
than the cheapest, yet will give you high-quality performance. They
are made with a much better water valve that does not use a questionable rubber washer. Some manufacturers use a tough ceramic disk;
others use a hard plastic mechanism. These are usually guaranteed for
five to ten years. You'll never need a valve-seat grinder to smooth
out the valve core to stop a leak.

If the valve seat does go bad, you merely replace it. That's a key
thing to remember when you buy: Purchase only faucets that come
with replaceable valve seats. These better faucets and trim are also
made with bodies of solid brass. Visit a plumbing supply showroom,

and the dealer can quickly show you the difference between tough, well-made brass faucets and the lightweight, cheapest kind. Though made of brass, the better variety will have a permanent copper-nickel-chrome finish. A tough protective coating is applied in the factory over the brass body. This gives a durable finish that will not tarnish and requires infrequent cleaning.

The exterior appearance still may vary. There is a wide choice of colors and degree of luster, suitable for virtually every decor—brushed satin, polished gold or chromium, or highly polished brass.

Most manufacturers do not stamp their names on their lowest quality products. Knowing this, you can avoid the lowest grade.

Good faucets for bathrooms include single-lever models, similar to those used in kitchens. Almost all have a replaceable valve. The really top-notch ones cost a few dollars more. One of the best is the Moen single-lever. When shopping, compare the length of the guarantee and how much repair work and expense are involved if the valve must be replaced. Styles and designs of single-lever faucets vary greatly. You will have no trouble finding one you like that fits the decor of your bathroom.

Stepping up to top-of-the-line, deluxe faucets is not worth the extra money just for extra operating quality. Most premium-price faucets are made mechanically identical to the middle-line faucets noted above. The extra price for deluxe faucets is chiefly due to their special styling and appearance. For the final word in luxury, there are even models that are gold-plated. Be prepared to pay as much as $300 or more for such styling and looks.

Incidentally, you need not accept a particular kind of faucet with a particular bathtub or sink just because you saw both together in a showroom. Nearly any other faucet set will be interchangeable and can be specified. (This is also true of shower heads.) They should, however, be sized to fit your tub and bowl, but your plumber can handle this. Standard dimensions prevail, so this is seldom a problem.

Shower nozzles

A good-quality shower nozzle will not clog or corrode. It has a flexible ball joint to adjust the spray direction. It should also have a control that enables you to obtain a fine or coarse spray or anything in between. There are new varieties of heads that deliver a water massage. If you have hard water, a self-cleaning head is another good feature. The cheapest kinds have a rigid head (which cannot be adjusted) and little or no volume control.

Because water, like energy, is becoming increasingly scarce and expensive, getting a shower nozzle that is not extravagant with water may be important. Nozzles that may look alike can spray as little as 3 gallons of water a minute or up to two to three times that much discharge. Obviously, that can make a difference in your water bill. So check water ratings, too. And be sure to specify an adjustable nozzle that will allow you to vary the water rate, as well as the spray. Ordinarily, an adjustable nozzle with a top rating of 3 to 7 gallons a minute is satisfactory.

SAFETY MEASURES IN THE SHOWER

You won't easily get burned in the shower if it's fitted with two desirable safety features: an automatic temperature control and an automatic diverter valve. The first will save you from water suddenly turning scalding hot, or ice cold, in the middle of a shower, a frequent result of somebody else in the house opening a tap drawing hot or cold water away from the shower.

The basic cause of this problem is low water pressure. It may be due to low water-main pressure on your street, an undersized water supply pipe and meter to the house, or undersized, clogged, old pipes inside the house. But correcting one of these may be impractical or too expensive.

You will never have this problem if the installation of a temperature-control valve is specified. The shower nozzle is automatically kept at a constant temperature; hot or cold water cannot suddenly spurt from it. One kind uses a special pressure control valve (which is what to ask for), while another more expensive kind is called a thermostatic mixing valve.

When you first step into a combination bathtub-shower with a manual diverter, you may be surprised by water cascading down from the shower head, instead of the tub spigot. That happens if the last person to shower forgot to reset the control. This must be done every time the shower is used. Otherwise, the shock of the unexpected water on you, even if it is not hot enough to scald, may cause an involuntary recoil that could lead to a fall and injury. Because the result of human forgetfulness can be serious, the manual diverter is a booby trap that should be outlawed. Unfortunately, many are sold and installed because they cost a little less than automatic ones that are much safer.

You should specify an *automatic* diverter control. This kind automatically switches the water supply back to the tub spigot each time the shower is turned off. It is obviously safer, but costs a little more.

NEW PLASTIC FIXTURES

These are rigid fiberglass and acrylic plastic lavatories, bathtubs, and shower stalls for houses.

Since introduced, they have proved that they can serve very well—provided you get a good brand. Rigid plastic bath fixtures are attractive, tough, and long-lasting. That's understandable since they're made of the same tough plastic used for boat hulls which withstand great exposure to water and hard knocks. Plastic units are also warm to the touch, are a pleasure in winter, and are much lighter in weight than traditional metal and china fixtures. Their light weight can cut installation costs and be a heaven-sent boon for do-it-yourself installation of a new bathroom.

One-piece plastic shower stalls and tubs for houses can cut bathroom costs not only because of their light weight (which speeds up the installation) but also because they provide a hard, waterproof wall at less cost than tile or any other kind. A stall for tub or shower is made in one piece with integral floor and sidewalls (this does away with leaky grouted joints). It has built-in fittings for easy pipe connections, it's shipped in a package, and it can be installed in a few hours. The walls have a low-gloss finish which is impervious to alkalis, molds, fungi, and household solvents. Two-wall models are available for corner locations, three-wall for the usual installation.

One possible catch is that some one-piece tub-and-shower units won't pass through the standard 32-inch doorway, so they can't be used to remodel an existing bathroom. (This can be a problem with a super-size but otherwise conventional tub, too.) If your plumber says his supplier doesn't carry a model that can be fitted into your bathroom, don't despair. Some manufacturers make compact one-piece stalls that will fit through almost any doorway, and others may introduce them. Or you can use a model that comes knocked down for assembly in place. Just have the plumber look a little harder. You may have to help out with a little shopping, which can be done on the telephone. At the least, a knocked-down unit (which means more than one piece to be assembled) can be had for almost any bathroom. Its one drawback, compared with a one-piece unit, is that it requires sealing of the joints between the separate parts to be assembled.

Beware of shoddy, low-quality plastic units. Be sure to get a good one. The quality varies because, as one expert puts it, "Practically anyone with a garage and a set of molds can turn out plastic fixtures, and dozens of guys are doing it. There's no quality control over their products."

To protect yourself when you get a plastic bathtub, stick with a brand that meets the stiff design standards of the American National Standards Institute, or ANSI Z 124.1–1974. A shower unit should meet the ANSI Z 124.2–1967 standard. These numbers may be found on the product or in the descriptive literature. A similar standard is being developed for lavatories, but until it's ready, buy only a plastic lavatory made by a well-known company that will replace it if something goes wrong. Another check is FHA (Federal Housing Administration) acceptance of a manufacturer's unit. Ask the dealer about this. Buying a product that comes with FHA acceptance is a good rule to use with many, though not necessarily all, housing products.

Plastic fixtures tend to be priced higher than the conventional kind but that's usually offset by lower-cost installation. A good plastic tub-wall unit, for example, may cost more than the lowest-cost enameled steel tub, but not more and maybe less than the same size top-of-the-line cast-iron model. And you don't have to spend more money to cover the surrounding walls.

DO-IT-YOURSELF TIPS

Professionals and do-it-yourselfers will find plastic fixtures, especially the new plastic tubs, much easier to work with. This can be quickly understood by anyone who has ever seen a plumber and his men wrestle a regular heavyweight metal fixture into place. It takes plenty of muscle—plus some. Plastic fixtures are lightweights. They make it child's play.

If you're remodeling, generally you just rip out the old fixtures and replace them with new ones. Whether you use plastic or regular fixtures, it's highly important that each new fixture fit the existing pipes and vents. If not, be sure you can compensate easily. In other words, when a new bathroom is installed, the roughing-in pipes, drains, and fittings must be absolutely true. Roughing-in dimensions and other requirements should come in the specifications with new fixtures and parts.

Installing a new tub is usually the toughest and most critical job. If you tackle this yourself, be doubly sure that the rough plumbing is true. Recheck other factors such as proper support and allowances for wall and tile overlapping before the tub is set in place. If a problem arises and the tub has to be removed for corrective work, the odds are that removal will make the tub unusable—you'll have to buy another.

A building permit is usually required for new plumbing and a new bathroom, and this work must conform with your local code. Find out about it from your building inspector before you start.

TILE WALLS

Even with a shower stall or tub with integral finished walls, other bathroom walls should have a hard waterproof surface that's easy to keep clean. Ceramic tile unquestionably has long been the top choice here and for bathroom floors. It is handsome, is available in a variety of colors, patterns, and textures, is easy to keep clean, and is so rugged that it will last as long as the house when properly installed. It should cover the entire wall and ceiling area around a shower stall or tub. The rest of the room usually needs no more than wainscot from the floor to, say, 36 inches high. This will protect the low, most vulnerable parts of your walls.

The old traditional way of making a tile wall was to have a good tile man put the tiles up, piece by piece, by what was called a mud job. The tiles are set in a portland cement backing which is virtually indestructible. The backing is important to be sure the tiles don't fall off later.

Expert tile men, however, are increasingly hard to find and expensive to hire. If your plumber cannot recommend a good one, or if his price is too high, all is not necessarily lost. There are good, tough laminated plastic materials, much the same as the tough plastics that countertops are made of, that are excellent for bathroom walls. They come in many attractive colors and patterns, withstand abuse well, and are easily wiped clean with water, though a detergent may be necessary to get rid of stains. They come in several sizes of tiles and sheets and lend themselves well to do-it-yourself installation. To get a good picture of what's available, visit a couple of home-products centers in your area. Don't fall for a low-price substitute; plenty of pseudo-tough plastic wall materials and paneling that should never be put in a bathroom are also sold. This includes ordinary wood wall paneling, which should be kept out of the bathroom.

No matter which kind of wall material is used, it can be applied over a gypsum-board wall. This will save money, but special care is required. The gypsum board should be primed with a top-grade waterproof sealant. The staff architect of the Tile Council of America told me for this book that a good marine varnish is one of the best sealers.

The gypsum board should not make actual contact with the bathtub or floor; there should be a ¼- to ½-inch gap between the top of the tub and the wallboard (which is later covered by tile). This is a moisture gap to prevent water from the tub rising up into the wallboard and ultimately ruining it. These two requirements—varnish sealer and clearance between gypsum board and tub rim—are essential for a permanent tile job on gypsum board. Specify them, and then make sure the work is done before your tile is installed.

Because water and water vapor are such troublemakers in a bathroom—and a major cause of rotted wood and exterior paint blistering—untiled bathroom walls should be painted with a special vapor-barrier paint, an alkyd paint, which is also a vapor barrier, or covered with plastic-coated wallpaper.

THE BATHROOM FLOOR

Look at an old bathroom floor, and you will often see signs of rot and deterioration, notably around the bathtub and washbowl. Of all floors this is the toughest to keep clean, attractive, and free from water damage. Many people prefer a ceramic-tile floor, for its good looks and rugged wearing qualities, or a floor of marble, terrazzo, or even flagstone. Drawbacks of these materials, as well as tile, are that they are cold on the feet, and they are death on accidentally dropped glass and medicine bottles.

For this last reason I prefer a resilient plastic floor of pure sheet vinyl, one of the best plastic floors for bathrooms. Though it is the most expensive kind of plastic flooring, pure sheet vinyl is one of the toughest, best-looking, and easiest to maintain.

You can save money with other resilient flooring, such as vinyl-asbestos tile, or with linoleum. But the loss in wearing quality exceeds the small savings in first cost. A sheet material is better in the bathroom than individual tiles of flooring because with the individual tiles the numerous joints are an invitation to water penetration and subsequent damage.

COMPARTMENT PLAN

A large bathroom for a large family can be compartmentalized, an idea heavily promoted by fixture manufacturers. Toilets, the shower, and sometimes the tub are fenced off by partitions which enable as many as three to five people to use the bathroom simultaneously with privacy. Partial partitions, dividers, or folding doors may be used. Two toilets are often found in rooms of this kind, each in its private enclosure. Two washbowls are mandatory; a second tub or shower stall is optional. A compartment bath is tantamount to having two or three bathrooms, but plumbing costs are lower as a result of grouping all the fixtures together. A space of at least 8 x 10½ feet is required to start with; 10 x 12 is better.

The merits of the compartment bath, however, are debatable. It has received much publicity, because the big manufacturers landed on it as a good way to sell more fixtures—two instead of one at a time. Partitioning off a toilet in a large bath coupled with double wash-bowls often can serve a family equally well at less expense. Or you may do better with a separate second bathroom elsewhere, especially in a large house.

WHAT COLOR BATHROOM?

Tread slowly here. Colored fixtures, tile, and floor covering should be chosen with care. Taste in colors frequently changes from year to year, and later you may be stuck with colors you will no longer like. Exotic-colored fixtures and tiles also tend to drop out of fashion as quickly as they came in. Colored fixtures, incidentally, generally cost about 10 percent more than white.

It's best to paint a bathroom with pastel colors or white, since dark colors make a bathroom seem even smaller than it actually is. Warm colors such as yellow and pink are good if the room gets little or no sun. Cool colors like blue generally should be limited to a bathroom with plenty of light and sunshine or else the room will feel cold.

If you wish to indulge your special color tastes, by all means do it, regardless of what anyone else may think. It's your pleasure. But when you sell your house, an esoteric taste could reduce the house resale value.

GARDEN PLAN

This luxury idea, popular in warm climates such as in Southern California, consists of opening up a wall of a bathroom to a private outdoor area by means of a large glass window or door. If there is no naturally secluded spot just outside, a fence at least 6 feet high, erected about 10 feet away, will create one. The idea, obviously a nice touch for bathrooms, is to let sunshine and light flood in. At the same time, you have given the bathroom the feeling that it is as large as all outdoors. You can lounge in such a bath amid glorious sunshine and plenty of light and air—if you can afford it, of course.

This idea is also practical for a bathroom with direct access to and from an outdoor swimming pool or sunning spot.

A bathroom should have a storage cabinet, ample shelves for towels, bathroom-cleaning materials, linen, and so on. Though not essential, an ample laundry hamper can be a boon; it could be built into the bottom of the lavatory unit. Divide it into sections for white, colored, and other soiled clothes, each of which may require separate washing. You could also install a chute leading down to a basement laundry area.

Install a large medicine cabinet and mirror. A cabinet built into the wall with sliding-mirror doors is both attractive and functional. The medicine cabinet should be at least 20 x 30 inches. For safety's sake, a small, separate cabinet put high up out of reach of kids is good for storing drugs and medicines that could harm them. A small locked-door section at the top of a bathroom linen closet is ideal for the purpose.

Good lighting is essential for emotional reasons, as well as for illumination. There should be a light near the mirror on the medicine cabinet and over the washbowl so you can see your whole face without shadows. Some cabinets can be had with concealed, indirect lighting on each side or with tubular lights on the sides.

A separate light is often needed over the bathtub and shower compartment. You may also want an overhead fixture for general lighting. The switch for the main light should be convenient to the doorway.

Other ideas: space for a makeup bench at the lavatory; a waterproof light over the tub or in the shower-stall ceiling; an auxiliary electric wall or ceiling heater for extra comfort if required (but keep it well away from the bathtub and shower stall for safety); a built-in electric outlet for shaving (which should also be well out of reach of the bathtub); grab bars for extra safety in the tub or shower stall; built-in towel and soap racks; clothes hooks; and shutoff valves at each fixture (so you will not have to shut off the main water supply to the house for a minor repair).

A few special features will please small children: towel racks within their reach; a foot bench for climbing into the tub or reaching the washbowl; a tilt-down mirror; a low shelf for holding bathtub playthings. Such things can be easily removed when the children outgrow them.

Manufacturers' catalogues display additional custom features. These include built-in towel and tissue holders; built-in scales; elegant towel bars and other trim; and, of all things, heated towel bars. Some manufacturers also promote the sale of bidets, widely used in Europe, for personal hygiene.

HOW TO AVOID THREE WIDESPREAD HEADACHES

Many people are harassed by three nagging troubles in bathrooms. They are toilet tanks that drip water on the floor, hot-water faucets that spurt forth with cold water for minutes, it seems, before the hot water at last appears, and bathtub crack.

The first problem results from very cold water inside the tank cooling the entire tank. Water vapor in the bathroom air then condenses on the cold surface and drips. The antidote is the installation of a hot-water mixing valve in the supply line to the tank. This allows enough hot water to be mixed with the cold to warm the tank above the point where condensation occurs. Another remedy is an insulated tank. Some new toilets can be had with insulated tanks, or a special insulation kit on the market can be bought for about $5 or $6 and installed in your present tank.

Cold water pours out initially from hot-water faucets after cooling off in the long pipe run from the water heater to the bathroom. Hot water does not arrive at the faucet until the water in the pipe has been drawn off. The remedy is what plumbers call a hot-water circulating line, which consists of a second hot-water line installed up to the bathroom and hooked up so that hot water circulates continuously back and forth from the heater and is therefore always present close to the faucets. Then you should have quick hot water. A partial and cheaper remedy for the same condition is insulation of the hot-water supply pipe.

Bathtub crack gradually develops at the joint between the bottom of the tub and the floor. Not only is it ugly, but it is also a hazard because water seepage through it can damage and ultimately rot the wood floor below.

Bathtub crack develops as a result of tub settling or constant small movements of the tub as people get in and out of it. It can be avoided if the tub is securely mounted; this in turn normally requires special L-bracket supports under the tub and bolted to the wall. In routine installations they are not usually provided, so you must ask for them or for comparable support.

Another tip: Have your plumber load the tub full up with water just before he locks it in place and makes his final connections. This will weigh the tub down to its lowest possible position, allowing little or no room for settling.

HIS AND HERS

Planning and executing a good bathroom may seem like a lot of work, but so is attaining anything good. Once finished and done, however, it can pay off in pleasure that you didn't realize. Here's how, in a few apt words from Ann David, woman's service representative of the American Standard Corporation. Miss David's firm is in the business of selling bathroom fixtures, to be sure, but her comments are of interest. She says:

> Sibling rivalry never gets such a clear expression than in the carryings-on of the child who is second in line to his sister in the morning use of the bathroom. And what a fiasco when mother and father go out at night. Powdering starts in the bedroom, shaving in the bathroom. Much running, hurrying, and switching of rooms go on until they can emerge coordinated and groomed . . . and exhausted. Heaven help the child who, in the midst of this crash program, has to use the bathroom . . . it's regarded as little less than sabotage. Add to this picture a guest or two for a short time, or a hot summer, and you have an absurd story—absurd because it is unnecessary.

Aside from the fact that one bathroom just cannot bear traffic for four people, let me review a few other reasons for at least two bathrooms. First, the bathroom should offer complete privacy. One bathroom should offer this for the adult; another for the child. With the heightened pressure of life and heightened activity, there must be more room to relax and be alone.

House designs allow for this generally—we have family rooms, dens, workshops, sewing rooms, children's play areas, etc. The same should apply to the bathrooms in the house. Two bathrooms are not a luxury, they are a necessity. If you figure that two adults share the master bathroom, and probably two or more children share a second bathroom . . . that's sharing enough. Some people still may think that a separate bathroom for children is paying too much attention to them. Believe me, it's not. Children have a sense of privacy and possession. You see it with their toys; you see how much they love their own bedroom if it's decorated with their books, their pictures, their heroes. I bet the legend that children have to be kept clean would have much less substantiation if children didn't constantly have to wash in their parents' bathroom.

I've seen lovely bathrooms, smaller and perhaps more modest than the master bathroom, decorated for children. Just as the master bathroom is no place for soap duck decorations, children could do with other than His and Hers towels. We all want children to take an interest in their grooming, and many books have been written on the importance of early training to encourage clean habits. The answer may not be in directives or washing schedules. It may be in a separate bathroom for the younger set. And besides the use of the second bathroom for children, it is very useful when you have guests, be they young or old.

Now to the master bathroom. Many a man will say all he needs is a small bathroom for a quick shave and shower. That's all right if, as I mentioned earlier, his wife isn't trying to powder her nose under his elbow. Besides which, his wife probably likes nothing better than a luxurious bath when her housework is done and the children are still at school. The decor can make the bathroom a place for quiet and relaxed washing and grooming.

I am not exaggerating the importance of this comfortable and attractive atmosphere. I've read articles by doctors and beauticians who say the best therapy for fraught nerves and tired limbs is a long and relaxing bath. The master bathroom is a place where the housewife escapes the perpetual motion of her household management, where she can enjoy the private application of as many beauty creams as she chooses to try. As dedicated as she is to the home, the family, and everyone's welfare and nutrition, there must be a spot where she can feel a dedication to herself, her femininity, and her grooming.

PART FOUR
Adding new rooms

This section deals with the most common kinds of new living space needed in houses. It presents basic design information about finishing off an attic, basement, or garage, adding or closing in a porch or patio, and obtaining a new family room.

In each case there are inherent pitfalls that can lead to serious drawbacks unless precautions are taken. There are also certain advantages related to a particular space which should be exploited.

CHAPTER 11

CONVERTING AN ATTIC INTO GOOD NEW ROOMS

Getting good new attic rooms requires solving three problems encountered in nearly every attic. They are how to get plenty of air, how to get good light, and how to make the space warm in winter and cool in summer.

Sometimes there is a fourth problem—not enough headroom. One solution is to lift the roof, but that can cost a small fortune. Sometimes you can raise the ceiling and provide walking space inside the room by adding dormers, though this can be expensive. A dormer, however, is not always essential. If you have enough headroom to start with, gable-end windows and roof skylights can provide just as much air and light at less expense. Opening up one or both gable ends of the attic with a large glass window and letting sunlight flood in can make an astonishing difference in the feeling of space obtained. All or most of it could be fixed glass, a lower-cost method than having complete window units that open and shut—and cost more. Ventilation can be provided with a second, smaller window that opens, or bubble skylights built into the roof can let air and light into the center of the space.

A warning about windows and skylights: Too much glass exposed to direct sunshine can make the new space insufferably hot, not only in summer but in spring and fall too. Good shading from hot sun should be provided initially for such windows; this means when the windows are designed and built, assuming you don't want to be a baked potato every summer. The same windows can let in welcome sunshine in winter to help you heat the room.

Because the windows you choose can make or break new attic rooms, their importance cannot be overemphasized. In short, try to put large window glass in the gable ends of the attic and you cut or eliminate the window glass needed to be built into the sloping roof. This can also eliminate the cost of a dormer. Attractive skylights built into the roof are another means of opening up a roof for window air and light without dormers. To save energy in winter and summer, locate your windows with good year-round exposure to the sun—facing south is best for reasons noted in Chapter 5—and provide summer shading for the windows.

All that is not difficult to accomplish. How I did it in a new attic room is described in the next chapter. The fundamentals of window exposure and orientation are given in Chapter 29.

IF DORMERS ARE NEEDED

A wide shed dormer is usually recommended over single-window dormers, which do not add enough headroom and light to be worthwhile. A shed dormer, of course, is simply raising the roof on one side of the attic.

The most common mistake with a new dormer is not extending it out far enough to the exterior wall of the house. It should extend to within 18 inches of the exterior wall, preferably to the wall itself. The depth of a dormer has a direct effect on the finished ceiling height inside the room. Unless it extends out to within 18 inches of the exterior wall, you could be shortchanged on interior headroom. This is a key point to check when bids are obtained for attic remodeling. What seems like a low price could be the result of cutting back on dormer extension. You don't realize the loss until too late. You can be sure of what you are getting by obtaining a plan in advance that shows the exact dimensions of the finished room, including an elevation view with ceiling heights.

When the roof is broken for a dormer extension, salvage all the good shingles that you can. Mixed in with new ones, and applied to the dormer roof, old shingles can provide a closer match than new ones alone.

Sometimes a roof can be raised bodily. It depends on the house. The simpler the roof, the easier it will be and the less it will cost. The expense involved may be worth the cost of obtaining as much as an extra floor of living space.

SPACE, ROOM DIVISION, AND STAIRS

The stairway location is decisive. A central stairway is normally required to attain two separate rooms in the attic. A stairway at either end almost always dictates only one room.

A feeling of space and openness can be had if partitions, storage walls, and closets are head-high. They need not extend fully to the ceiling. A clear space of at least a foot above the partitions gives you an open ceiling, and the room will seem large and pleasant.

Chimney, vent pipe, and heating-duct obstructions are real problems. Moving a brick chimney is usually out of the question because of the expense. Though a chimney is often boxed in, it need not be. Leave it there in naked splendor, and it can add to your room. Box it in only if it's unattractive, or combine it with a wall or closet. If any pipes or ducts are stubbornly in your way, check on the cost of having them moved. Nothing is sacred if you want a good room—and if the expense is acceptable.

The stairway to the attic should be 3 feet wide and rise at a 30- to 35-degree angle, no more, for safety. Tread width plus riser should add up to about 17 inches. Thus, 7-inch risers between steps call for a 10-inch-deep tread. Hand rails are best about 32 inches above the stair treads.

If a new bathroom is installed in the attic, piping costs can be reduced by locating it above another bathroom below. The important element here is a location that permits new piping vertically up from the existing pipes, plus convenient access to an existing plumbing vent stack (the large pipe rising through the roof for release of sewer gases).

New attic living space should, of course, conform with the requirements of your local code (and this can be a check on the adequacy of your plans), but some people choose to ignore the local code. They file no application for any remodeling in order to avoid an increased house assessment and consequent higher taxes. But they can hurt themselves by putting in a flimsy addition that, worst of all, could collapse. Obtain a copy of your building code early to be sure that your new structure is adequate.

A key requirement of the code is that the attic floor beams be strong enough to support new rooms. In general, 2 x 6 beams are the minimum size required, depending on the house and the span of the beams. Sometimes they must be 2 x 8s.

Yet many houses are built with smaller 2 x 4 beams, which can doom the whole project. But don't give up without a fight if your existing floor beams are not strong enough. A smart architect or contractor may come to the rescue with a comparatively inexpensive means of beefing them up, with special plywood covering or a steel girder, for example. Some codes also lay down rules for minimum ceiling height.

Because attics are naturally cold in winter and torrid in summer, use thick insulation all around the walls and ceiling of a new attic room. Its importance cannot be overemphasized, regardless of climate zone. The walls should be completely filled with good insulation. Because it's directly under the roof and therefore brutally exposed to heat and cold, the ceiling should get at least 6 to as much as 12 inches of insulation, depending on certain variables spelled out in Chapter 17. Good outdoor air ventilation is also essential under the roof ceiling of an attic room and around the outside portions of the room's wall structure. That's to keep dark structural nooks and crannies free of moisture, as well as to carry off excess heat in summer.

A source of heat is required in a new attic room except possibly in a warm year-round climate. If you have been generous with the insulation, chances are that the present heating system will have sufficient extra capacity to supply the new space. But new heating ducts or radiators are certain to be needed, and this can get expensive.

An alternative is the use of a separate gas or electric heater. This may be less expensive than tying in with the house heating system. A gas heater will require correct exhaust venting, plus an intake air vent to the room to assure adequate air for its combustion. Most communities have rigid codes applying to fuel-burning heaters. Be sure to observe them.

If you live in a relatively warm climate and the new space is well insulated, a few floor vents could be installed to let warm air rise up naturally from the floor below. But this also opens up extra paths for noise to travel in and out of the new rooms, and privacy suffers, too. Noise can be reduced if the vents and their short duct connections have a couple of right-angle bends and are lined with acoustical tile. This is a simple job that can be done at comparatively small cost.

CHAPTER 12
CASE HISTORY OF A NEW ATTIC ROOM

I was confronted with the same problems that face nearly everyone who wants to convert raw attic space into new rooms—only more so. How do you install good new windows in a dark, restricted space? How do you make it warm in winter and cool in summer, especially when the available window locations are difficult exposures? It took work. I made a few mistakes in the bargain, but the room came off well. Not only is it pleasantly cheerful all the time, but on a sunny day in winter the morning sun provides enough heat for virtually all day with little or no expensive mechanical heat required.

The windows were the toughest part to do. The space available was small, so I wanted big windows to make the room seem larger. The conventional wisdom today says to keep down the size of your windows to conserve heating and cooling energy. That's all right if you don't mind living in a cave and are willing to give up free solar heat in winter.

The windows I chose all used double-pane glass. This cuts the heat loss roughly in half, compared with single-pane glass. That also paid off in extra comfort. On the coldest winter days, when howling north winds lash the house, drafts and cold spots are not felt in the room. Because windows can get expensive, I used fixed-glass units (window glass that doesn't open) for all but one section, where a sliding glass unit was installed for ventilation and for an exit route in case of fire. Fixed-glass units are less costly than regular windows. The room is air conditioned, so there's no need for cross-ventilation.

In planning the room, there were only two places where new win-

A large new window contains a sliding window section in the center and fixed-glass panels on each side and the top. All are double glass for warmth. Facing east, the window lets morning sun and heat pour into the author's attic office. *James Brett.*

dows could be placed, unless I was willing to pay extra for tearing into the roof and installing a dormer or skylights, which I wanted to avoid. One location was in a gable facing east; the other, in a gable facing north. I decided on a big window in both. They are shown in the accompanying photos.

Here's where that happy bonus of free solar heat results. Enough warm sunshine pours in through the large east window on a sunny

This window contains three panels of fixed, double glass. It faces north, the worst exposure for weather. It is necessary to open up the room, though it could have been made smaller.

winter morning to keep the room as warm as toast virtually all day. That solar bonus comes about for two reasons. First, the double glazing, much better than ordinary single glass, lets direct sunshine pour in and retains the warmth. Secondly, heat is also retained inside the room because the ceiling is beefed up with 8 inches of insulation piled over it.

That much insulation is actually on the low side for a house with

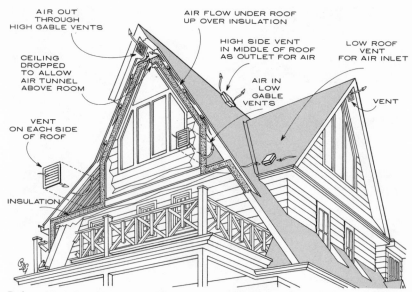

AIR OUT THROUGH HIGH GABLE VENTS

AIR FLOW UNDER ROOF UP OVER INSULATION

HIGH SIDE VENT IN MIDDLE OF ROOF AS OUTLET FOR AIR

LOW ROOF VENT FOR AIR INLET

CEILING DROPPED TO ALLOW AIR TUNNEL ABOVE ROOM

AIR IN LOW GABLE VENTS

VENT

VENT ON EACH SIDE OF ROOF

INSULATION

Before: Note the old window under the roof before a new attic room was built. *After:* Photographs and the diagram show how vents were located to permit natural air flow in low and flow out high for year-round ventilation under the roof. *Diagram reprinted from* Popular Science *with permission. Copyright © 1977, Times Mirror Magazine Inc.*

Two-by-three lumber was nailed on existing 2 x 6 roof rafters to provide enough space under the sloping roof for eight inches of insulation. Small 1-inch filler strips were nailed in between each pair of rafters to insure open space over insulation for air to flow up under the roof.

air conditioning in my winter climate of 5,000 degree days (not far from New York City). According to studies by the National Bureau of Standards (NBS), 6 to 8 inches of insulation will produce economies in a house with oil or gas heat and no air conditioning in this climate. But in a house with central air conditioning, and no matter what kind of heat is used, the studies show that as much as 12 inches of insulation will pay for itself in energy savings in a cold climate. The NBS people who did the study (scientist Steve Peterson and co-workers) turned out to be right, too. During hot weather in summer, when my air conditioning is working overtime, my new room under the roof gets hotter, especially near the ceiling, than the other air-conditioned rooms of the house downstairs. A little more ceiling insulation would have paid for itself in savings.

So much hot morning sun can pour through an east window in summer that even with air conditioning the room would roast, unless you installed a machine with twice the cooling capacity ordinarily needed. In short, even a large east window should be shaded from the morning sun to keep down the air-conditioning bills, as well as avoid one's being a baked potato. To shield the window from that sun, I installed a roll-down plastic shade on the outside that can be raised or lowered from inside. An outside shade keeps out twice as much heat as a shade inside. Incidentally, see-through plastic shades, or "screens," are available for keeping out hot sun rays but still let you see out.

CHOOSING THE HEATING

The room is heated with two slender electric baseboard units, one under each window. They give independent control over the temperature of the room and are thus independent; even better, they can be turned off entirely when the room is not being used. In this case, only one of the two heaters is enough to keep the room warm in winter. That was a surprise since standard heating calculations for the new room called for two heaters, but such calculations tend to be conservative. Next time I will see to it that there is enough electrical capacity for two units but install only one, adding a second one only if more heat is found to be needed in cold weather.

Instead of electric baseboard heaters, I could have had new radiators installed and connected to the old steam heating system that served the rest of the house. But extending its big pipe tentacles to the new room would have cost more than trim new electric baseboards. The new electric units are also much easier to turn off when heat isn't needed in the room, compared with steam radiators. For that matter, installing new electric units, or perhaps a new gas room heater, can often provide better heat than the existing heating system in the rest of the house.

Unlike the heating, the new room is air-conditioned by the same central system that cools the rest of the house. This was made possible by preplanning, for which I pat myself on the back.*

When the central air conditioning was installed a few years before, it provided capacity for future rooms that might be built in the attic. That advance planning paid off. Because the capacity was already there, it was easily installed. The special pains taken for other aspects

---

* Though I kick myself in another place for other things that I didn't think of!

of the new room paid off in other ways. Because of the double-glazed windows and extra-thick thermal insulation, minimal heating and cooling capacity is required to heat and cool the room, resulting in lower annual operating bills.

UNDER-THE-ROOF VENTILATION

This is essential in virtually every house with or without an attic room, unless you want the roof to rot away slowly. Such hidden-from-view structural spaces must breathe; besides, a good air wash under the roof is important in summer to get rid of excess heat.

Without ventilation, particularly in winter, water vapor rising from the house below (largely from the kitchen and bathrooms) can pass up right through the ceiling, like smoke through cloth, and condense out as water when it hits the cool underside of the roof. It's for the same reason that vapor condenses out as fog on cold window glass. That attic condensation can be minimized if a vapor barrier is installed with your ceiling insulation. Moisture can also get into the roof structure from other sources, such as a leak. Wherever it's from, it can cause wood rot, damage the roof, and dampen and hinder the effectiveness of your insulation.

The Federal Housing Administration (FHA) calls for a minimum of 1 square foot of net air venting for every 150 square feet of attic floor area—half as much if a vapor barrier is used (see Chapter 18) or if a combination of high and low vents is used.

Providing the necessary ventilation was a problem in my house because the 2 x 6 rafters (the size found in many houses) lacked depth to allow for thick insulation plus the air space needed for venting. My solution was to nail a 2 x 3 on the 2 x 6 to widen each rafter. To ensure an air space between the top of the insulation and the underside of the roof, I nailed 1- x 2-inch cleats to the underside of the roof between each pair of rafters.

To let outside air into this gap between insulation and roof, I installed intake vents near the eaves and outlet vents near the ridge. A natural air wash results, since warm air rises. The air flows up the outside of the insulation and out the top.

One other question should be cleared up. What do you do with existing insulation previously put in the attic floor when you build a new attic room above that insulation? The insulation is no longer needed with a new heated living space built above it. Because insulation prices have risen sharply, why not use it elsewhere where needed for the new room?

I left the existing insulation untouched to serve as a sound barrier between the second floor and the new room above. This has worked out fine. The insulation shuts off noise travel two ways, between the new room and the house below (a real blessing when someone is playing booming records downstairs but quiet is preferred above). If acoustical control is important to you, by all means leave the old insulation in the attic floor when you convert an attic into finished rooms.

CHAPTER 13

ADDING A NEW ROOM IN THE BASEMENT

This is a deceptive new room put in houses, and it's often a mistake. It's deceptive because you can be fooled by all that raw space underground just itching to be finished off and used. It's often a mistake because after you pour money and time into it, a new basement room is hardly ever used.

That's because an underground space with little natural light and air is not especially inviting. People don't gravitate to it. Observe finished basement areas in the houses of your friends. When is such space successful? The acid test is how often it's used voluntarily for the purpose intended. Do people, especially children, head downstairs to play without being told to do so? Are successful parties held in the basement? Or do people tend to stay upstairs, shunning the expensive, new, basement party room? Does the family naturally use the room and use it often?

In addition, what is the best use for your basement? It depends, first, on your needs. With children, a downstairs playroom can be a big help, if only for retaining your sanity. It is a natural spot for a workshop (though a ground-level garage puts necessary tools closer to their point of use).

It can be a laundry or utility space, if necessary (though here again a first-floor location will save much stair-climbing inconvenience). It can be an entertainment and party room, many people say, but this puts special emphasis on making it a cheerful and pleasant place. A basement can also be transformed into a truly pleasant living space of almost any kind *if* large new windows can be installed and *if* it is naturally dry.

PLANNING

When you've decided on the kind of room you want, draw a plan. Work with a scale diagram of your basement, including the location of stairs, heating equipment, and interior walls. Keep the plan as open as possible. Close off only those areas that require privacy or are unsightly. Make the stairway look airy and light by leaving the space under it open and running your floor covering into that area. That is, unless the same space is a natural for needed storage or for a built-in television set or record player.

The ceiling can be dropped to close in pipes, wires, and other unsightly obstructions. Gas and electric meters can be enclosed within cabinets, with hinged doors for access.

Paneling is often the desired cover for walls. There is a great variety of different kinds and a broad range of prices. Hardboard paneling is generally among the less expensive kinds, and it has rugged wearing characteristics. It comes ready to paint, with finished grainy surfaces, or with a hard plastic finish.

There is also veneered plywood, available in a wide range of finishes and designs and becoming more and more economical. You can get it with a factory finish or in unfinished grades. Often the factory-finished kind is a better buy, though it's a little more expensive. Figure your cost for finishing materials, brushes, etc., and you may be money ahead by choosing the prefinished paneling.

You could also use gypsum wallboard (dry-wall), which is about the cheapest wall cover of all. But it has to be painted; add this to the material cost.

Do *not* use any material that will be damaged by moisture or water in the basement. This includes some hardboards, fiberboard, and some playwoods and solid wood panels which may be particularly sensitive to water. Check on this before buying.

LIGHTING

Good lighting can make the difference between a really successful basement space and a dimly lit cave. You'll generally need plenty of lighting, not just a fixture or two. Special recessed fixtures can be installed in the ceiling. A variety of styles and types are available with fluorescent and incandescent bulbs. At the same time, strive for a bright, well-lit space by using light-colored or white walls and ceiling. The lighter the color of the surrounding surfaces, the more light-reflective they are and the less light absorbed, thus a higher overall light level.

NEW WINDOWS

Don't rule out new windows just because basement walls are of solid brick or masonry. This is the opportunity to open up a basement with genuine light and air, overcome the major drawback of basement rooms and obtain a new room that *is* truly inviting and therefore successful and really used by your family.

Punching a hole in a basement wall can be easier than it may sound and is eminently logical. Obviously, there should be enough exposed wall above the ground level for the window. With the usual 2 to 3 feet of basement wall rising above the ground level, a ribbon of wide horizontal windows can be installed with remarkable success.

Deeper windows can be installed where the ground may slope away from the basement walls by 4 or 5 feet. If the ground slopes off sharply from one end of the house, there may even be enough exposed wall for a large picture window. This can work wonders for a basement, almost single-handedly transforming it into a full-fledged room.

If very little basement wall is aboveground, attack the problem the other way—by excavation. In effect, the wall is raised above the ground level. With suitable terrain a private sunken garden can be located outside. At the very least, a small excavation can provide a well for a window.

A more ambitious scheme is extension of part of a basement wall, and only the basement wall itself, several feet out past the house walls. This can be an 8- or 10-foot portion of basement wall which is then roofed over with a glass skylight or greenhouse glass. Not only will it let sun and light flood into the entire basement, but with a southern exposure the portion under the glass can make an excellent sunning spot the year around.

OTHER SUGGESTIONS

A warm basement floor can be had by building a new wooden floor several inches above the cement floor. A vapor barrier (of heavy 55-pound roll-roofing building paper or plastic sheet at least 4 mills thick—that's what to ask for when you buy), plus 1 inch of insulation, should be installed under the raised floor.

Every basement should have a 36-inch-wide door to the outdoors for carrying large things in and out.

The basement stairway should become an inviting approach to downstairs. Vertical rails are mandatory along its length, particularly for the safety of children and old folks.

The basement should be inspected for termites and wood rot before it is finished off. Have it done, or you risk damage from these destroyers to your new walls, as well as to the basic house structure.

ACHIEVING A DRY BASEMENT

All bets are off if your basement is chronically wet. Converting such a basement into finished space is foolhardy unless the moisture problem is cured first. Even if the problem is minor, damage from wood rot can be serious. Eliminating dampness and water requires first tracking down its source.

Water entry is most often the result of poor groundwater drainage away from the house. The water sinks into the earth and then pushes into the basement through the walls. Waterproofing the inside of the walls is only a halfway remedy even with the best brush-on materials. The first precaution is to be sure that the ground outside slopes away from the house on all sides so that rainwater is shed away from the foundation walls.

Make sure that the vertical drainpipes from the roof gutters down to the ground are not clogged. When this occurs, the gutters overflow, usually dropping water on the earth next to the house wall. The water breaks through and into the basement. Roof drains (leaders) that spill their water directly onto the ground should be directed away from the house. Put a splash block below them so the water does not sink directly into the earth.

Sometimes a tile pipe drain is required in the ground all around the house exterior. This is about the only cure for a chronic wet basement condition. Unfortunately, a trench must be dug all around the foundation walls and the tile pipe laid in it. The pipe is put down at a depth equal to the basement-floor level. Its purpose is to catch groundwater, before it presses into the basement, and carry it away. The exterior wall surfaces could also be waterproofed with a good waterproofing material sold in paint and hardware stores. Obviously, all cracks and holes in the basement floor and walls should be filled in.

The basement floor is sometimes the source of dampness. Moisture from the ground below will rise straight up through ordinary concrete in the form of vapor. Lay a sheet of waterproof building paper or heavy aluminum foil directly over a portion of the floor, and weight it down. After a few days pick up the paper to see if its underside is damp. If it is, the floor vapor can be kept down by sealing the floor with a good vapor-barrier masonry paint. Another solution is to cover the floor with waterproof building paper (the 55-pound kind at least) and then to build a new floor above it.

If moisture is a persistent problem, a dehumidifier may be your solution. It removes moisture from the air and will keep the basement dry, provided the problem is not acute. A dehumidifier will remove from about 10 to perhaps 25 pints of water a day, depending on the type and brand. That's not much when you realize that an ordinary window air conditioner will wring out 100 to 200 pints of moisture every twenty-four hours.

Choose a dehumidifier with an automatic humidistat control so it will not run all the time. The control automatically turns the unit on or off as required, according to a preset humidity level. The water removed from the air settles in a pan or tank integral with the unit. You empty it by hand, unless you can locate it above a floor drain or have a pipe drain installed.

Unfortunately, there are no rules for choosing the size and capacity needed. Obviously, the larger your basement and the greater your moisture problem, the larger the dehumidifier required. Check manufacturers' ratings, especially the water-removal capacity, one against the other, and also discuss it with a good dealer. Since brand quality changes continually, look up dehumidifier ratings in *Consumer Reports* magazine.

THE SUMP PUMP SOLUTION

Plenty of water per se can seep up through floor cracks into a basement. Sometimes it may be considerable. That happened in my house when the ground below became saturated after very heavy rainfalls. The drainage system that was supposed to carry it away from underneath the house had clogged and stopped working. Groundwater like that can be removed by a good sump pump. The one I installed solves the problem and, in addition, gets rid of water that leaks in from elsewhere after a heavy rainfall.

A sump pump is an electric pump designed to lift water up and out of wherever the pump is placed. In a basement, it's put in a small pit lined with concrete or a rectangular piece of tile like a hunk of chimney flue. Water that finds its way into the cellar gravitates to the sump. An automatic switch on the pump starts it working when the water reaches a predetermined level, and the water is pumped out.

Sump pumps are made of corrosion-resistant materials, such as plastic, stainless steel, and bronze, since they are immersed in water much of the time. The best kind is bronze, which lasts longest and will virtually never rust or corrode. It costs more than other pumps but is worth the extra money.

CHAPTER 14

FAMILY ROOM AND LIVING ROOM, BEDROOMS, AND LAUNDRY

A NEW FAMILY ROOM

In recent years this has become one of the most popular of all new rooms in new houses. It's an informal living room, where you, your family, and your friends can relax.

It is also called a rec room, a game room, a Florida room, or even a lanai. The early colonists called it a keeping room. In the 1920s it was called the whoopee room and was usually located in the basement, where children played by day and adults danced the Charleston at evening parties.

The keynote of a family room is informality. Ideally, it is a household's center of gravity for a variety of family activities that relieve the formal living room of noise, clutter, and toys. It is for informal everyday living and entertaining, for watching TV, sewing, listening to records, reading, children's play, card games, hobbies, coffee with neighbors, or just plain informal talk and conversation. In short, it neatly handles those overflow activities that often occur by default in a crowded kitchen or formal living room, neither of these rooms being satisfactory as a genuine family room.

The first requirement

Some family rooms are hopeless failures, while others are great successes (sometimes by accident). The key to success is deciding in advance precisely why you need a family room. This depends on your family, and it is not so much what new activities you intend to use it for, but what your family likes to do that could be carried out enjoyably in a family room.

What will your family room be used for? Do you have children who need a play area (because they are either underfoot in the kitchen now or messing up the living room)? Do friends, neighbors, and relatives drop in frequently? Do you play bridge regularly, listen to records, or need an informal room to relax in, with the living room unsuitable for such uses?

Make a list of what your family likes to do and the activities that could be centered in a family room. This may sound like an unnecessary chore, but it can shed surprising light on what to do. For that matter, the list may show that you really don't need to spend money for a family room. A few changes in your dining room or living room may make one of these sufficiently versatile to take up the slack when for deceptive reasons these rooms are not carrying their share of the load.

This happened, for example, quite by accident in my house with a large dining room that was largely neglected except at dinnertime. We casually tried a couch in the dining room, and the transformation was remarkable. It became the natural spot for reading the paper and after-meal coffee, while often at the same time the children (ages five, two and a half, and one at the time) confined their play there, apparently finding it a secure place with parents unobtrusively present. They no longer left their toys and debris strung around the adjacent living room. We didn't need to build a new room.

Location is crucial

The best location is adjacent to the kitchen with easy access to outdoors. There are good reasons for this. A mother can keep an eye on children and be readily available in a crisis, and in addition, children, especially young ones, like to know that a parent is nearby. Being close to the kitchen also simplifies the serving of food and refreshments that would otherwise require a long trek through the house for delivery.

A location on the opposite side of the kitchen from the living room can be particularly effective. The kitchen serves as a buffer between adults in the living room and the noise of children in the family room; at the same time the kitchen can serve both rooms.

Do you have the space now? Look around your present kitchen.

The fireplace is the focal point of this new family room, formerly a garage. *Kranzten Studio, Inc.*

Can you convert a dining room, carport, garage, breezeway, porch, or even a patio into a family room?

Remember that a family room should be airy, bright, and exposed to plenty of daylight. This calls for at least one southern exposure, anywhere from the southeast to the southwest side of the house, especially in a northern climate. A southern exposure is less important in a warm climate. On the other hand, access to an outdoor patio or play area is virtually essential so that the family room can be a natural link between indoor and outdoor living.

The lowest level of a split-level house may be a good location. In a cold climate, however, the space is often so cold and poorly heated that it is off limits in winter. Adding insulation and improving the heat are usually required.

As a rule, avoid a basement location because it is inconvenient, it lacks plenty of light and air, and, as noted in the previous chapter, you may find everybody back upstairs after the novelty wears off. A basement playroom may be superb for the roughhousing of older children who do not need supervision or for a workshop, say. But its nature rules against the cheerful informality and convenience required of a good family room.

Size, decoration, and construction

A good size for a family room is about 14 x 20 feet, according to studies at the Small Homes Council, University of Illinois. This size simply was found to work well for typical families. Minimum size recommended is 12 x 14.

Choose light and gay colors to make the room feel large and cheerful. Cool shades of blues and greens are good in a warm climate. Warm colors like reds, browns, yellows, and oranges are better in a cold climate, particularly to make up for limited sunshine during winter. Wall and floor materials should be chosen for ruggedness, low upkeep, and easy cleaning. They'll take continual abuse. An acoustical tile ceiling is good for putting a damper on noise. It is not recommended, however, if you intend to listen to records because of its muting effect on music.

Plan for plenty of built-in storage. Make a list of everything you intend to store there, and then build the appropriate shelves, cabinets, and drawers. Freestanding storage partitions are excellent for separating the room into zones, as well as for providing built-in storage. Another good idea is a window seat with a hinged top. Toys can be tossed into it at night or when a quick cleanup is necessary, if, for example, guests are coming. Put the top down for extra seating capacity and instant neatness.

More good ideas

A nearby bathroom for washing up can be a boon. If you already have one conveniently near, fine. Adding one can be expensive, of course. If you will need a bathroom anyway but cannot afford it now, plan for it when the family room is being built, and have the necessary plumbing lines installed so that the bathroom can be completed later at minimum expense.

A fireplace is a good idea and can be had comparatively inexpensively with one of the neat little prefabricated fireplaces now on the market. As noted earlier, they can cost as little as $500 installed.

Don't forget a place to eat. If there isn't space for a regular table, consider a pull-down table or counter hinged to a wall. It can also serve double duty as a desk, card table, or game surface.

But don't load down the room with every conceivable feature. Think out in advance what you want most, and omit everything else. A pool table may be great for a neighborhood bar, but not necessarily for a family room.

A NEW LIVING ROOM

When you contemplate a new living room, analyze the good and bad features of your present one. Do you use it fully? Or do you find that it is hardly ever used, except perhaps when you have company? Why is it used or not used much? This is the crucial question. It may have an isolated location, stuck in the front of the house while your family gravitates to the rear and the backyard. Does it feel bright and pleasant with plenty of window light and air? Or is it dark and gloomy because of few windows and poor light? Summarize its good and bad features so the good can be repeated and the bad omitted.

What about location and traffic circulation? As noted earlier, a living room should be free of cross-traffic from one part of the house to another. It should be a dead end, not a major thoroughfare. Is it convenient to the dining room and kitchen so that there can be a smooth flow and relationship among these three rooms?

Is the new living room big enough? Are there good places for furniture and storage? Will it be bright and cheerful with plenty of light and air? Size depends much on personal requirements, and you can get an idea of its adequacy from the size of your old living room. A feeling of roominess and large size can be had with a high ceiling or a sloped cathedral ceiling, plus the judicious use of large windows (but not the usual foolhardy front picture window). A large glass area should look out on a private garden, patio, or pleasant view.

A sloped cathedral ceiling and large windows can, of course, mean high heating bills unless each is properly designed for conserving heat. That kind of ceiling under the roof demands extra-heavy insulation, as cited in Part 4, and large glass areas should have a good exposure and in all but the warmest climates be made of insulating double glass.

A living room should have at least two exposures, and its design should permit the furniture to face the three main focal points at once: fireplace, television set, and outside view. It's a nuisance when furniture has to be switched around every time you watch TV, enjoy the fire, or merely sit pleasantly with guests looking out the window.

Before and after photographs show this neat new laundry put in an old basement of a Tacoma, Washington, house. It's handsome and all of a piece. It was designed by architect Soo K. Kim. Water-resistant plywood was used for walls, cabinets, and shelving. *Courtesy, American Plywood Assn.*

NEW BEDROOMS

The same analysis of present bedrooms and the same tests for size, furniture placement, and a bright cheerful countenance apply to new bedrooms as they do to a new living room.

Bedrooms for adults should be large enough to hold a desk and chairs, as well as bedroom furniture. A child's bedroom needs space for study and play. Windows should be large enough to let in ample light and air. Windows in at least two different walls formerly were mandatory for cross-ventilation but are less important now because of air conditioning.

A common drawback is the use of high, ribbon bedroom windows for privacy. People feel just as compelled to draw curtains or shadows over them as over large windows. They are also particularly imprisoning in children's bedrooms, hard to see through, and hard to get out of in case of fire.

THE LAUNDRY

Like other rooms, the location of the laundry is important. Ideally, when it is near the kitchen and the bathroom, it will save many steps. A location near the bathroom eliminates steps in gathering soiled clothes and putting away clean ones. It also eliminates the need for clothes chutes and requires little additional plumbing cost.

In a two-story house, a location on the first floor gets the nod over a basement. It makes laundering much simpler, and you are not burdened with the chore of getting a clothes basket up and down the basement stairs. Putting the laundry in the kitchen has become a popular idea. But it draws fire from people who dislike the idea of soiled clothing in an area where food is prepared. A hall location is also increasingly popular but too often is small, cramped, and lacking in adequate light and ventilation.

The total amount of space needed for a laundry depends on your equipment. The smallest space recommended with an automatic washer, dryer, and ironing-board area is about 6 x 12 feet.

There should be a cabinet or shelves for storage of soap, detergents, iron, and so on, counter space for sorting, and a space for a clothes rack, no longer so important for drying, but a convenience for ironing.

Equipment sequence

The equipment should be arranged for all movements in one direction toward where clothes are dried: from hamper, to sorting counter, to sink if necessary, washer, dryer, and ironing counter. The normal sequence for a right-handed person is right to left, which means the dryer should be to the left of the washer when they are side by side.

Like the recommended kitchen fixture sequence, this sequence is also the result of studies by home economist experts, but not everyone agrees. The opposite sequence may be agreeable or necessary (owing to your space) for you. If the sequence is important to you, experiment beforehand for yourself. What is your present laundry arrangement, and how does it work for you? This is not exactly of earthshaking importance, but it could matter to you.

The decision also puts special emphasis on having the doors of the washer and dryer open in the right direction. For the recommended right-to-left washer-dryer location, the washer door should, of course, be hinged at the right or at the bottom; the dryer door at the left or at bottom. The opposite is required for a left-handed person.

The dryer should be located near an outside wall to permit easy venting to outdoors. A vent is essential, for without one, much moisture, heat, and lint will be blasted into the house. Some dryers, however, have drainpipe attachments for carrying away their exhaust; they do not need an air vent.

An excellent laundry planning booklet is available for 25 cents from the University of Illinois's Small Homes Council, Urbana, Illinois 61803.

CHAPTER 15

CONVERTING A GARAGE INTO A NEW YEAR-ROUND ROOM

Probably no other enclosed space under a roof offers a more tempting opportunity for an inexpensive addition than a ground-level garage attached to your house. Construction costs are sharply reduced since the basic floor, walls, and roof are already in place. This assumes, of course, that new shelter for the family carries higher priority than the family car and that a new place for the car is available.

Converting a garage may also be misleading, and it could be a major mistake, as noted in Chapter 3, ending up a distressing misfit, with the whole house suffering. First, be sure that the new room will fit naturally into your floor plan as if it were an unmistakable part of the original house. If it will always look like a converted garage, beware. Secondly, don't forget the family car. If you care not about leaving your wheels out in the cold forevermore, that's all right, provided you also care not about possible loss of resale value of your house in the future because of no garage and no place to put one later.

Next step: What kind of space do you need? A garage can be turned into a family room, bedroom or two, guest room, playroom, a versatile covered patio or porch in summer, or even a new and better location for kitchen, dining room, or living room.

Its location usually dictates its best use. Close to the kitchen, it can be a natural for a family room or playroom or even a new master bedroom or study. Bordering on the side or rear of the house, it almost always can be used as an adjunct to an outdoor patio or play area.

Indeed, one of the most logical garage ideas is to open it up with windows, screens, and sometimes sliding glass doors so it becomes a cool, sheltered retreat in summer for children's play or adult relaxation and the outdoor area just outside turned into a private patio. The same idea, of course, is eminently practical for a carport. In winter, summer furniture is stored away and the space turned back to shelter for the car.

Privacy from the street and neighboring houses is essential. It is usually easy to achieve merely by leaving the front door of the garage closed in summer and breaking through a rear wall or sidewall so that the new space for living opens up on a private outdoor area. At the very most, a discreet fence can be erected to screen a new carport living area or patio-garage from the street.

Regardless of what you do, new windows are inevitably needed, and the garage door opening may be a problem. New windows are usually easy to install, but they should conform in style with the rest of the house windows and also line up with adjacent windows in the house. If the door opening faces a potentially good view, not just the street, it can take a large window or sliding glass doors with the apron outside turned into a private patio.

The garage floor, usually lower than the rest of the house, should be raised, if practical, to the same level as the house floor to avoid the hazard of steps. Often the ceiling is sloped high to its peak, and leaving it open will give you the expanse of an open-beam, vaulted ceiling in the new room, a much nicer idea than putting in the usual flat (and uninspired) ceiling.

If you tackle a garage conversion job with your own do-it-yourself labor, remember that this improvement, for inexplicable reasons, tends to bring out the worst six-thumb results in workmanship. No one knows why, it just does, to judge from the results seen in many houses. Obviously, special care may be necessary to avoid this trap. A word to the wise here is all I can add.

A NEW CARPORT OR GARAGE

Its location may take a little juggling, depending on your requirements. It should be located close to the kitchen for convenience and speedy grocery unloading. On the other hand, the closer it is to the street, the lower the driveway cost. These two requirements may clash, and compromise may be necessary. The garage need not be attached to the house. If it is set off 10 to 20 feet from the house, it can sandwich a patio or breezeway between it and the house.

In a cold climate, try to locate it, if possible, on the north side of the house, where it will shield the house from cold north winds in winter. Next best in the North is a location on the west to shield you from hot sun in summer. A western exposure is obviously best in the South for protecting you from the sun on hot days.

Before the work is launched, check your building and zoning code for setback and driveway restrictions. This is extremely important because minimal space for off-street parking may be required by law, in addition to the space needed for the new carport or garage.

CHAPTER 16

CONVERTING A PORCH INTO A YEAR-ROUND ROOM

The location of a new porch or patio should provide a natural link between the house and the outdoors. A location on the side or back of the house with a private view is obviously better than one facing the street. If located close to the kitchen or dining room, a porch or patio can be a convenient and delightful place for summer meals, as well as a retreat from summer heat. The same location also can be a play area for children.

Consider the porch or patio exposure to sun and winds. With a southern exposure and turning its back to cold northern winds, a porch or patio can be a delightful spot in fall and winter. This is especially true for the patio designed to catch the sun during these seasons but roofed over to keep it cool in summer.

If summer cooling is your chief consideration, a porch should be located so it will receive the prevailing summer breeze where you live. The direction of the breeze can be obtained from the nearest weather bureau office or airport. In a hot and humid climate, however, even the best new screened porch does not offer much relief from muggy humidity. The same money spent on central air conditioning may be necessary if being cool and comfortable during hot, humid weather is important to you.

PRIVACY IS ESSENTIAL

Will you have privacy? If you feel exposed to passing traffic or neighbors, you will not enjoy the place as much as you'd like. This is particularly important when you spend a lot of time in summer dining

Formerly a screened porch, this room retains its airiness as a year-round room with sliding glass windows. It's toast warm in winter because of insulation, double-glass windows, and baseboard radiators below the windows. Glass window units can be removed in summer if desired, with screens remaining.

The porch, before remodeling, had half walls and a few screens, period.

outside, entertaining, or just relaxing in welcome coolness. It even can be close to the street or the next house, but privacy can be built in by adroit location of a wall or fence to screen you from view.

You will want a light or two and a couple of electrical outlets. At least one outlet should be connected in heavy-duty wiring capable of handling a coffeemaker, electric frying pan (for morning pancakes outside), or other cooking appliances.

Use rugged waterproof materials, not only because they will resist rain (and snow, too, in the North even with an enclosed, screened porch), but also so that you can hose down the walls and floor. The floor should slope to outside and have openings to let water drain away. Screen the openings so bugs cannot enter.

A new patio can be built for as little as $750 (without roof). Cost of a new screened porch starting from scratch and roofed over generally runs at least $1,250 and up, depending on size and how much existing house wall the porch can borrow.

TRANSITION PORCH

If a new porch is to be a transition step, later to be made into a fully enclosed year-round room, the walls, floor, and roof should be insulated when they are built. Use plenty of insulation; its cost is a lot cheaper if it is installed while the structure is being built, compared with adding insulation afterward. Make provisions for heating for the same reason; heat outlets can be added later.

Design the screen openings for the kind of window you will want. Windows can be installed later with a minimum of expense. This and other ideas for a transition porch are perhaps best illustrated by an actual example which also shows how an existing porch can be converted into a year-round room.

CASE HISTORY: CONVERTING A PORCH INTO A YEAR-ROUND ROOM

Many families, to be sure, want a porch that is a porch, and it doesn't make sense to give up a cool summer porch for a regular year-round room. The airy benefits in summer are much too desirable to lose. You can have your cake and eat it too if the new room is properly designed to retain its coolness for summer use as before and simultaneously be a truly warm and comfortable room in winter.

I was torn by this problem with a screened porch on a small house we once lived in. It was a delightfully cool retreat in summer with a lovely view of a small lake. At the same time new year-round living space was urgently needed (because of a new baby), and the porch was the logical place for obtaining it at the least expense. It seemed reasonable to convert the porch into a warm winter room and design it so it could be turned back into a cool porch in summer.

Starting point was a small screened porch only 9 x 12 feet in size. It had three exposed walls and was attached to the house at its fourth wall. It had a cold concrete floor built on the ground and continuous screening around the three exposed walls.

After mulling over a variety of ideas, I decided to replace the screening with a ribbon of glass windows. Horizontal, sliding wood windows were chosen because they come with matched screens and storm windows, and, highly important, the window glass units could be removed easily in summer, leaving only the screens. It was the ideal solution and worked perfectly when the hot weather came. In fact, not all the windows had to be removed in summer to let in enough breeze for cooling.

Replacing all the screening with glass gave another big advantage. That much glass made the small 9 x 12 room seem much larger than it actually was. Even on the coldest and gloomiest days of winter, the large expanse of glass made the room remarkably pleasant because of the view and the feeling of great space. In summer, too much glass getting hot sun can turn a room into a hothouse. Since this porch exposure was chiefly north and east, it did not receive that much summer sun.

Keeping warm in winter

Of all things, the new room also turned out to be the warmest, most comfortable room in the house in winter, though this took a little doing. The original porch had been built a few years before. I had full-thickness insulation installed in the new walls and roof at that time, knowing it would pay off later. The combination of a lot of window glass, a cold concrete floor, and a cold northern exposure obviously demanded special attention to insulation and heating. Three things were done.

First, rigid insulation board was installed all around the exposed perimeter of the floor slab. This is an absolute necessity for concrete floors in the North. Secondly, a built-up wood floor, including a layer of insulation board, was installed over the concrete. Thirdly, hot-water baseboard radiators were installed around the three exposed walls of the room. A heating boiler was used to heat the rest of the house, and the new radiators were simply connected to it.

These things may sound unnecessarily expensive, but their cost is low. Without any one of them the room could easily have been cold in winter. There were also the storm windows to reduce heat loss through the glass. But storm windows were not required on all the windows for the room to be remarkably warm in winter; cold downdrafts from the glass were virtually eliminated by the rising heat from the baseboard radiators. At the height of winter, storm windows were essential on two sides of the room to shield it from icy cold winds bearing down on the house from across the lake. They were not required on the third side.

Common mistakes made

A separate heating control should have been provided for the new room. Because it wasn't, the room overheated when it was flooded with early-morning sunshine in spring and fall. Its radiators were controlled by the single house thermostat in the living room. If this thermostat was turned down, the rest of the house (not well insulated) got too cold. I had discussed the need for a second thermostat (zone control) beforehand with two different heating contractors. Like many unthinking men, both dismissed the idea, saying it was unnecessary.

The cost of remodeling the porch came to $150 over the original estimates, a total cost of $1,645. The extra cost was due to two new doors, which required much extra installation labor because they were ordered too large by mistake. Both the inside and outside doorways had to be enlarged for the new doors. It was an expensive personal oversight that I paid for.

We also forgot that new doors require hardware, like doorknobs and latches, and overlooked this cost. I subcontracted each part of the work myself, and the cost added up as follows:

Cost of ready-made windows and doors, including storm sash and screens	$625
Vinyl-asbestos floor tile and mastic	42
Electric wiring (four outlets)	48
Edge insulation, mastic, and related materials (labor by owner)	30
Heating (materials and labor)	310
Carpentry labor for floor, windows and doors, and floor tile	590
Total	$1,645

The cost for a similar new room may run more or less than above, according to local labor rates and how much prices go up (or down, I hope) since that room was done. These figures above not only give you the cost breakdown, but also show the various cost items to consider during the planning stage.

PART FIVE
How to reduce your home energy bills

Home heating accounts for by far the lion's share (64 percent!) of the average family's annual energy bill, according to the U.S. Dept. of Energy (DOE). So cutting it down clearly offers the fattest opportunity for making large-scale energy savings.

With one exception the next best place to save energy is your home water heater, the second largest energy guzzler in American homes. It accounts for 18 percent of family energy consumption, according to the DOE. The exception is in houses with central air conditioning, particularly in the warm South, where air conditioning can rank as the first or second largest energy user.

From here on down, saving energy is mopping up energy waste in cooking and household appliances. Obviously, you will save the most by giving priority to the areas where the largest energy paths are, as shown in this table of average home energy use in the United States from the DOE:

Home heating	64% (less, of course, in the hot South)
Water heater	18%
Cooking	6%
Refrigerator-freezer	3%
Air conditioning	3% (more in houses with central air conditioning)
Lighting	2%
Clothes dryer	1.5%
Other	2.5%

In terms of getting the greatest savings for the least expenditure in time and money, that big energy bill for heating can be cut the most by insulating the ceiling of your house, followed by installing tight storm windows and doors, weatherstripping and calking windows and doors, insulating the walls and floor of the house, tuning your heating unit for maximum operating efficiency, thus least waste. This section tells how to follow through on each of these energy savers, plus more.

CHAPTER 17

WHAT EVERY HOME OWNER SHOULD KNOW ABOUT INSULATION

Insulating a house properly not only can plug up major energy leaks and save you big money, but substantially helps make a house warmer and more comfortable than one with little or no insulation. It is the king of all energy-conservation measures for houses.

Tests by scientists at the U.S. National Bureau of Standards showed that insulating the walls, ceiling, and floor of a typical one-family house cut the total heating bills by 32 percent, the largest single saving. This figure is on the conservative side. Actual savings from insulation would have been greater than 40 percent except for two major insulation savings knowingly excluded from the NBS final figures, as noted later in this section.

The next largest saving made in the house—25 percent—was made by putting storm windows on the twenty-six windows in the house.

WHAT INSULATION IS
It's any material that substantially reduces heat flow. A pot holder protects your hand from a hot pan because it insulates; in other words, it virtually stops heat flow from hot to cold. In a house, insulation is any material that, stuffed into the outside frame of the house, keeps heat inside in winter and out in summer.

Early American colonists found out about insulation for their houses when frigid winter gales from the Atlantic, lashing at their

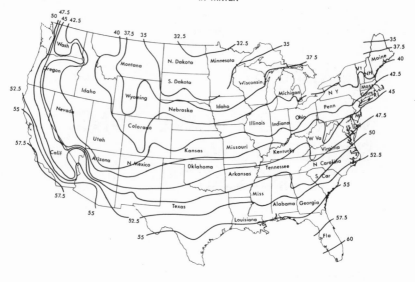

AVERAGE OUTDOOR TEMPERATURE
IN WINTER

Source: National Weather Service

The average annual temperature in winter is useful in determining heating needs and potential savings.

houses, made things inside a bit chilly, to put it mildly. Experimenting around, they found that dried-out seaweed stuffed into the walls of their Cape Cod houses worked like an outside overcoat, keeping them warm inside by stopping the wind and conserving precious house heat.

Special materials made today are much better than seaweed by being fire- and bug-resistant, as well as being more efficient at stopping heat flow. A good insulation material put over your ceiling, like a blanket, will reduce the amount of house heat leaking up and out of the house through the ceiling by 90 percent. In other words, nine out of every ten units of heat provided by the furnace and leaking out through an uninsulated ceiling will be held inside to keep you warm. That much less heat must be provided to replenish the heat lost through the ceiling. Similarly, insulation sharply cuts heat leaking out through the walls, and insulating glass or storm windows cut the heat leaking out through the window glass.

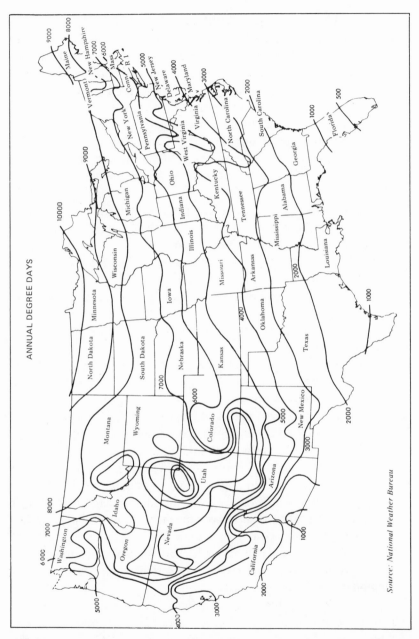

ANNUAL DEGREE DAYS

Source: National Weather Bureau

Degree days is a measure of heating needs and severity of climate. The greater the number of winter degree days, the colder the climate. Degree days are figured by subtracting the average temperature of each day from 65 degrees F and adding up the total for all the days in a year. Total annual winter degree days for different parts of the country are shown here.

THE WALL CHILL FACTOR

Insulation also saves more heat and cuts heating bills considerably more than many people realize because it minimizes what I call the wall chill factor. On a cold day in winter inside a house with little or no insulation, you will lose body heat by radiation to the cold surrounding walls. On such a day the interior surface temperature of the walls may range from about 65 degrees F to less than 60 degrees, depending on the outdoor temperature. You feel cold and chilly for the same reason you get goose bumps standing in front of an open refrigerator. The cold drains heat from the skin faster than your blood can make it up.

In a house with cold walls, we compensate by turning up the heating thermostat to be warmer. Thus the thermostat in poorly insulated houses is usually found set at from 75 to as high as 80 degrees. That much overheating is required to counteract the cold-chamber effect, or chill factor, of an uninsulated house.

Consider the same house after its walls have been insulated. The inside wall surfaces are much warmer. They are within a degree or so of the interior air temperature. What is technically called the mean radiant temperature is significantly higher, and less heat is now drained from your body to the surrounding walls. Most important, people inside are more comfortable at a lower interior air temperature. Less heat is required for comfort. In a house that is well insulated, including double-glass windows, the thermostat can be set as low as 68 to 70 degrees F and most people will be comfortable. Insulation is clearly essential for human warmth and comfort in houses.

In addition, the reduced thermostat setting brings you a bonus heat saving. You save from 3 to 5 percent of your total heating bill for every degree that you can reduce your thermostat setting. Reduce it from, say, 76 degrees formerly with no insulation, down to 72 degrees, a 4-degree drop, and your winter fuel bill drops by 12 to 20 percent, depending on your climate. This saving is a straight-line ratio proportionate to the average outdoor temperature, according to the National Bureau of Standards.

Let's say, for example, that your house is not well insulated and your thermostat is kept at 76 degrees indoors. Say, further, that you live in a city like Boston, New York, or Kansas City, where the average outdoor temperature is 44 degrees in winter. On an average winter day of 44 degrees you could save 100 percent of that day's heating bill by lowering your thermostat from 76 to 44 degrees, or 32 degrees in all. You'd save 100 percent because the house would be in balance with the outdoor temperature.

If you insulated the walls of the house, you probably would be comfortable by lowering the thermostat setting at least to 72 degrees, a 4-degree drop. You would then save 12.5 percent of your total heating bills (4 divided by 32) because you reduced your heat requirements inside the house by one-eighth of the way down to 44 degrees (where you would save 100 percent). That's a saving of 3.1 percent (12.5 divided by 4) for each degree the thermostat is lowered. The saving per degree in any other city is calculated in the same way on the basis of the average winter temperature in the area, as shown in the accompanying map.

Insulating your house ceilings, your window glass, and any other portions of the house shell that are ordinarily cold also reduces the overall chill factor of your house. It makes you comfortable inside at a lower thermostat setting, compared with no house insulation. Because the outside walls tend to be the greatest surface surrounding you in a typical house, the wall chill factor tends to be the greatest source of discomfort. In short, wall insulation is crucial for comfort and savings. Single-pane window glass will also get cold, and windows should therefore be protected with double glass. But according to government figures, windows in the average U.S. house account for only 15 percent of the total outside wall surface.

Similar savings come to you in an air-conditioned house for the same reason in reverse. Insulation keeps the walls, ceiling, and everything else from getting overheated and excessively hot and uncomfortable as a result of heat radiated from outside in. That's why it can be so hot and uncomfortable sleeping in a second-floor bedroom under a hot attic roof and attic in summer. You are being bathed in heat radiated down from the hot ceiling above, which is behaving like a radiant heater. That radiant heat can be stopped by proper insulation of the ceiling.

INSULATION MYTHS

Many people refrain from insulating their houses because they are unwitting victims of certain widespread myths, such as the following: *Thick walls of solid stone or brick are protection against winter cold.* "Look at those hefty walls," people say. Their fuel bills are likely to be hefty, too, because heat leaks out through stone, brick, and other masonry faster than it does through ordinary wood walls.

Actually, twice as much heat will leak out through a solid stone wall 2 feet thick as through an ordinary uninsulated wood frame wall only 8 inches thick. You would need a stone wall over 10 feet thick to give you the same heat-retaining protection you would get from an ordinary frame wall with 2 inches of insulation. Brick, concrete, and cinder-block walls are almost as leaky as stone. Yet for years it has been common (and penny-wise) practice to omit insulation from masonry walls. Masonry walls require insulation even more than wood walls.

Thick concrete block and other masonry wall should not be insulated because masonry stores cooling in summer and keeps a house from getting hot. More nonsense. The myth originated in the Southwest, where in summer it's extremely hot during the day but quite cool at night. Old adobe houses cool down considerably at night, and the thick, cool adobe indeed helps keep the houses cool well into the next hot day when the temperature is again soaring.

But in most other parts of the country, including the humid South and most of the North, the nights do not get very cool in summer. When a heat wave sends temperatures soaring in most of the country, the nighttime temperature generally does not fall below 70 degrees. A house with masonry walls does not cool off much and therefore does not help ward off the heat the next day.

No matter where you live, the walls of any house with air conditioning should be fully insulated. The walls of any house in a cold climate should be insulated against heat loss regardless of what they are made of. About the only time masonry walls need not be insulated is in a climate with mild winters where little or no heat is needed and where summers are very hot and dry.

The air space inside hollow walls helps insulate a house. Wrong again. At most, an air space can provide a little bit of extra insulation if it is at least ¾ inch thick. Widening the air space increases the insulating value very little. For example, a 3½-inch air space in a typical frame wall has little more insulating resistance to heat flow than ¾-inch space. A space less than ¾ inch thick has practically no insulating value, according to the *ASHRAE Guide,* the technical bible for thermal insulation data. It's published by the American Society of Heating, Refrigeration and Air-Conditioning Engineers.

Any person who says that the big, thick walls of his house have large air spaces inside and don't need regular insulation is full of beans. That myth is costing him dearly in wasted energy. If you doubt this, put your hand on the interior surface of a masonry wall

The closed walls of virtually any existing house construction can be insulated, assuming there is an open cavity space within. Mineral wool insulation is being blown into this brick wall.

during a cold winter day, and you'll quickly feel how cold it can get.

Insulation is more important over the ceilings than in walls. After all, heat rises, doesn't it? That's true, but even more heat will leak out of the walls of a house because the walls add up to a large chunk of exterior house shell that's exposed directly to the outdoor cold and to cold winds in winter. The wind is a major factor in winter heat loss from houses. On the other hand, the wind has little or no chilling effect on the ceiling because the ceiling is shielded from it by the roof and attic. Besides, the attic is considerably less cold than the outdoors and thus drains less heat from the ceiling than many people realize. Wall insulation is every bit as important as, if not more so than, ceiling insulation.

Insulation causes paint peeling. This half-truth keeps many people from insulating their houses because they fear that the exterior paint will blister and peel. Yet it is a scientific fact that insulation per se does not and cannot by itself cause paint peeling, with one main exception.

Paint peeling is caused primarily by moisture trapped inside walls. It is made worse by the wrong paint or defective paint. Occasionally, though experts say it is rare, the paint on a house may be on the verge of peeling and suddenly does so after walls are insulated. Very few of the hundreds of thousands of buildings that have been insulated have developed such problems, according to a top building authority. This small number would not have suffered, he says, if the chief cause of the problem, moisture, had been properly eliminated. The moisture stems from such causes as kitchen cooking, bathroom showers, a wet cellar or crawl space under the house, a leaky roof, or an unvented clothes dryer. It gets into your walls, with or without insulation, and plays havoc with the outside paint. Most of us need not fear paint peeling with insulation if we do not have it without insulation.

The exception to insulation by itself not causing paint peeling is urea-formaldehyde insulation, which when foamed into a house contains a great quantity of water. That water, no longer wanted, can cause trouble, such as paint peeling, when it later tries to force its way out from inside the house structure. More on this later in this chapter.

To play safe when you insulate an existing house, track down and eliminate sources of indoor moisture. Make sure gas heaters, stoves, and clothes dryers are vented to the outdoors. Use vapor-barrier paint when you redecorate interior walls and ceilings. If necessary, have little wall ventilators installed on the outside of the walls. When you remodel, using vapor-barrier insulation is one of the best safeguards against paint peeling.

How vapor barriers work and when they are needed is discussed in the next chapter.

Aluminum-foil insulation radiates back 95 percent of the heat in a house, thus cuts down heat leakage by that much. Foil, unfortunately, is widely misapplied owing to this misconception. A single sheet of foil will bounce back much radiant heat, the kind of heat that jumps across a space, like the sun's rays.

But inside the house structure, a sheet of foil is much less effective because heat leakage from the house is a sneaky business. Much of it occurs by means other than radiation—for example, by air currents within the walls (called convection). Foil by itself does not prevent these other kinds of heat leakage. Thus, a single sheet of foil does little good in your walls or roof in winter even though it is superb for

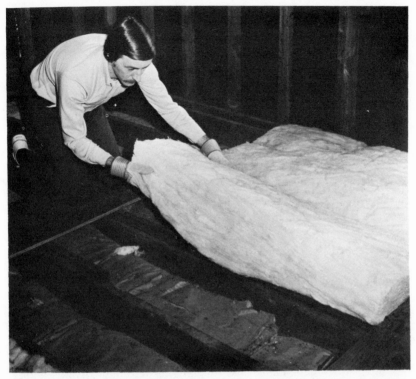

Because of sharply increased energy costs, beefing up the attic insulation will pay in most houses. Super-thick insulation is put down here over lean 3-inch insulation installed before the energy crisis.

baking potatoes in an oven. Foil can help a little when it is on one side of insulation, though its principal purpose there is to serve as a vapor barrier. It will give you a little extra insulating effectiveness sometimes if it faces an air space of at least ¾ inch. It can also be used directly under a roof to radiate back heat waves emanating down from the roof in summer.

THE MAIN KINDS OF INSULATION

Mineral wool is one of the most common kinds and in general the most recommended. It has a relatively high performance rating and is inorganic, naturally fire-resistant, rotproof, bug-resistant, versatile, and not high-priced. It includes rock wool and fiberglass materials. It is made in different forms and can be used almost anywhere. One of its few drawbacks is with fiberglass, which is made from small particles of glass. These can stick in your skin and be bothersome if inhaled. Installing it therefore calls for gloves and a face mask.

Cellulose insulation, also widely made and used, is a little cheaper than mineral wool and has a good performance rating. But it's an organic material made by mashing old newspapers, cardboard, and other such waste. In principle, that's all right, provided that it is chemically treated to make it fire-resistant and bug- and rotproof. The catch is that the chemical treatment is often inadequate and insufficient; with some brands it is practically nil.

Hundreds of companies are making cellulose insulation; new ones are springing up every week. Some of them are literally turning out the material in a garage with little or no quality control. The resulting product is understandably questionable, to put it kindly, and pretty hazardous stuff, to put it frankly. In short, you can't necessarily tell what you will get when you buy cellulose insulation. That's even if your local insulation contractor says he sells a top brand from a major manufacturer. "Look here," he adds, "the federal standard is marked right on the package." But that, too, is no guarantee that the stuff inside the package conforms with that standard. The material could still catch fire easily, rot, or for other reasons not last inside your house.

Until a truly dependable test for gauging its quality comes along, cellulose must be considered questionable. If you still want to use it, do these simple tests. First, put some in a pile, and try to set it afire. It should not burn. Next, wet it down. It should not soak up very much water and should dry fairly quickly. This test should be done on a batch of the actual material to be installed in your house, not on a salesman's special sample.

Urea-formaldehyde foam insulation (uf foam) could be the ideal insulation of the future. It's a chemical plastic that comes foaming out of a nozzle like shaving cream. It spreads quickly throughout the space being insulated, reaching virtually every nook and void inside a closed wall, for example. Practically nothing is missed, if the applicator knows what he is doing. The foamy material sets like a cake within a minute or so and completely cures and stabilizes in about three weeks.

But, unfortunately, all is not peaches and cream with uf foam. It still has troublesome bugs. Its effectiveness is subject to serious question until the following problems are solved.

Shrinkage is the biggest problem. After foam is put in a house it

Urea-formaldehyde foam insulation is gunned into an existing house much like mineral wool or cellulose insulation.

literally cracks and shrinks while curing. Manufacturers claim that the shrinkage is no more than 3 to 5 percent, but independent tests show greater shrinkage. For example, the walls of houses insulated with uf were opened up by the Minnesota State Energy Agency; the shrinkage ranged up to 10 percent.

Incidentally, uf foam is chiefly a wall insulation with occasional use only in other closed spaces. It is not recommended for use in any open space such as an attic where exposure to free-flowing air currents can cause extreme shrinkage and possible disintegration of the material.

Under ideal laboratory conditions, uf foam has an R-value of 4.2 per inch of thickness, according to U.S. government studies. Some manufacturers claim an R as high as 4.8, but that figure cannot be believed. Even the R value 4.2 should be discounted by 28 percent because of shrinkage, say officials of the Federal Housing Administration (FHA). In Europe and Canada the R value is discounted by 40 percent because of shrinkage. Thus the effective R value of uf foam comes down to 2.5 to 3.0, which can make it less efficient than mineral wool, including fiberglass, and cellulose insulation. Some foam makers may claim that they have developed nonshrink uf foam, but this is still to be confirmed by independent researchers.

UF foam, being a chemical plastic, can be highly temperamental. Unless it is installed carefully, it will not spread evenly and fill up every nook and cranny the way it is supposed to in the space being insulated.

Of all things, the maximum temperature and humidity that uf foam can withstand are still unknown. Tests by the National Bureau of Standards show that three of four brands of foam crumbled and disintegrated when exposed to 100-degree F and 95-percent relative humidity, but that's as far as the NBS tests go. True, that's an extreme condition encountered only in a few parts of the United States, such as southern states bordering on the Gulf of Mexico. Foam should not be installed in houses in these areas. Because of the lack of follow-up tests, it may be discovered that uf foam disintegrates at lower temperature and humidity conditions that have not been ascertained when this book was published.

Foam is roughly two-thirds water when it is put in a house. This can cause trouble when the water later evaporates and leaves the foam. During cold weather, the great quantity of water escaping (literally thousands of pounds) has caused paint peeling and blistering in houses. Put into an air-conditioned house during hot weather, all that moisture could conceivably cause the interior wall paint to peel off. That's because the moisture from the fresh foam can be sucked into the house as a result of lower vapor pressure inside with air conditioning. Here again, little is known about this possible problem, which should be investigated. The interior wall paint peeled in my house, which is air-conditioned, after uf foam was put in the walls in early summer.

A house with air conditioning should not be foamed with uf insulation prior to the start of hot weather or when the air conditioning is on. That's because the water in the foam takes as much as two months to evaporate and escape. To avoid possible trouble, until more is known about foam problems with air conditioning, don't turn on the air conditioning for two months after uf foam has been put in a house.

True, condensation and paint peeling are not likely in all houses insulated with uf foam, but you never can tell. The only sure way to avoid such a problem is not to use uf foam in a house, particularly in winter and in a cold climate. If a uf foam dealer disputes this and you decide to use the material, get a written guarantee from the company saying that it will pay the cost of repainting, if necessary, after your house is foamed.

In addition, good exit routes should be provided to let the foam water out easily when a house gets uf foam, in winter as well as in summer. How to do this is described in the Condensation section in the next chapter.

UF foam can cause a formaldehyde odor problem in houses. UF's competitors say, "It stinks, and shrinks." They say that the odor is dangerous, but this charge is exaggerated. In a few rare cases, a really botched installation of uf foam has caused a serious formaldehyde odor in houses. It can make one's eyes smart and sting. But there is no real scientific evidence that the odor is a real health hazard. It can be painful, but that's about all. Besides, formaldehyde has been used for years in structural plywood in millions of new houses, with no known detrimental effect to the humans inside.

Most brands of foam, by the way, have a shelf life of sixty days and should not be used if older. That applies to the so-called "wet" foams. The date that the foam was made and bottled should be marked on the container. There is also "dry" foam, which is a powder with a shelf life of one year. But dry foam has its potential Achilles heel too. Mixing it with its foaming agent when it is put in a house requires the kind of precision control encountered in a laboratory, and you can't necessarily depend on it in the field.

Summed up, uf foam may have great future potential, but its present relatively unproven stage of development makes buying it like buying a pig in a poke. In addition to shrinkage, a questionable R value, no scientific knowledge about its maximum tolerance to heat and humidity, and a possible water problem, it requires highly skilled applicators to assure a good job; unfortunately, some people installing it are not as skilled as they should be.

If you have uf foam put in your house, have it done only by really top people who have been in the business for some time. For self-protection, be sure that there are no serious voids and missed places before you make the final payment. This is done by drilling random holes in your walls to be sure there's foam all over. Better still, have an infrared camera check the whole house, as noted later.

Polystyrene is one of the best all-around insulations for houses because of its high insulating value, ruggedness, and durability, but its relatively high price limits it to special needs. Two of the main brands are Styrofoam and Scoreboard. It comes in sheets and boards with a very high insulating efficiency. It is particularly good for insulating a concrete floor, foundations, and basement walls. Because it is a rigid material, it can be put up flat on walls. Because it is inorganic and a good vapor barrier, it is impervious to water damage, rot, and bugs. It is a neat white material which can also be cemented to the inside of a masonry basement wall, for example, and easily plastered. That's in addition to using it on the outside of foundation walls for houses built over a concrete slab and with no basement. A 1-inch thick sheet of Styrofoam or other polystyrene gives you the equivalent insulating effectiveness of roughly 1½ inches of mineral wool or fiberglass.

Sheets of polystyrene also can be used in other parts of a house where there is little space and a lot of insulation has to be squeezed into a limited space.

Urethane is the most efficient of all insulation used in construction. It is roughly 50 percent better than polystyrene and two to three times better than the other insulations noted above. It is made in sheets and boards, and a mere 1 inch of it will give you the same protection that requires 2 to 3 inches of another insulation. That makes it excellent for use where space is limited, such as under a flat roof. But it's also two to three times more expensive than other insulations; that is why it's not used much in houses.

Urethane also can be foamed into closed spaces, but this is not recommended for house walls because it may expand and cause a wall section to buckle.

Perlite and vermiculite are metallic kinds of loose insulation, like gravel. Each has a lower insulating value than rock wool and fiberglass. Perlite is roughly 20 percent more efficient than vermiculite. To get the same insulating protection provided by 6 inches of rock wool insulation at your attic floor, some 7 inches of perlite and almost 9 inches of vermiculite are needed.

HOW INSULATION IS MADE AND APPLIED

It is made in four main forms: blanket, loose fill, board, and foam.

Blanket insulation is made in pads up to 8 inches thick and up to 24 inches wide. It may be bought in precut pads called batts, usually

4 feet long; and in rolls up to 50 to 75 feet long. You choose the width that will fit between the floor beams of your attic or between the studs of your walls (commonly 16 inches wide).

Loose fill insulation is, as the name suggests, loose insulation, like chopped-up pieces of wool, that comes in bags. It is dumped into the spaces between the floor beams and spread around with a rake to the desired thickness. It can also be blown into a space with a mechanical blower; that is how insulation contractors install it.

Board insulation is pressed into stiff boards or sheets chiefly for lining a wall or under a flat roof.

Foam insulation is a chemical plastic, like uf foam, that foams out of a cylinder, expands in a given space, and then solidifies.

On the whole, blanket or batt insulation is best for houses because it can fit any accessible space, it has a relatively higher R value, it will not settle or shrink, and it is also available with a vapor-barrier cover on one side.

INSULATION R VALUE

If all the different types of insulation were, like apples, basically the same, choosing insulation would be easy. But one kind of insulation can be twice as good at stopping heat as another, while a third is only half as good. So you can't buy insulation willy-nilly, taking what's easy to get and lowest in price. You must go a step further and gauge what you're getting by its R value.

That stands for resistance to heat flow, the way insulation is rated. R value is actually the inverse of the "conductivity" of an insulation, the rate at which heat will flow through a piece of material 1 square foot in size and 1 inch thick in one hour. For example, suppose the conductivity of an insulation is 0.30. Its R value is therefore 3.3 (1 divided by .30).

Here are the *approximate* R values for common insulations from the American Society of Heating and Air-Conditioning and Refrigeration Engineers (ASHRAE), the top industry authority in the field, and from U.S. government ratings. The higher the rating, the higher the insulation efficiency (though insulation should not be chosen only according to these ratings; other factors come into play). For example, a low-rated insulation may be better for some uses because its lower price enables you to buy more than a higher-rated material. The values can vary according to type and brand.

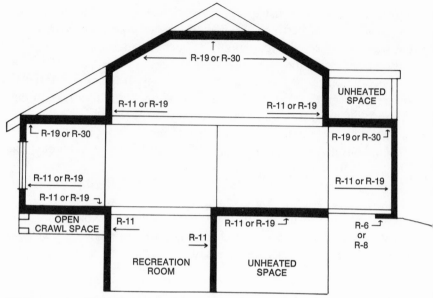

Different parts of a house require different amounts of insulation. The greater the R value, as shown here, the more the insulation recommended. This diagram shows the insulation needed for virtually every part of a house in a typical climate. More or less insulation than shown may be recommended in some houses, as noted in the text. *Courtesy, National Mineral Wool Insulation Association.*

Insulation	*R value per inch of thickness*
Polystyrene board and sheets	3.8 to 5.6
Urea-formaldehyde foam	3.0 (based on 4.2 initial value minus 28 percent to allow for shrinkage, according to FHA)
Mineral wool, rock wool, fiberglass batts and blankets	3.2 to 3.7
Mineral wool, rock wool, fiberglass loose fill	2.2 to 3.0
Cellulose loose fill	3.2 to 3.7
Perlite	2.5 to 3.7
Vermiculite	2.4 to 3.0

To determine the approximate R value of insulation more than 1 inch thick, multiply the thickness by the R value per inch. For example, 3 inches of a fiberglass batt with an R per inch of 3.3 will give you a total R value of 9.9 (3 times 3.3). Some brands, however, will give a little higher or lower total R value, so you must check the total R value of any insulation you may buy. But that should be easy because it's usually marked on the package. If not, don't buy it.

To determine how much insulation is needed to give a specified R, such as R-19 at your attic ceiling, divide the R value needed by the R value per inch of the insulation used. Suppose you use blanket rock wool at your attic ceiling, and the package says it has an R value of 3.2 per inch. To get R-19 at your attic floor, you would need 5.93 inches of it (19 divided by 3.2). Or use batt or blanket insulation that says it is R-19.

The important point: No matter what insulation you use, it should be specified and bought according to its R value. Then you can be assured of getting reasonably good protection. Any insulation that is not R-rated should be rejected, no matter what a salesman says.

HOW MUCH INSULATION FOR EACH PART OF YOUR HOUSE?

R values make it easy to choose the right amount of insulation for all parts of your house. The accompanying diagram shows the R value of insulation recommended for each part of a house in the United States. These recommendations are based on using insulation that will pay for itself in fuel and energy savings in five to ten years.

Naturally, the insulation recommended will vary according to such variables as climate and the kind of heat energy used (because fuel costs vary). Thus, the colder your climate and the costlier your heating fuel, the higher the R value needed to save on energy. A house with central heating and central air conditioning ordinarily should have more insulation, thus a higher R value, than a house with heating only.

INSULATION RECOMMENDED FOR A HOUSE WITH GAS, OIL, OR ELECTRIC HEAT WITH AND WITHOUT CENTRAL AIR CONDITIONING

Choose insulation with this R value (thermal resistance):

New addition or new construction	Ceilings	Walls	Floors over vented crawl space	Floors over unheated basement	Walls between heated and unheated parts of a house
Annual degree days of your climate					
Over 5,500	R-30	R-18	R-19	R-19	R-11
3,500–5,500	30	13	19	11	11
Under 3,500	19	11	19	11	11
Central air conditioning, all climates	30	18	19	11	11

Existing houses	Ceilings	Walls	Floors over vented crawl spaces	Floors over unheated basement	Walls between heated and unheated parts of a house
Annual degree days					
Over 5,500	30	11	19	19	11
3,500–5,500	30	11	19	11	11
Under 3,500	19	11	19	11	11
Central air conditioning, all climates	30	11	19	11	11

Special notes: *The R values in this table are stiff recommended standards especially for houses with electric heat and air conditioning. They can be occasionally lowered in a house with gas or oil heat, which costs less than electric heat. For example, even in the coldest climate (over 5,500 degree days), the walls of a house with gas or electric heat could be made with an R value down to 13 with little sacrifice in savings, and the R value for the ceilings of a house with gas or electric heat in any climate could be as low as 19 with minimal savings sacrificed.*

NEW RECOMMENDED *INSULATION LEVELS IN
SIX U.S.A. HEATING AND COOLING ZONES

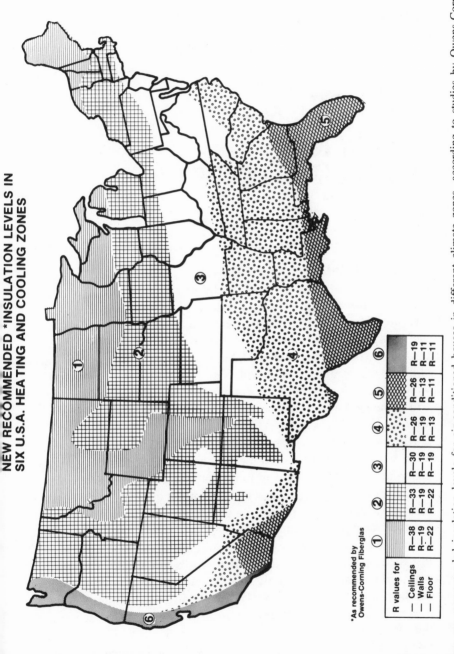

*As recommended by
Owens-Corning Fiberglas

R values for	①	②	③	④	⑤	⑥
— Ceilings	R—38	R—33	R—30	R—26	R—26	R—19
— Walls	R—19	R—19	R—19	R—19	R—13	R—11
— Floor	R—22	R—22	R—19	R—19	R—11	R—11

Here are recommended insulation levels for air-conditioned houses in different climate zones, according to studies by Owens-Corning Fiberglas Corporation. Less insulation than given above may be used in houses with central heating only.

CHAPTER 18

HOW TO INSULATE A HOUSE

START WITH THE CEILING

More total energy and money can be saved per dollar invested by insulating the ceiling of a house than by any other energy-saving measure. Most ceilings can be insulated quickly and inexpensively merely by putting a layer of insulation at the attic floor. It can be an easy do-it-yourself job, completed in a day or two. Except in a warm climate, the insulation cost will come back to you in fuel savings within a year or two. Hire a contractor to do it, and the increased cost will come back in savings within three years. The savings every year afterward are all gravy.

Attic insulation should not be put under the roof at the top of the attic. It goes there only when the attic has been converted into rooms and when that's the only way to insulate the ceilings of each room.

Insulation always goes at the floor of an unheated attic for two reasons. It permits the rest of the attic to be ventilated in winter and summer. That's important to keep the whole space under the roof free of moisture and condensation damage. And if the attic floor is well insulated, the loss of heat from the rooms below will be too small to matter. In summer good attic ventilation will wash out excess heat and help keep the house below cool; with air conditioning that means lower electric bills. R-19 insulation, *at least,* should go at the attic floor in all houses except those in the warm South without air conditioning, where less insulation may be used. On the other hand, more than R-19 is recommended for houses with air conditioning. This is noted in the table in the preceding chapter.

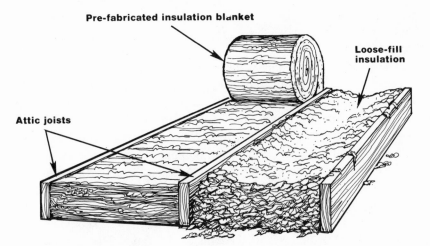

Pre-fabricated insulation blanket

Loose-fill insulation

Attic joists

"BLANKET" INSULATION

- Pre-fabricated by manufacturer into uniform densities or "R-values."
- Easy to install; simply unroll and lay into place.
- Offers greater assurance of in-use performance.

"LOOSE-FILL" INSULATION

- Must be carefully machine or hand poured to achieve a given density or R-value.
- Can settle over period of years.

You can obviously tell if insulation is needed over the ceiling by going up and looking for it between the attic floor beams. It may be a tight squeeze in some attics, but it is usually possible. If there's flooring in the attic, prop open a few of the floorboards, and look inside. Is there insulation? Is it enough? If it's less than recommended for your house, add a second batch of insulation over what you already have to bring the insulation up to par.

New blanket insulation is better than loose fill insulation for the attic floor. The blanket kind may cost a little more, but it gives more uniform coverage and a higher R value. Merely unroll the blanket insulation, and cut it to fit the length of each space. Its width is initially chosen to fit when it is bought. The cost generally runs about 1 cent per square foot for each unit of R value—i.e., 19 cents per square foot for R-19, installation, plus labor.

If you have a wood floor in your attic, the insulation still should be installed under the floor between the floor beams. This is done in either of two ways: Remove enough of the flooring to put the insulation below it, and then renail the flooring back in place, or blow loose fill insulation into the spaces below the floor with an insulation blower. Sometimes the blowers can be rented ($30 to $50 a day). If not, and if you can't do it yourself, the insulation will have to be blown in, a job for a contractor. But then you could probably hire a teenager to pull up the floor, blanket the area with insulation, and replace the floor for less money.

The floor of an attic that is difficult to reach or otherwise not easily accessible must generally be insulated by blowing in bags of loose fill. Insist on a contract that clearly states the number of bags of insulation the contractor will provide when he does this work for you. You must check that the total volume of insulation provided will give you the R value needed. Figure the number of square feet of area to be insulated; then multiply by the thickness required (in fractions of a foot). This gives the total cubic feet of insulation needed. Then count the empty bags used after the insulation was put in.

If mineral wool fill insulation is used, each bag should bear a legend that it complies with Federal Specification HH-1-1030A for mineral wool insulation. If cellulose insulation is used, it should conform with Federal Specification HH-I-515C, though this may be revised, to 515D, for example. Only properly marked insulation should be used.

Insulating the ceiling of a new addition to your house is done much the same way as it is on an existing ceiling but is usually easier, just as insulating a new house during construction is easier. Because new construction is easier to insulate, insulation with a higher R value can be installed, as recommended in the table on page 191.

A ceiling that is to be insulated will also benefit if it is lined with a vapor barrier at the same time. Some kinds of blanket insulation come with a vapor barrier lining on one side. If loose fill insulation is used, a sheet of vapor-impermeable plastic is put down on the attic floor first, before the insulation is poured. More on vapor barriers is given later in this chapter.

INSULATING THE WALLS OF A HOUSE
New walls for a new room or addition are easy to insulate. The insulation will pay for itself in fuel savings within two or three years in nearly every house with central heat. In colder climates, where heating costs more because larger amounts of fuel are consumed, the more the savings mount and the faster insulation will pay for itself.

Thick blankets of mineral wool insulation, pressed or stapled in between the wall studs, is usually best for insulating new walls being built. A vapor barrier should be used if your average January temperature is less than 35 degrees F. See the map on page 192.

It almost always pays to fill the walls with insulation. In a very cold climate, especially where high-cost electric heat is in use, additional insulation may be wise. One way to make it possible is by building the walls thick to provide a cavity for 6-inch insulation. But the higher cost of the walls, plus construction complications that arise, makes their value questionable, and the extra benefits that result are comparatively small. Besides, virtually as much extra protection can be obtained from standard 2 x 4 fully insulated walls with insulating sheathing board, instead of the ordinary noninsulating type on the outside. Sheathing is the sheet material that is nailed on the outside of wall studs before the outside wall skin (clapboard, stucco, brick, etc.) is put on. (The type that is insulated has a comparatively high resistance to heat flow.)

INSULATING CLOSED WALLS OF AN EXISTING HOUSE

This is one of the biggest needs in existing houses. Its cost ranges from about $750 to several thousand dollars. Fuel savings will usually repay the cost in from two to eight years.

Are your walls already insulated? to find out, remove the cover plates from a few electric switches and outlets and peer inside the wall with a flashlight. Don't fail to turn off the electricity by removing the appropriate fuse or turning off the circuit breaker. Or drill a few ¾-inch holes at random in the walls if you cannot otherwise see right away. Close them later, of course. Another good place to look is in a closet with an exterior wall, where openings will not leave a conspicuous scar.

The walls of houses built prior to the late 1950s and early 1960s were generally not insulated during construction. If your house was built earlier, its walls were probably not insulated, and if it was built about that time, the insulation is likely to be not enough by today's standards.

Another way to learn about the insulation in a wall is by the palm test. Hold the palm of your hand flat against each exterior wall of your house. In winter it should not feel colder than an *interior* wall. If it is colder, it means the wall is losing excessive heat to the outdoors and insulation is needed. The same test for ceilings and floors, particularly around the perimeter of rooms with outside walls, will reveal other unsuspected cold sources. Though not infallible, the palm test is a handy way of spotting problem areas.

How warm do you have to keep your house in winter? If you are comfortable with the thermostat at 70 to 72 degrees, you probably don't need insulation. If you have to set the thermostat from 75 to over 80 degrees, you probably need insulation, since a high thermostat setting is a tip-off to little or no insulation. You have to heat the house air warmer to compensate for the loss of body heat to the cold structure.

Still another indication of insulation or the lack of it is snow retention around the house. Does the snow remain piled up around the exterior walls of your house? Or does it melt for about a foot away from the house skirt while it remains on the ground elsewhere? If it melts away, you are paying to heat the snow, as well as the house. Excessive heat is leaking out through the floor or the low sidewalls. This is also a good indication of whether or not you have adequate floor insulation in a house without a basement.

The closed walls of any house can be insulated comparatively easily if there is an air space inside the walls. Loose insulation or foam is pumped into the cavity through holes drilled in the wall. This can be done to a brick, stone, or stucco wall, as well as to conventional wood frame walls. The cost ranges from about 50 cents to $1 per square foot of net wall area; it varies according to the kind of insulation used and the type of wall. Cellulose insulation is the cheapest, mineral wool generally costs a little more, and uf foam costs the most. The average three-bedroom house has about 1,400 square feet of wall surface, so the contractor price for insulating the walls can range from $700 to $1,400.

A skilled do-it-yourself person could install the same insulation and save a good part of that bill by renting a blower to install it. There can be complications, however, so consult an insulation contractor before you plunge in. Pay the contractor for his advice by buying the insulation and possibly renting the blower from him.

If you hire a contractor, sometimes savings can be made by drilling the holes in the walls before the contractor arrives to blow in the insulation and by closing them up afterward. Depending on your house construction, this could save as much as one-third of the contractor's regular price. If the saving is important, discuss it with contractors when you get bids.

Another do-it-yourself way to insulate the present walls of a house is by adding sheets of a high R value insulating board over the present surface; the best would be Styrofoam. An inch or two of this new interior insulating wall surface is not as effective as full wall insulation, but it can be a big step forward.

Incidentally, the addition of new aluminum or vinyl siding on the walls of a house is no excuse for not insulating them, even if the siding is allegedly insulated. This type of siding comes with a mere ½ inch or so of insulation, and that's like trying to stop a Sherman tank with a rifle. Real wall insulation is still needed, no matter what a salesman says. The siding would have to be beefed up with considerably more insulation (to R-11 at least) before it can do any real good. A good time to have the walls fully insulated, however, is when new siding is put on a house.

HOW TO BUY WALL INSULATION FROM A CONTRACTOR

An insulation contractor once told me that he does home insulation jobs only because "insulating the house walls is a nice clean business. It's difficult for the customer to tell when you've made a mistake," he said. Unlike Superman with his X-ray vision, the usual homeowner can't tell if the walls were completely filled with insulation or if any spaces were missed. When the job is finished, the contractor is paid and generally never again hears from the customer.

That's fine for the contractor but not for you, the homeowner. Human errors are made, but some home improvement contractors are careless, or shoddy, or even outright crooks who may shave the quality of their work deliberately. Since insulation is hidden inside the walls, an improperly done job is hard to spot (except by your heating unit, which must use extra fuel). It's your job to catch them, whether the deficiencies are accidental or not.

To be sure of getting a good wall insulation job, start right and deal only with a good, experienced contractor. He should be one who's been in business for more than a year or two. Literally thousands of new people have entered the business since the energy crunch began, and many are still green and learning, not to mention the inevitable fast-buck operators among them. So don't be a guinea pig. Get price bids from at least two or three, but don't necessarily buy the lowest in price. And check on the contractor before signing, as suggested later in Chapter 36.

When the contractor comes to insulate your walls, not only count

Left: An infrared picture is not only an excellent way to tell if a house needs insulation, it's also an excellent way to tell if new insulation has been properly installed in a house, particularly within the enclosed walls. Warm, uninsulated parts of a house show up as bright spots on this infrared photo, which was taken before the house was insulated. The most heat leaked out around windows before the house was insulated. *Right:* After storm windows and insulation were put in, the heat loss from the house is considerably less than before. Virtually no heat is now leaking out through the ceiling and the roof, which is black.

This is the Bowman test house located on the grounds of the National Bureau of Standards, Gaithersburg, Maryland. Insulation and storm windows installed in this house cut the heat losses by more than 50 percent, as noted in the text. *Photos courtesy the National Bureau of Standards.*

the bags of insulation used, but also stand outside and watch the men work. Don't be shy about this. Watch that insulation is fed into every part of the walls. You still cannot be sure that every stud space in the walls was filled up all the way, so another check is necessary afterward. Many people don't make their final payment until they have drilled small holes at random in the walls around their house to be sure that insulation fills up every space. This is easily done on the inside of a house and, of course, must be patched later. If necessary, the contractor is called back to fill the missed voids. Many homeowners assertively carry out this check, and a surprising number of them find voids in their walls.

Another check is the use of an infrared camera or gun to scan the walls of a house after they have been insulated. These devices register heat which you can see when one is aimed at a house. Areas like window glass, as well as uninsulated portions of a wall where heat is rapidly escaping, show up on the device. This tells you where insulation was left out.

Some insulation contractors, in fact, say that they use an infrared camera or gun to check on their work and assure you that the job will be well done. Ask the contractors about this before you buy. An infrared camera and gun, however, will work only when there is a difference of at least 10 to 20 degrees between the indoor and outdoor temperature. So you cannot count on the test during mild spring or fall weather or in the summer unless you have air conditioning. Take this into account if you buy insulation at such a time and the job is subject to an infrared check.

INSULATING THE FLOORS OF HOUSES
WITHOUT BASEMENTS

This includes houses built over a crawl space—i.e., a space between the ground and the first floor just large enough to crawl into—and houses with a concrete slab floor built on the ground. The first floor of a crawl-space house should be insulated. Blanket insulation is stapled up in between the floor joists. The insulation may have to be supported with chicken wire, for example, to prevent sagging.

Floor insulation over a crawl space is sometimes omitted because of the erroneous notion that a tightly shut crawl space makes insulation unnecessary. That's a mistake because the usual crawl space requires ventilation in winter, as in summer, to keep it free of moisture, wood rot, termites, and vapor travel up into the house. Much water vapor and moisture can get into the space from the earth below. Ventilation is essential. Insulation is therefore required under the floor, and it should be backed with a vapor barrier (on its top surface facing up toward the house).

A good vapor-barrier cover should also be laid over the crawl-

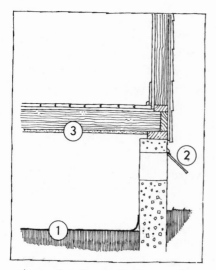 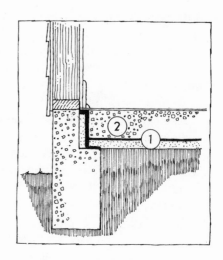

A new first floor built over a crawl space should have 1) a vapor barrier over the ground; 2) vents to air the crawl space; 3) insulation under the floor. A concrete floor on the ground should have 1) a vapor barrier between the floor and the ground; 2) edge insulation, built into the concrete around the floor perimeter.

space earth to prevent the rise of ground vapor up into the house. This can be polyethylene plastic sheet (at least 4 mills thick) or 55-pound roll-roofing building paper. A vapor-barrier seal over the earth is unnecessary only if the crawl space is well ventilated the year around. With no vapor barrier the crawl space should have at least four vents and 1 square foot of vent opening for every 150 square feet of crawl-space area.

Sometimes a crawl space is heated (usually when the heating unit is located there) and ventilation is not required. The crawl space is kept shut, insulation is applied on the inside surfaces of the crawl-space walls, and a vapor-barrier sheet is essential over the ground.

INSULATING A CONCRETE FLOOR

A concrete floor needs insulation all around its outside edges where it is exposed directly to outdoor cold and snow. This type of insulation is called perimeter or edge insulation. It is generally placed around the floor perimeter (usually in boards or sheets) before the concrete is poured. It stops floor heat from draining out all around the outside.

Incidentally, the underside of a concrete slab normally doesn't require insulation because the ground below, being protected, rarely gets cold enough to warrant it.

Does your present concrete floor need insulation? If it feels cold, particularly around the edges, and if snow quickly melts away from it, the answer is probably yes. It's possible that some insulation was installed when the house was built, even though it isn't visible, but if you have these telltale signs, it probably wasn't enough.

New edge insulation is applied to a slab floor simply by putting it flat up against the outside edge of your floor all around the house. The insulation sheets or boards are placed vertically in the ground extending to the frost line or below, which generally means 2 or 3 feet below grade. Because edge insulation is usually soft and can be bruised easily, it should be covered with a hard skin, such as asbestos cement board, that will protect it.

A good rotproof inorganic insulation should be used, which calls for a mineral wool or a foam plastic, such as polystyrene or urethane. Use a thickness that conforms with these R values:

R VALUES FOR EDGE INSULATION FOR A CONCRETE HOUSE FLOOR

Climate: heating degree days per year	Thermal resistance, or R value needed with gas or oil heat	electric heat
Over 8,000	R-8	R-10
4,500–8,000	6	8
Under 4,500	4	6

WHY VAPOR BARRIERS ARE IMPORTANT

Vapor barriers for houses go hand in hand with insulation. As noted earlier, they have long been highly recommended, if not essential, for nearly all houses in the northern United States and all Canada where the outdoor temperature in January drops below 35 degrees. That's roughly the northern two-thirds of the nation. A vapor barrier is a material that is impermeable to water vapor travel, such as aluminum foil, sheet plastic, and asphalt-treated paper. Its purpose is to keep the walls, ceiling, attic, and other structural guts of a house dry, much the way plastic and foil wrapping keeps food from going bad.

Vapor barriers can be installed the easy way by using blanket insulation that comes with an integral vapor-barrier lining (such as foil or kraft paper skin) on one side. With one exception, insulation should be installed with its vapor-barrier side facing the *interior* of the house. In other words, attic insulation should have its vapor barrier on the bottom facing down and toward the living quarters below.

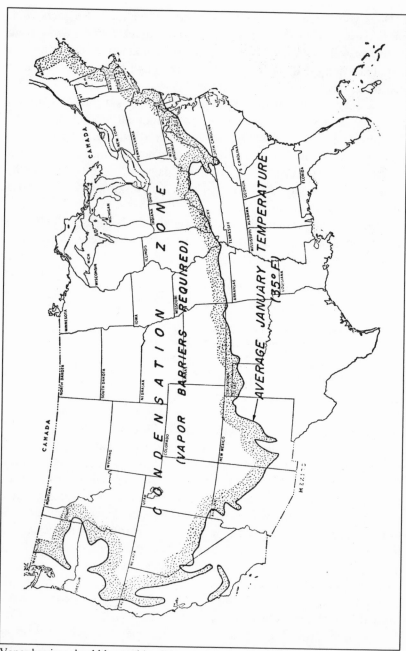

Vapor barriers should be used in all houses located where the average temperature in January is 35 degrees F or lower. *Forest Products Laboratory, U.S. Department of Agriculture.*

Wall insulation should have its vapor barrier facing in and toward the house interior. To prevent errors, the barrier side of insulation is clearly marked. Nevertheless, mistakes occur, resulting in improperly installed insulation with the vapor barrier facing outdoors. When this happens, condensation can wet the insulation, making it ineffective, the same way a damp pot holder no longer insulates and can burn your hand.

The exception to this rule is in air-conditioned houses in the hot, humid areas of the South, such as around the Gulf of Mexico, where winters are mild. Here vapor barriers are installed facing outdoors. That's to prevent water vapor from the high-humidity outdoor air from being drawn *into* the house in summer. That's the result of the interior vapor pressure's being lower than outdoors when the air conditioning is operating.

Vapor barriers, however, are used chiefly to prevent moisture and condensation troubles in a cold climate in winter. One of the more common troubles is blistering and peeling on the outside house walls. It is often conspicuous on walls outside kitchen and bathrooms because both are large producers of moisture. In winter, in a house with no vapor barrier, the vapor sails right through the walls, inexorably pulled outdoors, because the vapor pressure of the cold outdoor air is lower than that inside the heated house, and like water seeking its level, vapor must equalize itself. It flies right through an ordinary wall structure like cigarette smoke through a handkerchief.

A coat of oil-base paint is impervious to water vapor and therefore acts as a barrier. If it is the first such barrier that vapor meets on its way outdoors, the paint stops it dead in its tracks. Then the vapor is likely to condense out as drops of water on the cold interior side of the paint, just as vapor striking a cold windowpane condenses and fogs up the window. When it condenses and bubbles up underneath the paint film, it pops the paint and causes blistering and peeling.

That happens in houses irrespective of whether or not the walls or any other parts of the house are insulated, assuming that no vapor barrier exists to stop the movement of vapor in and out of the house. Once in a while, when a house is insulated, the new insulation will trigger vapor condensation, but only when the problem was on the verge of happening before.

In short, the problem is basically caused by water and moisture, not by insulation, as noted in the previous chapter. It sometimes happens after a house has been insulated, when all the conditions for vapor condensation were already present, and insulating the house walls, for example, was the final nudge. Because insulation keeps house heat inside, the outside walls are colder than before. Hence, when the vapor, still pushing its way to the outdoors, hits the cold outside walls, it condenses. It did not condense before because the outside walls were warmed just enough by heat leaking from the house. In other words, the insulation keeps the heat in and the temperature of the outside walls below the dew point at which moisture condenses.

HOW TO STOP CONDENSATION AND PAINT DAMAGE

The colder the climate, the greater the likelihood of condensation in the house structure. Paint blistering generally can be avoided by the use of latex paint that "breathes," rather than an impermeable oil paint that does not.

Here are other ways to avoid condensation problems. Provide an escape path for vapor by opening a window or two slightly in the kitchen and bathrooms, particularly during high vapor periods (cooking, taking showers, etc.). An exhaust fan is even better, especially in the kitchen. The clothes dryer, another major vapor producer, should be vented outdoors even if it is located in the basement. It spews out great clouds of vapor that can be destructive and should be got rid of fast. If necessary, paint your *inside* house walls with a vapor barrier. Two coats of an alkyd semigloss interior house paint will give a permeability of one or less. That is an indication of the rate of water vapor travel through a material, with a rating of one or less being the definition of a vapor barrier. Special vapor-barrier paints are expected to be introduced by 1979, so you might also ask your paint supplier about their availability.

When insulation is blown or foamed into walls, the insulation contractor could also provide paths for water vapor to escape so it is not bottled up in the walls. For example, the paint cover underneath each course of wood siding could be narrowly cut with a knife. Or small circular metal vents for the purpose could be inserted in the outside wall, particularly outside the kitchen and bathrooms. Making allowances for water vapor migration from a house is virtually mandatory when urea-formaldehyde insulation is used, for the reasons noted in the preceding chapter.

CHAPTER 19
STORM WINDOWS, DOORS, AND WEATHERSTRIPPING

Five times as much heat leaks out of a house through a single-pane glass window as through the same area of uninsulated wall. Twenty-five times as much heat will leak out through glass as will through the same area of insulated wall. Window glass is clearly the biggest cause of heat loss from a house, short of the mass exit of heat through an entrance door left open.

Obviously, windows should be "insulated." An insulated window is one having at least two parallel sheets of glass separated by an air space. According to tests at the University of Illinois's Small Homes Council, insulating glass can mean "fuel savings of 20 percent or more," depending on your climate zone and the amount of glass in the house. The 20 percent savings resulted in an experimental house with twenty double-hung windows in Springfield, Illinois.

In a house with a well-insulated structure and a small ratio of glass to overall wall area, fuel savings with insulating glass may amount to only 10 or 15 percent a year. In a house with a great expanse of glass the fuel savings may approach 40 percent. And as mentioned earlier, storm windows added to the twenty-six windows in the National Bureau of Standards test house mentioned earlier cut the annual fuel bills by 25 percent.

Ordinary single-pane windows get quite cold—put your hand on one on a day when the temperature is low. In addition to cold down-drafts swirling into rooms, cold glass causes chills and goose pimples by drawing off body heat from your skin, and it fogs up with moisture because of condensation. Insulating glass combats these defects because the inside glass pane stays warmer. That means

Double-pane insulating glass does not frost or fog up in winter. The frosted windows at right are ordinary single-pane glass. *Pittsburgh Plate Glass Co.*

a warmer room, lower fuel bills, and no window condensation.

Insulating glass includes storm windows, which give double protection. They consist of a second window installed over the first. The storm window shields the inside window from wind and cold and cuts the heat loss through that window roughly in half.

There is also commercially made double glass, like Thermopane and Twindow, two national brands. Each consists of two sheets of glass with a sealed air space in between. Sealed double glass also cuts window heat loss by roughly one-half, sometimes a little more, depending on the type. The latest twist is triple glass, consisting of three parallel sheets of glass with two inert air spaces. The heat loss through triple-pane glass is one-third that of single-pane windows.

STORM WINDOWS VERSUS SEALED INSULATING GLASS

Which is better? The main purpose of storm windows is to insulate existing windows in an existing house. They are sold in standard

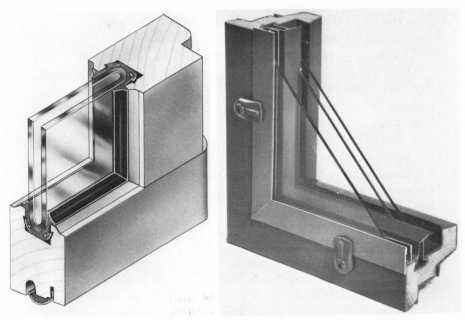

Left: Sealed double glass in windows cuts heat loss by 50 percent, compared with single-pane glass. Tinted glass is also available to cut sun heat entry in summer in air-conditioned houses. *Right:* Triple-pane glass cuts heat loss by roughly 35 percent, compared with double-pane glass. *Andersen Corp.*

sizes to fit standard windows, and they can be custom-made to fit nonstandard windows.

The most versatile storm windows are triple-track units which include screens for window ventilation in summer. Triple-track units need not be removed in spring and put up again in the fall, as do ordinary storm windows. A storm door, of course, is a great deal like a storm window, a second door to protect the first from winter cold.

Sealed double- or triple-glass units are better when new windows are installed in a house. Compared with storm windows, sealed insulating glass offers these four benefits:

1. Convenience, since double glass does not have to be put up and taken down every year, as do some storm windows;

2. Reduced maintenance, with only two glass surfaces to keep clean instead of four;

3. Easier ventilation the year around with double-window units;

4. Neater, better appearance.

HOW DOES INSULATING GLASS PAY OFF?

With gas or oil heat, double-glass windows will pay for themselves in fuel savings, as well as increased comfort, in a climate with at least 3,000 degree days of winter, with electric heat down to 2,000 degree days, according to National Bureau of Standards studies. Triple insulating glass will pay off in savings and comfort in a climate of 5,500 degree days or more.

If you have home air conditioning, storm windows can be left on the year around, as they work just as well in reverse, so to speak. Insulating glass reduces summer-heat entry from hot outside *air* into a house by roughly 50 percent. Only half as much outside air heat will enter through a square foot of either kind as will enter through the same area of single-pane glass.

Reducing sun heat in summer, however, is another matter. Despite popular belief, nearly as much solar heat will enter through double glass as through single glass, and solar heat is by far the bigger heat problem. In other words, if you live in the South, spending extra money for sealed double glass or storm windows will generally not pay for itself in reduced cooling costs. A shading device is the only way to keep out sun heat. Like storm windows, double glass pays off most in increased comfort and reduced fuel bills in a cold climate.

Summed up, sealed double glass is generally worth its cost in a cold climate when you remodel. Window openings should conform to stock-size double-glass units. These are commonly used glass sizes, available quickly, and lower in cost than other sizes not kept in stock.

BUYING STORM WINDOWS AND DOORS

There are many hundreds, if not thousands, of storm window manufacturers in the country and—here we go again with our "buyer beware" warning—you enter the market for getting well-made ones with the odds against you. Many are poorly made; they'll quickly pit and corrode and not last very long. When new, however, they're as shiny and attractive as the best-made units, and it takes an experienced eye to tell the difference. The problem, of course, is the same with much other merchandise. The very low price advertised for questionable storm windows is an enormous tug for buying them, and at the moment of truth we conveniently forget that low price generally means low quality.

Some of the incredibly low-price ads for storm windows and doors are outright bait ads, often for windows that are not even available. Answer such an ad, and a slick salesman will confidentially tell you that the windows in the ad are so shoddy and poorly made that he doesn't have the nerve to sell them to you. They're junk, he says.

With a highly persuasive buildup he switches you to much more expensive combination units priced three to four times as high. One New Jersey couple actually signed up for the cheapest windows advertised. The salesman said, "Of course, you'll have to rub them down once a week with steel wool, but they still may pit and corrode." The couple was alarmed.

The salesman poured it on. "But you'll never need to wipe these really good windows. They never pit, never discolor. The screens and glass are better made. The frames are guaranteed for a lifetime." An hour later the husband and wife tore up the old contract for a set of windows at $149.95 and were talked into signing an outrageously overpriced $559.95 order.

This example of the gyps' tactics may make us smile sadly. We feel that it can happen to others but not to us. Actually, it happens to many people, though perhaps not so blatantly. The initial offer may be for $21.95 windows, which aren't that bad; but before we know it, we are up to $50 windows, which may sound like the very best but are not worth more than $25.

For good-quality aluminum storm windows, look for windows with an AAMA label on them, which means the windows conform with the certification and labeling program of the Aluminum Architectural Manufacturers Association. Windows with this seal have been tested for compliance with the standard. There's one possible catch. Only a small percentage of the many manufacturers of aluminum storm windows and doors participates in this certification program. That may make your shopping quest a little longer, but it's worth the extra time.

The other way to be assured of getting good storm windows is to buy—yes, still again—from a reputable dealer. Or get a good national brand, though this is not always easy to do. New manufacturers seem to enter the field all the time, and old ones leave. One of the few national makers who have been making good storm windows for a long time is Rusco.

DO-IT-YOURSELF STORM WINDOWS

Window kits run the gamut from clear plastic sheets that you cut to size and staple or tack up around an existing window to prefabricated window frames and moldings with which permanent storm windows and screens are made. But again you must shop to see what's available in your area. The various kinds sold vary from year to year, and improvements in them are continually being made.

Some are made for inexpensive installation on the inside of a window; this is practical in a rented house or high-rise apartment. Once installed, some cannot be opened. Later, when the storm window is removed in summer, little or nothing of it may be reusable the following winter. Still others provide a permanent frame that can be reused year after year, though new plastic must be bought and installed each year. These are things to check before you buy, especially before falling for a storm window kit with an almost irresistibly low price. Kits for full-fledged aluminum frames or moldings from which you can make a complete professional storm window are sold by at least one national manufacturer, Reynolds Metals Company, Richmond, Virginia 23261.

WEATHERSTRIPPING

This, of course, is the material that is used to plug up the cracks, crevices, and openings around a window or doorframe to keep warm air from escaping and cold air from entering. Many windows and doors fit loosely, some of them leaving gaping openings through which jets of cold air zoom into a house. Weatherstripping seals off such leaks.

You can find these leaks easily on a cold, windy day by moving a hand around door and window frames, at the bottoms of doors, and also across the middle joints of double-hung windows. Do it on the windward side of the house.

Various kinds of weatherstripping are available. You can see a good selection at a lumberyard, at a hardware store, or in the Sears, Roebuck catalogue.

Incidentally, old windows should be weatherstripped *before* new storm windows are installed. Failure to seal a loose old window can open the way for troublesome condensation on the inside face of the new storm window. Water vapor from inside the house sails into the space between the two windows and condenses on the cold inside surface of the storm window.

Tests at the University of Minnesota show that weatherstripping can reduce total heat loss from a house as much as 37 percent. This is close to the extreme saving. By and large, fuel savings may run closer to 10 or 20 percent, compared with having no weatherstripping at all. Equally important is the sharply increased comfort that results when leaks are plugged, and air jets stop blowing into the house.

CHAPTER 20

HOW TO STOP
FUEL WASTE AT
THE HEATING SYSTEM

Everybody talks about insulation as if it was the only way to cut fuel bills. But it is not, of course. A lot of energy and money can also be saved merely by being sure that your heating system, that mechanical oven down in the cellar, is perking along in fine, uninhibited, and healthy fashion.

It's like an auto engine. Give it a little loving care once in a while, keep it happy and in tune, and it can save a lot of expensive fuel that would otherwise be wasted.

Not so long ago a big utility company in the East decided to investigate the efficiency of the heating systems in several hundred houses chosen at random. The findings were appalling. In more than three-quarters of the houses, 25 percent or more of the fuel being consumed was wasted. That much heat was going up the chimney rather than into the house.

Yet in most, only routine tuning, cleaning, and adjustment were needed to eliminate that waste and have the equipment perform efficiently. All the systems tested were oil burners, which are the most wasteful of all when neglected. Gas and electric heating systems, however, can also benefit from periodic checks and adjustments.

A second way to cut fuel costs at the heater depends on the kind of heating you have. If it is fueled by electricity, merely switching to gas or oil heat can often cut annual heating bills by 50 to 75 percent! Gas and oil cost that much less than electricity in many parts of the country. Switching from oil to natural gas can cut fuel bills by 25 to 50 percent, depending on your local gas cost. The cost of switching is repaid by the operating savings. (More on switching fuels later.) Here is a checklist of how to keep a heating system well tuned, reduce fuel waste, and cut fuel bills significantly.

1. *Test your heating efficiency.* A serviceman does this with oil or gas heat by checking the combustion efficiency. He does what's called a carbon dioxide (CO_2) test of the blue gases going up the chimney and takes the flue-gas temperature. This tells right off if the fuel is burned efficiently. A CO_2 content of 9 to 10 is fair to good; 11 to 14 or higher is excellent—strive for that.

If your serviceman cannot raise your CO_2 value that high by adjustment, one or more of three likely causes should be corrected: A) Air is leaking into the furnace combustion chamber, which should be sealed; B) The draft up the chimney is too high or low and should be corrected; C) The air mix with oil is not right for good combustion. These problems sometimes can be corrected by adjustment or modification, but sometimes a new burner may be needed.

The flue-gas temperature (temperature of the gases going up the chimney minus the furnace-room temperature) should be at least 400 degrees F to as much as 700 degrees F—the higher the better. A temperature of 400 to 600 degrees F is average for original equipment, and 600 to 700 is average for a replacement oil burner. Other checks on heating efficiency include taking the "smoke spot number" and the stack draft. The smoke spot number should be 0 to 1, which is excellent, and no higher than 2. A higher reading is poor and indicates an untuned or obsolete unit. Stack draft is a measure of pressure in inches of water on a gauge. It generally falls between 0.04 and 0.06 for nonforced draft equipment (what most house units are).

Write for the free pamphlet "How to improve the efficiency of your oil-fired furnace," DOE/OPA-0018 (1–78) from the U.S. Department of Energy, Office of Public Affairs, Washington, D.C. 20585.

Oil burners should be cleaned and tuned at least once a year to rid them of accumulated carbon soot, which reduces their efficiency. Yet as obvious as this may seem, many haven't been cleaned and tuned for years! No wonder some people spend a small fortune for fuel! Gas burns more cleanly than oil, and as a result, a gas heater needs to be checked only every three or four years.

2. *Be sure that the burner nozzle is sized right for your house.* This critical device is like an automobile carburetor; it feeds fuel to the combustion chamber. If not the right size for your house, it could be feeding too much fuel. This is a fairly widespread condition because so many houses have been reinsulated and weatherproofed after being built. Less fuel is now required to heat them, but since the nozzle is still the same large one originally installed, it is inefficient and wastes fuel all the time.

A properly sized fuel nozzle is important for both oil and gas heating units. If a new, smaller one is needed, it will pay for itself. The nozzle should be replaced by a good serviceman; sometimes your local gas company will provide one.

3. *Keep all moving parts well lubricated.* This includes the water circulating pump of a hot-water heating system and the blower motor and fan of a forced warm-air system. But don't drown them in oil; only a few drops are normally needed. Apply the oil through the small fittings or holes provided for the purpose. Some devices are permanently lubricated and sealed in the factory, and additional lubrication is unnecessary. Check your heater instructions for information about this, as well as for periodic lubrication. The fan blades of a forced warm-air blower should also be kept clean. Blades caked with dirt lose blowing efficiency, a hindrance often overlooked. At the same time the blower belt (like a car fan belt) should be checked for proper tension. It should be tight enough so that it doesn't give more than an inch when pressed. Also inspect for cracks, fraying, and other signs of wear.

4. *Clean the air filter in forced warm-air heating systems at least once every month or two.* A dirty filter chokes off heat supply and is a common cause of inefficient heating. The furnace and blower have to work overtime to force through enough heat to the house; this obviously means higher fuel bills. Pulling the filter out and cleaning or replacing it is a simple job that nearly anyone can do.

5. *Install a clock thermostat.* It will automatically reduce the house temperature while you sleep and turn it up before you awake the next morning. Overall fuel savings range from 8 to 17 percent, depending on your climate. Cost of the thermostat runs from about $50 to $100, and installing it is an easy do-it-yourself job. If you're cold in bed at night, use a down quilt or an electric blanket. Both keep you warm at considerably less cost than heating the whole house.

6. *Periodically clean the electric contacts inside the thermostat.* Remove the thermostat cover, and slide a 3 x 5 card or equivalent between the contacts to get rid of dirt. If the thermostat uses a mercury bulb contact, be sure the bulb is absolutely horizontal when it's supposed to be. It's simple. Just put a level on it to tell, and adjust if necessary. See the instructions that came with the thermostat.

7. *Set the thermostat for the lowest possible temperature to keep you comfortable.* Fuel savings range from 3 to 5 percent for every degree you lower the thermostat and house temperature.

8. *With warm-air heat, have the blower adjusted for continuous air circulation (CAC).* A warm-air blower is often set so that it goes on and supplies air to the house only when the thermostat calls for heat and the furnace is firing. When enough heat has been supplied to satisfy the thermostat, the heat stops, and the blower also stops running. That's inefficient.

With CAC operation, the blower does not go on and off at the same time as the furnace. Instead, the blower is adjusted to operate much of the time in mild weather, most of the time in cold weather, even through periods when the furnace is not heating. A uniform supply of warm air is supplied in bucketful quantities rather than a truckload blast of warm air once an hour and nothing during the long intervals. Continuous air circulation by itself often can turn a sluggish heating system into a top performer. Only a few changes in the furnace control and blower setting are required.

Increased fan operation will, of course, cause somewhat higher electric bills, but this is offset by a far more comfortable, easier-to-heat house and often lower fuel bills, too. That's according to considerable testing of CAC operation in houses by the National Warm Air Heating and Air-Conditioning Association.

8. *Close off unused rooms, and turn their heat off.* This is easily done with electric heat and on separate thermostats in each room. With hot-water or steam heat, individual radiators must be turned off all the way. Turning them off halfway is no good. It's done, by the way, merely by turning the radiator hand valve down, or clockwise as far as it will go. Warm-air heat is turned off by closing the supply-air registers in rooms where heat is not desired.

9. *Back up the radiators in your rooms with a sheet of reflective aluminum foil placed between the radiator and the wall behind it.* The foil can be stiffened by being taped or pasted on cardboard or a thin wood board. Radiant heat from the radiator is then reflected back into the room, rather than lost to the outside wall. The foil, in short, reduces heat loss.

10. *Paint radiators with an oil-base or flat latex paint, not with a metallic aluminum or bronze paint.* Metallic paint reduces heat output by about 10 percent. If your radiators are now covered with metallic paint, a new nonmetallic paint can be applied without scraping off the old metallic paint. The final paint coat makes the difference, not what's underneath. The new paint may be any color, since the output variation from color to color is slight. So it's feasible to paint radiators any color desired to match your room decor.

11. *Periodically bleed hot-water heating radiators to release trapped air.* Put a bucket under the vent cock at the side of the radiator, and open the vent. Drain off a bucket or so of water. This is also the prescription for treating balky radiators that do not heat. Air trapped inside prevents hot-water or steam circulation. Bleeding releases the air. If a radiator still does not heat properly, drain off more water. Don't be afraid of releasing too much. It is replaced by a water-supply valve at the boiler.

There are three kinds of bleed vents for radiators: the manual, disk, and automatic float types. Most radiators have the manual kind, which sticks out near the top of one end of the radiator. It's circular in shape and about ½ inch long. It has a slot which you open with a radiator "key" (sold in hardware stores) or merely with a dime. Turn it open until water comes out; then close it.

The disk vent looks like the manual kind but contains a series of fiber disks. It is semiautomatic in operation in that it lets air out when necessary. The disks swell up when wet, which is when water, not air, is in the radiator, as it should be. If air gets in, the disks contract, opening the vent to let out the air. Sometimes the disks get worn or dirty and drip water on the floor. Replacements are sold in hardware stores and by heating dealers. The disk vent costs a little more than the manual vent.

The automatic vent is highest in price. It uses a small tank-and-float device much like a toilet tank float, but on a smaller scale. Water in the radiator keeps the float up and the vent closed. Air, instead of water, in the radiator will lower the float and open the vent, which lets the air escape. The automatic vent seldom needs attention and does away with the periodic need to bleed radiators. Of course, it can go bad after a number of years, and then you must replace it.

12. *Keep radiators clean.* Dust and dirt that accumulate inside the sections or between the fins inhibit heat flow. A once-a-month vacuuming prevents it. Cleaning is important for long, low baseboard radiators, as well as the regular stand-up kind. With some baseboards the cover must be removed first.

13. *Cover large windows with inside drapes or shades.* Insulated drapes pulled across the inside of the windows can save the most heat. They are especially recommended for thin, single-pane windows that let heat leak out fastest of all windows.

14. *Use the lowest-cost energy.* Natural gas was still the cheapest heating fuel in the latter 1970s even though its price began to rise sharply after the energy crisis broke. But gas started out much lower in cost for home heating than oil and electricity. The price of gas could still rise substantially more in future years before it becomes as expensive as oil or electricity. Based on 1978 average energy prices nationally, the cost of heating a house with gas was roughly two-thirds the cost of heating with 50-cent oil and roughly 30 percent of the cost of heating with electricity at 4 cents per kilowatt-hour.

If you now have oil or electric heat, you might save a lot of money by switching to natural gas, assuming it is available for your house. Installing the new heating equipment will require money, to be sure, but this cost is repaid in operating savings. How long it takes to be repaid depends on your local cost for each energy and the cost of switching the heat in your house.

First, of course, be sure that a switch is attractive. The table on page 208 showing comparative energy prices will give you an indication of the possible savings.

The table gives the equivalent prices for each heat horizontally across each line. For example, electricity at a cost of 3 cents per kilowatt-hour (kwh) for heating is equivalent to heating with oil at 86.1 cents a gallon, natural gas at 61.5 cents per therm (100 cubic feet of natural gas), and LP (propane) gas at 56.6 cents a gallon.

If your local cost for oil is less than 86.1 cents a gallon or gas is less than 61.5 cents per therm, heating with each of these will cost less than electricity at 3 cents per kwh. If oil costs, say, 45 cents a gallon, oil heat will therefore cost almost half the cost of heating with 3-cent electricity. If gas heating costs you 30 cents a therm locally, it therefore will cost you roughly half the bill for heating with 3-cent electricity.

Be sure that you use accurate local prices for the fuels being com-

HOW FUELS COMPARE IN COST

Electric, central heat cost, cents per kilowatt-hour	No. 2 fuel oil cents per gallon	Natural gas cost, cents per therm	LP (liquid petroleum) propane * gas, cents per gallon
0.5	14.3	10.2	9.9
1.0	28.7	20.5	18.9
1.5	43.0	30.7	28.4
2.0	57.4	41.0	37.7
2.5	71.7	51.2	47.3
3.0	86.1	61.5	56.6
4.0	114.8	82.0	75.4
5.0	143.5	102.5	94.3
6.0	172.2	123.0	113.1
7.5	215.2	153.7	141.4

Source: The Small Homes Council, University of Illinois
*To determine the price of butane LP gas, use the price of natural gas per therm from the table.

pared. If your fuel prices vary according to the quantity used each month, determining your energy price should be based on the unit price you pay or will pay each month for the total quantity used. You can determine the actual price paid for electricity, for example, from your last electric bill. Divide the monthly total price charged for electricity, your total electric bill, by the total number of kilowatt-hours consumed. Both amounts should be given on your bill. The energy price used in calculating heating costs should not be the cheapest price given with your bill.

To determine equivalent fuel costs at prices not given in the table, interpolate. For example, electric heat at 3.6 cents per kwh is just over halfway between 3 and 4 cents in the table above and is therefore equivalent to heating with oil at $1.03 a gallon, or just over halfway between 86.1 cents and 114.8 cents and natural gas at 73.8 cents per therm.

A detailed description of fuel costs and other facts about heating energy is given in Circular No. G3.5, "Fuels & Burners," available for 25 cents from the Small Homes Council, 1 East Saint Mary's Road, Champaign, Illinois 61820.

SWITCHING FROM OIL TO GAS HEAT

This change is usually easy and relatively cheap where gas is available. The oil burner section of the heater is merely replaced by a new gas burner. The rest of the furnace or boiler is retained as is. The total cost should run from about $400 to $500, more or less. Switching in reverse, from gas to oil, will cost more because an oil burner costs more and a new oil storage tank is also required.

Switching from electric heat to oil or gas usually offers the greatest potential operating savings, and it will be easiest if your present electric heat is provided by an electric furnace, blower, and air ducts. If the duct distribution system will work equally well with a new gas or oil furnace, only the furnace must be replaced with an oil or gas furnace. This should be determined in advance, obviously, by a good heating contractor (who should also guarantee it). The cost will range from about $1,000 to $2,500, depending on the type of heat desired and how much installation work is required for your house.

Switching from the more common electric radiant heat to oil or gas generally requires the installation of a complete new oil or gas heating system—i.e., a new distribution system of ducts or pipes and radiators installed, in addition to the new heating unit. The cost can vary greatly, depending on the house, and you must get estimates.

Obviously, the key figure to know in advance is the estimated operating savings that a fuel switch will bring. This puts special importance on making accurate computations beforehand. On the whole, a switch from electric heat to gas or oil is most likely to result in the greatest savings, provided the installation cost of the new heat will be repaid in savings within three to five years.

There is also what is called the heat pump, a machine that provides central air conditioning in summer and operates in reverse in winter. It provides heat via electricity in winter at roughly 25 to 50 percent less cost than regular electric heat from the same amount of electricity used. It is an alternative to regular electric heat, but it makes sense only if you are installing new central air conditioning at the same time and only in a winter climate no colder than that of Washington, D.C. (4,333 degree days). Air-conditioning manufacturers and heat pump partisans claim that the heat pump will work satisfactorily in colder climates, but I am skeptical of such claims. See Chapter 25.

CHAPTER 21

HOW TO CHOOSE AND BUY NEW HEATING FOR A ROOM OR WHOLE HOUSE

What's the best way to heat a new room or two added to your house? Should you hook it up to your existing central system or install new room heaters?

What about replacing an old heating unit that has finally conked out? How can you be sure of getting a good replacement? Here are answers to heating questions like these.

THE THREE MAIN KINDS OF HOME HEATING

They are forced warm air, hot-water (sometimes called hydronic), and electric heat.

Forced warm air

Forced warm air is by far the most common central heat in American houses and generally the most likely for heating a new addition to a house. It consists of a furnace, air ducts (usually made of sheet metal), and a blower for pushing the air through the ducts to each of your rooms.

Some people, particularly in the Northeast and parts of the Midwest, distrust forced warm air. They don't think it heats well, particularly after having had unhappy times with an old, obsolete, gravity warm-air (no blower) system, or with a poorly installed warm-air system. Actually, warm air can be perfectly good in any house, provided a good furnace is used and the *system* is properly installed.

A big advantage today of warm air is that central air conditioning can be easily added, if the heating ducts are large enough for cooling, which requires larger ducts than only for heating. This must be specified when a new heating duct system is installed, or it will be no good later when air conditioning may be desired.

Other advantages: Warm air responds quickly to calls for heat from the thermostat, and a filter at the furnace cleans the air. Its drawbacks: Openings may have to be cut in rugs or carpets for air outlets in the floor. Furniture placement may be restricted to prevent interference with warm-air discharge from the outlets. And air noise may be bothersome, though this is a problem mainly with a cheap, poorly installed system. Warm-air furnaces can be operated with gas or oil and in a pinch with electric heat.

Hot-water heat

Water is heated in a boiler and flows through pipes to radiators in each room. A circulating pump is located at the boiler to force the water around under pressure. An old system may lack a circulator pump.

Hot water is less susceptible to design and installation errors than warm air (a piece of pipe is a piece of pipe, but air ducts must be sized and hand-fabricated for each house); hot-water boilers are generally smaller and more compact than furnaces, thus require less room; you get more basement headroom because pipes take less space than ducts; some people simply prefer the kind of heat given off by radiators; and a new hot-water system is often easier and cheaper to install in an *existing* house, particularly a multilevel house (because pipes are easier to run through walls than ducts).

On the other hand, hot water cannot filter the house air; the cost of central air conditioning can run 25 to 40 percent more in a house with hot-water heat than in one with warm-air heat; and a hot-water system must be drained or given a dose of antifreeze if you leave the house for a winter vacation, or else freezing can burst pipes. Like warm-air heat, hot-water heating also can be fired by gas or oil and sometimes with electricity, though electric hot-water heat is inefficient and expensive and therefore not recommended.

Electric heat

Electric heat can be an excellent way to provide heat for a new room or two when it is impractical or impossible to use the existing house heating system. Individual room electric units are simple, relatively inexpensive, and efficient. They operate independently of the rest of the house, and because a new room can be well insulated, their operating cost should not be prohibitive. Heating a whole house or large new addition with electricity is, on the other hand, not recommended because of its high operating cost, its chief disadvantage.

The main advantages of electric heat are low cost of installation, compared with warm-air or hot-water systems, and the energy that can be saved with a thermostat installed in each room, allowing heat to any of them to be turned on or off easily.

There are six kinds of electric heat: (1) long, slender electric radiant baseboard units, which look and work much like hot-water baseboards except that the heat source is electricity; (2) units designed to be built into a wall, which contain an integral fan for circulating warmed air around the room; (3) glass panel units recessed in a wall, which radiate heat; (4) radiant panels, usually located in the ceiling, for providing radiant heat with surprising efficiency and comfort; (5) electric furnaces, which, like conventional furnaces, supply warm air to rooms through ducts, but are different in that the air passing through the furnace is heated by electricity instead of gas, oil, or coal; and (6) the heat pump, discussed later.

Electric baseboard units give pleasant uniform heat, but certain types must be cleaned regularly to keep them free of dust and lint. Wall units with built-in fans provide excellent warm-air distribution, but some people are bothered by the on-and-off swish of the fans. Glass panel units are recessed in a wall, like the wall units noted above, but they radiate heat instead of circulating it with a fan. Radiant ceiling panels can also be highly satisfactory, but they cost more because of the installation required. They are generally limited to new houses or additions where they can be installed when the ceiling is being built.

A new electric furnace is limited, as a rule, to new houses and new additions because of the ductwork it requires. It can be a good way to combine electric heating with central air conditioning, with the same ducts handling warm and cool air supply to rooms. On the other hand, it is even more expensive than conventional electric heat, because a fan must be operated, in addition to the electric heating. And it does not lend itself easily to individual room control of heat, which is a big feature of conventional electric heat.

HOW TO PROVIDE HEAT FOR NEW ROOMS

First determine if a branch can be easily extended from your present house heating system. This may be relatively easy if the new space is close to a main supply pipe or duct of the existing system.

Of course, your existing heating system should have enough spare capacity to provide heat to the new space. If insulation or storm windows were added after your house was built, it's likely the total heating demand was reduced enough to provide heating capacity for the new space. And if the new space is well insulated, it will require a minimum of additional heat from the house unit. The real test is how well the system heats during the very coldest weather. Does it keep all rooms satisfactorily warm? If not, and especially if a heating contractor figures that the system has little or no spare capacity, new room heaters will be needed for the new space.

There's one other alternative. If the rest of the house needs storm windows or insulation for the walls, for instance, fulfilling such a need could reduce the heat load on the central heating system enough so that it will have heat to spare for the new living space.

Get bids for adding room heaters for a new space being added, as well as bids to extend your present central heating system to it. New room heaters could be any of the electric room heaters noted earlier—I like electric baseboards best, followed by a gas or oil wall furnace. With a gas or oil unit, an exhaust vent to outdoors is required, and allowance for this must be made when the room is being built.

On the whole, new individual heaters are generally recommended when new living space is added to a house, compared with extending the existing heating system, particularly if it is an old steam or hot-water system, which could be knocked out of kilter when asked to heat new rooms.

INSTALLING NEW FORCED WARM-AIR HEAT

A new forced warm-air system is usually the best way to provide central heat for a large new addition or when remodeling a whole house. Its cost is significantly lower than hot-water heat, and air conditioning can be added to it most economically. Design of the ducts is the key to a good warm-air system and is crucial to its efficiency. A poor duct job more than any other thing is why many warm-air heating systems do not heat well and get bad reviews.

The best duct system is the perimeter kind. The warm-air discharge outlets are located around the exterior walls of your house (the house perimeter), preferably under windows. Warm air from the furnace is discharged into rooms at the source of the greatest cold—the key to good heating.

As a rule, at least one warm-air outlet should be located under every exposed wall, except perhaps in the kitchen and bath, where more than one exterior location may be impossible. Two or three air outlets should be spread out below a long wall, particularly under large windows in a living room. The warm air rising up counteracts cold downdrafts from the windows. This spells the difference between comfort and chilly discomfort.

You should request at least two warm-air outlets in bedrooms with two exposures, especially in children's rooms. A perimeter duct system is essential for a house in the cold North that lacks a basement, if the curse of cold floors is to be avoided; it is decidedly preferable in other climates.

The usual and generally second-rate alternate to perimeter ducts is a system with air outlets located high on interior walls. The warm-air supply has to travel all across the room to the critical exterior windows and walls, by which time it has dispersed much of its heat. Spotty heating results. In the cold of winter you cannot sit comfortably near an outer wall. You complain about the heating furnace, but in reality your exasperating discomfort stems from poor air distribution.

An uninformed heating man may stoutly advocate that the supply-air outlets be located at your interior walls, rather than at the exterior walls. You should also get, he may say, return-air registers under the windows. The cold downdrafts from the windowpanes, he'll say, are sucked back to the furnace through these intakes before they can spread into the room.

Unfortunately, it doesn't work that way in practice. Supply-air outlets on interior walls are recommended only in a house with very well-insulated exterior walls, coupled with double-glass windows, or in houses in the South. Perimeter ducts may cost a little more, but they'll pay off handsomely in warm comfort ever after. (You automatically get perimeter heat with radiators located around exterior walls and under windows.)

THE WARM-AIR FURNACE

There are furnaces and there are furnaces. Know how to get a good one. A furnace, by the way, heats *air* and is the heating contraption that provides warm-air heat; a boiler heats *water* and is used for hot-water or steam heat. A good warm-air furnace, the top-of-the-line model, carries a twenty-year guarantee but should last longer. There are also low-grade furnaces with a five- or ten-year guarantee (made chiefly for the low-cost tract-house market). The good furnace made for gas fuel also will have electric ignition, rather than a more costly gas pilot light. If you need an oil-fired furnace, it should be the same model made for gas heat with electric ignition. The difference is that it's made to burn oil instead of gas.

These two features—twenty-year guarantee and electric ignition—are two of the principal differences between a good furnace and the cheapie kind. The good furnace can be guaranteed twenty years because it has a thicker, better-made heating chamber. Brand name means little because most manufacturers make both a cheap unit and a high-quality model. A really good furnace costs only about $50 to $75 more, on the average, than the cheap kind.

Two other facts about furnaces: If it is a gas-burning unit, it should show the approval emblem of the American Gas Association (AGA), a must for safety. If it is oil-fired, it should carry the UL seal of the Underwriters Laboratories and also bear a tag saying that it conforms with U.S. Government Standard CS-195-57.

Suppose the furnace being replaced is an old gravity kind, generally a large, bulbous furnace with octopuslike ducts rising up from its body. It has no air blower; its heated air rises to the rooms above by gravity flow owing to the difference in weight between warm and cold air.

Should you replace it with a new gravity furnace or with a new, forced warm-air kind containing a blower? If the old gravity unit heated the house satisfactorily, then the same kind should do equally well. But the usual gravity furnace is not the best performer. If in doubt, it's best to order a forced-air furnace, even though there may be additional expense for new ductwork.

SPECIAL FEATURES WITH WARM-AIR HEAT

Check on these when you order the system. The air filter should be located so it can be removed easily for cleaning, or you will have trouble. Can you remove it and replace it easily? Filters require periodic cleaning. Clogged-up filters are a major cause of poor heating. You should not have to call a judo expert every time cleaning is necessary.

To avoid noisy operation—the rattling and banging of ducts every time the heat goes on and off—a short canvas collar should connect the ductwork with the furnace or every clang will be transmitted throughout the house. This is another touch that distinguishes a good heating job from a poor one. And insist that the system be adjusted for continuous air circulation (CAC), also called comfort air circulation, described in the previous chapter.

If central air conditioning will be wanted later, a few simple provisions made when a heating system is installed can simplify the future installation and save money. Because cooling requires larger ducts than heating, be sure that the heating ducts are initially designed for cooling, as well as for heating. Allow for space for the cooling equipment next to or on top of the furnace. A cooling-coil plenum, an empty sheet-metal box, is installed at the same time as the furnace. Later the cooling coil can be easily slipped into place here with a minimum of fuss and expensive alterations. This may cost an additional $50 or so when the heating is installed; later the same work could otherwise cost $250 or more.

HOT-WATER HEATING

The boiler is the heart of the system. There are two kinds: cast-iron and steel boilers. Know which you are getting. The cast-iron kind may cost more, but it is decidedly superior. It is ordinarily guaranteed for twenty to twenty-five years (but should last about forty years) and is virtually obligatory if your water is hard. Steel boilers are susceptible to rust and corrosion from hard water and are usually guaranteed, therefore, for only a year. Don't use steel if you have hard water unless you also have a water softener. (Steel, however, is perfectly good for warm-air furnaces because air, not corrosive water, is being handled. Nearly all furnaces are steel.)

A good cast-iron boiler will carry the seal of the Institute of Boiler and Radiator Manufacturers (IBR), which indicates that its heating output has been confirmed by stiff tests. A steel boiler should carry the seal of the Steel Boiler Institute (SBI), which is assurance that a steel boiler will deliver its rated capacity. Both cast iron and steel should carry the small "h" insignia of the American Society of Mechanical Engineers (ASME). This indicates that the design and construction conform to strict standards. Look for all these seals on the nameplate. Like warm-air furnaces, cast-iron boilers for gas fuel should carry the American Gas Association (AGA) emblem; an oil-

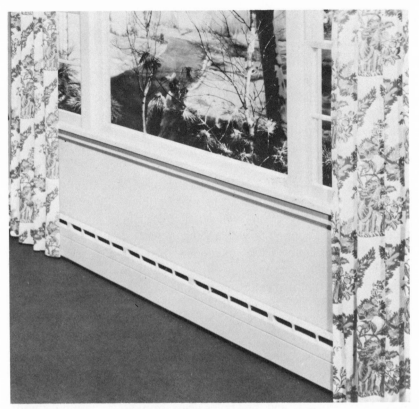

This low-slung baseboard radiator is clearly a major improvement over old-fashioned stand-up radiators. *Better Heating-Cooling Council.*

fired unit should carry the Underwriters Laboratories (UL) approval emblem.

Incidentally, if your heating unit lacks a nameplate it generally indicates a cheap, low-quality unit. All the better units have nameplates.

JUDGING NEW RADIATORS

The best radiators are baseboard radiators—long, low, spread-out units 7 to 9 inches high. They are neater and better-looking than the old-fashioned stand-up variety. There are two main kinds: the cast iron and the nonferrous (aluminum or copper). The nonferrous is identified by the presence of metal fins along its length.

Like cast-iron boilers, cast-iron baseboard radiators cost more but give better service over the years and provide more uniform heat. Nonferrous (aluminum and copper) baseboard radiators are often noisy. Regardless of type, every baseboard radiator should conform to the standards of the IBR. This is not marked on the radiator; you have to refer to the manufacturer's literature, which will mention it. If the IBR standards are unmentioned, the radiators should be rejected. And by all means, reject old-fashioned stand-up radiators unless you are the 1 in 100,000 who gets a rare new steam heating system. Baseboard radiators are far more efficient and far less of an eyesore.

Suppose you are stuck with old-fashioned radiators with your present heating and are unable to replace them. Can you improve their looks? Radiator covers will obscure their ugliness but will also reduce the heat supplied to your rooms. Covers should have as many openings as possible. There should be an opening at the front and particularly at the bottom for good air circulation, as well as a large opening at the top for heat discharge into the room.

MODERNIZING AN OLD GRAVITY HOT-WATER SYSTEM

Many old hot-water heating systems are called gravity systems because they lack a pump. The hot water from the boiler flows to the radiators by means of gravity flow, the hot water naturally rising to the radiators upstairs and the cooler water from the radiators naturally falling back to the boiler to be reheated.

Most gravity systems can be converted to a forced circulator system by the mere addition of a pump. This raises the system efficiency and is recommended if a gravity system doesn't heat the house well. Another advantage of forced circulation is that you can obtain zoned control by means of two or more circulators or zone valves, each supplying separate parts of your house (discussed later).

STEAM HEAT

Like hot-water boilers, steam boilers are either cast iron or steel. The cast-iron is preferred, especially when you have hard water. Regardless of whether it is cast iron or steel, it should show the ASME seal on the nameplate.

Steam heat is rarely put in houses today except for replacement of old equipment; this means that expert servicemen for it are rare. If your old system is still performing well and all you need, say, is a new boiler, by all means get one and spare yourself additional expense. But if the pipes and radiators, as well as the boiler, are rundown, then get bids on a complete new hot-water or warm-air system. If the old pipe system and radiators are still good, hot water should cost less.

Can you convert an old steam system to modern hot-water heat? This depends on whether you have a one-pipe or a two-pipe steam system. With the one-pipe system, the line that carries the steam to the radiators also returns the condensed steam (water) to the boiler. A two-pipe system has a second, separate pipe for the return leg. The system can be converted to hot-water heat only if it is a two-pipe job. Unfortunately, the one-pipe system is far more prevalent, and chances are that you have one and cannot convert unless new piping is installed.

RADIANT HEAT

The same kind of boiler used for hot-water heat is required when you replace the boiler of a radiant-heating system; thus, the same rules for hot-water boilers apply. The boiler supplies hot water to pipes embedded in the floor (usually a concrete floor in a house with no basement) which heat the floor and then the house.

Radiant heat had a brief spell of popularity after World War II. It can provide great warmth underfoot, and in theory at least, it is a splendid idea for doing away with eyesore radiators. Unfortunately, its idiosyncrasies can cause anguish. Some banks, in fact, will no longer give a mortgage on a house with radiant floor heat, and this alone raises a red flag for not using it.

If the boiler is good, but there's trouble within the floor-embedded pipe system, expensive repairs may be needed. This is a major drawback of radiant heat. If a floor pipe springs a leak or is gutted with corrosion, the floor may have to be dug up, a messy job at best. At worst, a complete new heating system may be required. Depending on the house, the existing boiler plant may be salvaged; it can be disconnected from the floor pipes and hooked up to a new system of baseboard radiators installed around the exterior walls of the house. The old pipes are left buried in the floor.

Other times, however, the big expense of a new system may dictate that you limp along with a sick radiant-heat system. Small auxiliary room heaters could be installed to take the chill off excessively cold rooms.

Before you do this, the addition of insulation to the walls, the concrete floor perimeter, and to the ceiling and the addition of storm windows might bail you out. New insulation can be the tonic for reducing the amount of heat demanded of the heating system and reducing cold drafts and chills that the heating system could not combat by itself. The use of thick perimeter-edge insulation, described in Chapter 18, could by itself considerably improve comfort in a radiant-heated house.

Another trouble with radiant heat is that it tends to overheat the house, or it cannot provide heat fast enough after a sudden dip in the outside temperature. The entire concrete floor has to be heated up first, and this may take an hour or two. If the sun abruptly breaks through again and you no longer need heat, there is little you can do; the floor will continue to radiate unwanted heat even though the boiler has gone off.

This calls for an outdoor temperature sensor located on an outside wall. It senses changes in the outdoor temperature and relays the appropriate message to the heating boiler so the heat will go on or off ahead of time, as needed. In other words, it takes into account the time delay necessary for the whole floor to heat up or cool off and starts the process going immediately. If not now in use with a radiant heating system, a new sensor control could improve its operation.

On the whole, all the potential troubles with radiant heat make it too risky for new heating. If you already have it, rooms being added sometimes can be easily heated with baseboard or other radiators hooked up to the existing house boiler. This assumes that the boiler has enough capacity for the new addition, as well as the main house. Otherwise, a separate heating system is required.

WHAT SIZE HEATING SYSTEM?

Heat capacity can vary greatly from house to house and from city to city, depending on climate. It is figured for a house by what engineers call a heat-loss computation. This takes into account the wall, roof, and glass area, type of construction, air volume, and so on.

The heating dealer should make a heat-loss computation to determine the size heating plant needed. If an old heater is being replaced, its capacity (usually marked on the nameplate) can give you a good idea of the new unit size required. But that's only if your old unit performed satisfactorily and no changes were made to the house since it was installed. If insulation, storm windows, and other heat-saving measures have been installed in your house, a smaller new heating unit should do the job. A new heat-loss computation should be made to avoid an oversized new unit.

New rooms or a complete house (in the North) with good insulation should have a heat loss of about 30 to 40 Btu's per square foot of heated living space per hour and preferably less. It's the heat needed to keep the place warm and thus the amount of heat that the heating unit should provide—i.e., the heater size.

The heat loss of a house or new room is computed according to what is called the outdoor design temperature in winter, the lowest temperature experienced in an area. For cities like New York, Philadelphia, St. Louis, and others with the same weather, the winter outdoor design temperature is 0 degrees F. For every 1,000 square feet of new living space, you will therefore need new heating with a heating output of 30,000 to 40,000 Btu's per hour, somewhat more in the very cold northernmost parts of the country. If a heat-loss computation shows that you require more heating capacity, go over the design. More insulation or insulating glass could reduce the heat loss, thus permit a smaller heating unit.

ZONE CONTROL

A common problem in houses is that some rooms are too hot while others are too cold, and it's difficult to make peace between the two. It's common in two-story houses where, because heat rises, the second-floor rooms are hotter than the first. If the house thermostat is turned down, the first floor gets too cold. It's also common in one-story houses with many exposures.

One owner, long plagued with this problem, was unable to get his heating man to correct it. Taking matters into his own hands, he "ordered" his heating man to "split" the heating system. He had hot-water heat. The hot-water supply pipes leading to the second-floor radiators were separated from those to the first floor. A second circulator pump was installed so there would be one for each floor level. (A circulator pump starts running when the thermostat calls for heat and pumps hot water to the radiators.) Then a second thermostat was installed upstairs to control the heat supply to this half of the house. Cost of the change was about $200 and worth it. Uniform heating resulted throughout the house for the first time. Heat was provided upstairs or downstairs only when needed there.

The man, though no engineer, had simply hit on the principle of zone control. His heating contractor should have known about it but did not. It means a second and even third thermostat for a new addition to a house, as well as for any part of the existing house that has heating needs different from the rest of the house. A national survey by a large manufacturer showed that nine out of ten houses costing more than $30,000 need either two or more thermostats or a split heating system with one furnace for the living areas, another for the sleeping areas.

The survey, made by the Honeywell people, found that zone control was needed in about 50 percent of all houses in the $50,000 to $60,000 price class and in only one of every five houses costing less than $40,000. Honeywell, of course, sells heating controls, so perhaps the study indicates that more houses need zone controls than might actually be the case. But with allowances made for their possible exaggeration, zone controls could still bring better heating benefits to many homeowners.

The principal condition requiring zone control is "a spread-out floor plan," the Honeywell people said. This causes widely differing exposure problems under one roof. It explains why the lower the price of a house, the less likely its need for special controls—i.e., the smaller the house, the less spread-out the floor plan.

Other conditions requiring zone controls, according to Honeywell experts, are (1) rooms with large glass areas; (2) finished basements; and (3) rooms over a garage. The last two were found to be a chief cause of chronic heating problems in split-level houses. Uneven heating occurs in houses regardless of the kind of heat used.

Zone control of warm-air heat is accomplished in much the same way as with a hot-water system. The main trunk ducts are each fitted with an automatically operated damper. Each damper opens to let air through or closes to shut it off, according to thermostat demand in each zone. If one part of the house begins to get cold and the thermostat there calls for heat, the appropriate damper opens, and the furnace goes on to supply the heat. If the other zone is warm enough, heat is kept from it by its damper remaining shut. If all parts of the house call for heat, all dampers open.

THE THERMOSTAT LOCATION

A good thermostat location is necessary for efficient heating. This applies to your present thermostat, as well as one installed in a new addition. The thermostat should be on an interior wall, out of reach of drafts from outside door openings. Drafts from an open door can cause a false alarm, prompting heat to be produced when it is not really needed.

Other bad locations are near a window with the thermostat exposed to sunshine, in range of radiant heat from a fireplace or of cooking heat from the kitchen, over a radiator or heating outlet, on a wall that contains warm-air ducts inside, and near light lamps. The heat from each of these can satisfy the thermostat while the rest of the house gets cold, thus producing erratic control and poor heating.

The best thermostat location is usually on an interior wall of the living room or dining room that is free of the above hazards. It should also be representative of the heat needs of the rest of the house.

GAS VERSUS OIL VERSUS ELECTRIC HEAT

The greatest difference among these three main kinds of heat is, as noted earlier, operating cost. Natural gas is usually the cheapest of all and is likely to remain so for some time, oil is next lowest in price, and electricity will generally cost two to three times more than gas or oil.

Besides operating cost, oil and gas are virtually interchangeable for warm-air or hot-water heat. In other words, warm-air and hot-water heat can be had with either gas or oil fuel. Other than the burner, the cost of the heating system is the same whether gas or oil is the fuel. The purchase price of buying and installing an oil system is higher than that of gas because an oil burner costs more than a comparable gas burner mechanism and needs a tank for oil storage; no tank is needed for gas. Because an oil system demands annual cleaning and adjustment, whereas gas requires less frequent service, the annual maintenance bill for oil heat is also higher. But from the standpoint of heating comfort, the use of oil or gas makes no difference; a good warm-air or hot-water heating system will perform well with either fuel.

The installation cost of electric heat is lowest of all. A chimney is unnecessary, and the cost of wiring a house for electric heat is less than for installing a heat distribution system for either warm-air or hot-water heat. But electric heat's low initial installation cost is quickly offset by its higher operating cost. An exception is the use of electric heat for one or two new rooms for which the operating cost is not so great, especially if the new living space is very well insulated.

The heating comfort of electric heat is roughly on a par with a good heating system fueled by gas or oil.

CUTTING THE COST OF GAS HEAT

Consumers are usually charged for gas on a sliding scale. The more used, the lower the unit price. This can make a welcome cost difference when considerable gas or electricity is also used for other household purposes. A typical family may consume about 800 cubic feet of natural gas, or 8 therms a month for cooking, plus another 2,000 to 3,000 cubic feet (20 to 30 therms) a month for water heating. After this much consumption the price you pay for additional gas falls to the next cheaper heating bracket.

If, however, gas is used only for heating, you are charged for the first 2,000 to 3,000 cubic feet each month at the higher end of the scale, so heating bills will be higher. A six- or seven-room house with insulation will use about 20,000 to 30,000 cubic feet of natural gas a month for heating in a climate like that of New York, Pittsburgh, or Kansas City with approximately 5,000 degree days per winter.

In a given house, using gas appliances, particularly the water heater, kitchen range, and clothes dryer, will cost less when you also have gas heat than if gas was not used for these other purposes.

Electricity also is often billed the same way. Electric company people like to point this out because it is one of the few positive things that can be said today to offset its high cost. It therefore follows, they say, that it pays to have an all-electric house, using an electric range, water heater, and dryer in addition to electric house heating.

But that's highly questionable. Even if you're stuck with high-cost electric heat, you may still pay less for other things by using gas for your kitchen range, water heater, and clothes dryer, since gas usually costs substantially less than electricity. That assumes that gas is available for those other uses.

Electricity is a fine, upstanding patriotic energy when it is used to operate a *motor*-driven mechanism, like a refrigerator compressor, food mixer, and vacuum cleaner. But it is highly inefficient when it is used to provide *sheer* heat, as needed for a range, water heater, dryer, and house heater, as well as for things like coffee makers and hair dryers. To save energy, beware of *heat*-making appliances that work with electricity.

AVOIDING THE TEN MOST COMMON TROUBLES IN HOUSES

The National Warm Air Heating and Air-Conditioning Association, a trade group of manufacturers, spent more than ten years investigating heating complaints in actual houses throughout the country. It used a mobile laboratory truck equipped with an expensive variety of instruments, and its experts spent as long as two to three weeks tracking down complaints about heating in actual real-life houses.

The association's experts found that nearly every heating problem boils down to the following common troubles. Understanding them can help you improve the efficiency of your heating plant and also avoid similar troubles when you install new heating. Some have already been noted but deserve repeat mention.

1. *Little or no thermal insulation.* The association's engineers made it official. Insulation is essential not only for cutting home heating bills, but also for a warm and comfortable house. With little or no insulation, the walls are cold; this causes chilly drafts and drains body heat, as I described earlier in the section on the wall chill factor. Even the most expensive heating system cannot counteract the ill effects of inadequate insulation and the cold-chamber discomfort that results.

2. *Dirt-clogged air filters.* This is one of the major reasons for poor warm-air heating. The house gets colder and colder as not enough heat gets to rooms. This happens often both in new houses and in old ones and after a new addition has been built. Reason: The air filter is clogged with building dust and shavings. Little or no air can pass through the filter, and the heat supply is sharply reduced. The same thing will happen in any house with warm-air heat as the filter soaks up dirt and dust removed from the house air unless it is periodically cleaned or washed.

3. *A too big or too small heating plant.* As many as 80 percent of all houses get an improperly sized furnace, experts found. One reason is that many heating contractors persist in figuring the size needed by hasty rule of thumb, scribbling a few figures on the back of an envelope. Or a skimpy furnace is used to save a few dollars. Still another reason, at the other extreme, is that many people believe in an oversized unit just to have reserve capacity.

An example, discovered in a Texas house, involved a heating installation that was practically perfect. Although the house heat loss was 97,000 Btu's, an oversized 157,000 Btu furnace had been put in.

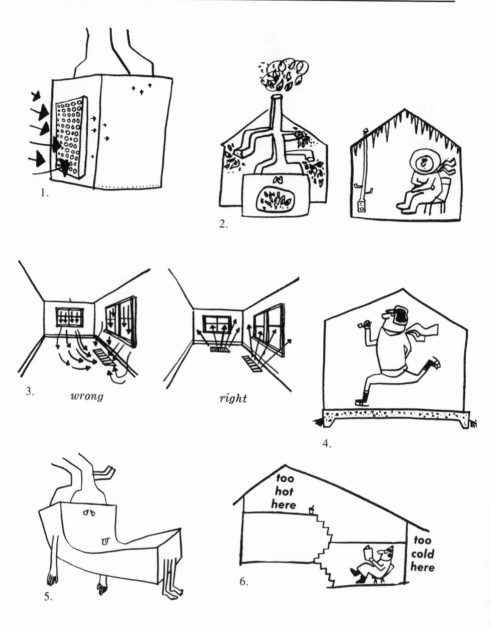

1. Dirt-clogged filters sharply slow up air circulation.
2. Heating plant is too big or too small.
3. Not enough warm air outlets in the right places.
4. Cold floors in concrete floor houses.
5. Heating plant starved for oxygen.
6. Uneven heating in split-level houses.

The supply air to the house got too hot, room temperatures fluctuated greatly, and uniform thermostatic control was impossible. The main lesson here is to insist that the heating contractor make an accurate heat-loss computation and match the equipment size to it.

4. *Erratic heating owing to an unbalanced heating system.* This is because many heating men omit the final adjustments necessary for apportioning the proper amount of heat to each room. As a result, some rooms get too much heat, others too little. The furnace blower, duct dampers, and room registers must be adjusted for good heat distribution.

5. *Improper control settings.* This results when furnaces are not set according to the principle of continuous air circulation, mentioned earlier in this chapter.

6. *Not enough warm-air outlets in the right places.* To help combat chilly downdrafts from cold window glass, the experts stress the great importance of proper heat discharge into a house; e.g., at least one warm-air outlet (or radiator) should be located under the windows at every outside wall.

7. *Cold floors, particularly houses with a concrete slab floor and no basement.* The two preventives: (1) thick edge insulation around the concrete floor perimeter, and (2) perimeter warm-air ducts or radiators which supply heat directly to the critical house perimeter.

Cold floors are also a problem in houses with a crawl space (built above the ground with no basement). Adequate insulation is required, as spelled out in Chapter 18.

8. *Heating plant starved for oxygen.* This occurs chiefly in new houses or newly insulated houses. They are so tight that you cannot count on outside air leaking in around doors and windows. As a result, the heater does not get enough oxygen to support combustion. The trouble is compounded when you have other air-consuming devices like clothes dryers and exhaust fans, which put a premium on the little air available. Incomplete heating-plant combustion may result, causing the release of lethal fumes into the house. Air must be made available to the heater. A small window opening or vent may be necessary. If the heater is in a closed utility room, a small duct to carry outside air to the equipment room is essential.

9. *Poor heating in split-level houses.* The biggest problem here is the lowest-level room, usually a playroom. It gets so cold that it is out-of-bounds in winter. It's a difficult problem because its floor and walls are generally below ground level, and the only heat supply is often a small duct discharging warm air into it from ceiling level. The floor and lower wall surfaces are not properly heated.

This kind of room should be treated like a house with a concrete slab floor; i.e., heat should be provided at floor level and around the outer edges of the room. This can be done with either perimeter floor ducts or baseboard radiators. Insulating the walls and floor can also help greatly.

At the same time the highest rooms in a split-level house get too hot because of the natural rise of warm air. One solution is cutting down on the heat input to the high rooms; another is the installation of a separate thermostat and zone controls to provide heat upstairs only when needed.

10. *Cold ducts.* Supply ducts from the furnace to the house may pass through a cold attic, garage, or crawl-space area and thereby cause so much heat loss that little or no warm-air supply reaches the rooms. This happens when the supply ducts in such spaces are not insulated. A supply-air duct is one with warm air flowing from the furnace to the house. There are also ducts that return cool air from the house to the furnace for reheating; these do not need insulation when they pass through unheated spaces.

CHAPTER 22

HOW TO CUT THE COST OF HEATING HOUSEHOLD WATER

Although that docile-looking water heater in the basement gulps down 18 percent of the average U.S. family's energy use, it accounts for 20 to 40 percent of total annual energy use for some families. That's among the two of every five American families with high-cost electric water heaters. It is the second largest energy user in the house.

The cost of operating an efficient, low-cost water heater for a typical family should run no more than $10 to $15 a month. With a high-cost unit, the cost of heating the same water each month, for your kitchen, bathroom, and other hot-water spigots, can run as much as $60 to $65 a month. Here are good ways to cut the water heater bill by as much as a third to a half each month.

Don't overheat the water. If the water from your spigot is so hot it scalds and must be mixed with cold water, you're obviously wasting energy at the water heater. That's common, the hot water often being heated to 160 degrees F or more. Turn your water heater thermostat down to 125 degrees F, more or less, and it will generally be hot enough. That's about the hottest water human hands can tolerate.

The water temperature is lowered at the thermostat dial, which is usually located at the bottom of the water heater. With some tank water heaters it's located inside a panel. If you can't find it, check the instruction manual or ask your plumber or utility company. A little experimenting may be necessary, turning it up or down a little over a few days' time until you get the lowest temperature that's satisfactory for kitchen, bathroom, and clothes washer use. There's one possible catch, however. Many automatic dishwashers need hotter, 140- to 160-degree water, and lowering the water heater temperature setting may cause a few dirty dishes to come out of the dishwasher. You may have to increase the water temperature at the heater to get cleaner dishes or put up with reduced dishwashing efficiency. If you don't mind a little inconvenience, you can turn the water heater thermostat up a half hour before turning on the dishwasher each time and turn it down after the dishes are done.

Reducing the hot-water temperature may not be easy if your water is heated inside the same boiler that provides hot-water or steam house heat for your house. Then you sometimes can turn the aquastat control on the top of the heater down to about 190 degrees F, but check this with your heating serviceman beforehand.

Wrap your water heater tank with an insulation overcoat. Two inches of fiberglass insulation wrapped around the tank can cut hot-water losses by 10 to 15 percent. Do-it-yourself water heater insulation kits are sold for this purpose at lumberyards, at hardware stores, or by mail-order companies. Installation is simple. I fitted one on my own water heater in less than an hour.

Insulate the exposed hot-water supply pipe from the water heater to the kitchen and bathrooms. Use at least ½-inch-thick fiberglass wrapping, cellular sleeves, or pipe insulation sized for your pipe.

Draw off a gallon or so of water from the bottom of your hot-water heater every month. That gets rid of sediment that otherwise cakes up at the bottom of the tank and cuts heating efficiency. It acts as an insulator between the water in the tank and the burner below. The harder your water, the more sediment and the greater the need to drain it regularly. Simply open the nozzle at the bottom of the tank, and let the water drain into a pail. Do it first thing in the morning before anyone has used hot water and churns up the sediment as a result of the heater's going on.

With a gas water heater, look in and check the flame color. As in a gas heating furnace, the flame should be clear blue with a flash of yellow occasionally visible. If more than a little yellow is seen, it probably should be readjusted and reset. A good serviceman can do this.

If you have an oil-fired water heater, have it checked, cleaned, and adjusted at least once a year, as recommended for oil-fired house heaters. Soot buildup inside the critical parts sharply cuts efficiency and wastes oil. Some of the better high-efficiency oil-fired water heaters and house heating units may not have to be adjusted and cleaned that frequently.

Take showers rather than tub baths. A shower uses about one-third the hot water of a tub bath.

Use cold water to wash clothes. Hot water is required only when germs must be killed, which means chiefly for handkerchiefs, underclothes, infant wear, and a sick person's wash. Use cold water for washing other garments, and cut the cost of heating 35 to 50 gallons of water for every cycle of wash. Cold water washes everything else just as well. All right, this may be hard to accept, but try it and see.

Turn the water heater off when you leave home for more than a day, especially when you are away on vacation. Turn it off at the thermostat, though the pilot light may stay on. Turning off the pilot, too, will save more, of course, but you should know how to relight it when you return. Instructions for this should be on the water heater. If, however, you'll be away during cold weather, when there is a chance of freezing, don't turn the pilot light off if there's no heat in the basement or wherever it's located. Ordinarily, the house heater should be left on at its lowest thermostat setting when one is away in winter, to prevent freezing water and pipes. If in doubt about the water heater's being exposed to freezing, leave its pilot on. Turning off an electric water heater when you're away from home is easily done at its switch. This can bring big savings. As with a gas water heater, if there's danger of water freezing in the electric heater while you're away in winter, leave it on at its lowest heat setting.

Install a tempering tank in the supply line to the water heater. This is a method of getting something for (almost) nothing. The temperature of water entering the house may be as low as 35 degrees F, no doubt desirable for a refreshing drink on a hot August afternoon but less than ideal for domestic hot-water usage. Think of how much less energy it would take to heat that water to 125 degrees if it started off at 60 instead of 35. A tempering tank is an ordinary water tank with about the same capacity as the heater. It is hooked into the line so that water destined for the heater first passes through the tempering tank, where it may remain long enough to be warmed up 10 to 25 degrees, depending on the surrounding air temperature, thus saving 10 to 25 percent of the energy ordinarily used to heat it. Not a bad idea. You can estimate your total energy savings by first taking the incoming cold water temperature in winter. This is used to figure the energy savings you will reap with a tempering tank.

HOW TO SAVE WITH AN ELECTRIC WATER HEATER

Hook an electric clock timer up to your electric water heater circuit so that, like a clock thermostat on home heating units, it will turn the unit off at bedtime and turn it on again in the morning before you awake. Like a clock thermostat that turns down the furnace at night, a timer cuts out unnecessary water heater operation at night when you sleep. Set it to go on half an hour before you wake, and plenty of hot water will be ready for morning washing and cooking. This seems an eminently sound idea, but for unaccountable reasons neither the government nor the electric utilities have promoted it. It could be that utilities prefer not to discourage nighttime electric use when they have loads of power to sell because demand is lower than in daytime.

On the other hand, some electric utilities offer attractively low rates for off-peak-hours use. These low-rate periods may vary from one utility to another, but for the water heater they are generally from noon to 3:00 P.M. and from 8:00 P.M. to 8:00 A.M. The utilities that offer these special rates for water heaters do it by having your water heater connected to a radio-controlled electric circuit (shades of the twenty-first century). This can control your water heater operation and confine it to such periods, as well as monitor its operation. Check on off-peak rates with your electric company. But be wary about the savings possible. You may have to give up too much for savings of no more than $100 a year.

SWITCH TO GAS OR OIL

One of the very best ways to save with an electric water heater, as with electric house heat, is to get rid of it. Put in a gas or oil water heater. According to studies by the government's Oak Ridge National Laboratories and the Rand Corporation, heating water with electricity costs twice as much as heating with oil and four times more than with gas. The exact differences in energy costs for you may be a little more or less, depending on your local cost for each.

Switching from an electric water heater to gas can therefore cut your water heating bill as much as 75 percent. Switching to an oil water heater can save 50 percent. The cost of installing a new gas or oil water heater will range from about $300 to $400 for a gas unit, more for oil. Besides the cost of the heater, its installation requires an exhaust gas vent to outdoors and, with oil, an oil tank in addition. This money can come back to you within a few years because operating savings can easily hit $200 to $300 a year, if not more. The cost of oil and gas in particular may rise in the future, to be sure, but each has a long rise ahead before it costs as much as electric water heating.

CHAPTER 23

HOW TO BUY
A NEW WATER HEATER

One may be needed when you remodel a house, when you must replace an old one that has died, or when you replace an electric water heater with a lower-cost gas or oil type.

When you buy, keep three main suggestions in mind: Choose a gas-operated water heater unless you cannot because, for example, there is no gas supply to your house. Buy only a *high-efficiency model*, which will mean the lowest operating costs. And get the right capacity for your house and family.

I'm talking, by the way, about the self-contained water heater and storage tank that sits quietly in the basement by itself and operates independently of the house heating unit. It is the most common kind of water heater, though used chiefly in houses with warm-air or electric house heating.

There is also what is called the tankless, or indirect-coil, domestic water heater. It is used only with hot-water or steam heat. This kind of water heater is located inside the house heating boiler, and its water is heated by the same fire that heats water for the house radiators.

That may sound like an efficient way to provide two different heating functions from the same source, but actually it is not. In winter, when the heating boiler is running most of the time, it can indeed heat the spigot water with little extra effort. But during the three to five months of warm weather every year, asking the heating boiler to rev down and heat only your spigot hot water is like calling on a bulldozer to straighten up your backyard. It's too big for the job. Heating

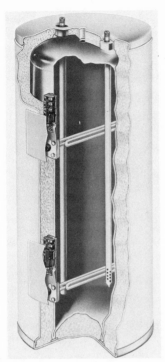

Super-thick insulation cuts heat loss and water-heater bills in new high-efficiency water heaters. *A. O. Smith.*

only your spigot water and not the house means inefficient operation. On a full twelve-month, year-round cycle, a tankless water heater built into the house heating boiler costs 10 to 15 percent more to heat hot water than a separate storage-tank water heater for the same house. So even if you have hot water or steam heat, buying a separate independent tank water heater is recommended.

BUYING THE LOWEST-COST WATER HEATER
A water heater fueled by natural gas is clearly the most efficient and inexpensive to operate. It also costs the least to buy and needs the least service. As I have noted several times elsewhere, gas prices may indeed rise in the future, but they have a way to go before they are on the same level with oil and a very long way before they reach the high-price level of electricity.

If natural gas is unobtainable for your house, consider using LP (liquid petroleum) gas. It's provided by tanks located next to the house, and LP dealers periodically provide refills. See the fuel price comparison table in Chapter 20 to determine if LP gas can save you money.

After gas, oil water heaters are the next lowest in operating cost. They are sold by fuel oil suppliers and plumbers.

Finally, there is the electric water heater. Because the cost of electricity has risen sharply since the energy crisis erupted, electric water heating, like electric heating, is recommended only for the profligate rich, for dummies, or if you generate your own electricity.

THE HIGH-EFFICIENCY WATER HEATER

This new water heater was introduced in the mid-1970s as a response to the high cost of energy. It's a conventional water tank in basic design and looks, but it's made with much better insulation, a better combustion mechanism, and finer controls. It's the first major improvement in water heaters in some twenty-five years.

Naturally, a new high-efficiency model will cost more than a conventional water heater. The first price runs 10 to 15 percent more than a good-quality conventional water heater. According to a U.S. government study, the extra purchase price will come back to you in operating savings within a year or two. In ten years your total saving will range from about $300 to as much as $750, depending on the fuel used. The savings are greatest, the study found, with a high-efficiency electric water heater, compared with using a conventional electric water heater.

OTHER GRADES OF WATER HEATERS

Besides the high-efficiency water heater, other, lower-quality water heaters are also sold by most manufacturers. At the bottom of the line, the cheapest water heater is sold with a mere one-year warranty. If anything goes wrong a year and a day after you bought it, that's it; it's also the least efficient and shortest-lived unit. Only a person with a hole in the head would buy one. You can also get a conventional water heater with a five-, ten-, or fifteen-year warranty. These are made better and cost more. Water heaters with a ten- or fifteen-year warranty were formerly the best, or top-of-the-line, models sold by manufacturers until the new high-efficiency units were introduced.

A new high-efficiency water heater, whether run by gas, oil, or electricity, is the only kind to buy now. Buying a cheaper model is penny-wise and pound-foolish. Besides letting you save big on operating costs, a high-efficiency unit will last much longer and provide better performance than all other water heaters.

WHAT SIZE WATER HEATER FOR YOUR FAMILY?

Size has to do with the amount of hot water a unit can deliver for you. It is related to the capacity of the storage tank, and it determines whether or not you will have enough hot water for shower baths, dishwasher, clothes washing, and the like. If you care about not running out of hot water in the middle of a shower or halfway through the dishes, then be sure you get an adequate size. Sizes range from mini-models with tanks of only 20 gallons of capacity up to giant models with 120 gallons of hot-water storage capacity.

The larger the family and, therefore, the more people taking baths and the greater the need for hot water in the kitchen and elsewhere, obviously the larger the water heater required to meet your needs. Here is how to choose a gas water heater according to the important variables.

SUGGESTED GAS WATER HEATER SIZE
FOR FAMILY NEEDS

Number of bathrooms	Number of people in family	Automatic clothes washer	Size in gallons
1	1 or 2	No	30
		Yes	40
2	3 or 4	No	40
		Yes	50
2	4 or 5	No	50
		Yes	75
3	5 or more	No	75
		Yes	100

Source: The American Gas Association.

Oil-fired heaters can be somewhat smaller than gas units, since oil heats hot water faster than gas does. The minimum oil size should be a 30-gallon tank, and from here up oil could be a size or two smaller than shown in the table above for gas. But verify this with the recommendations of the manufacturer of the unit you buy.

An electric water heater, on the other hand, must be as much as 50 percent larger in tank size than a gas unit, since electricity takes longest to heat new water. Electric water heaters range in tank capacity size from 50 to 120 gallons. As with the other units, the size of an electric model should be verified with the manufacturer's recommendations or your electric company.

Here are suggested sizes "usually considered adequate," according to the Edison Electric Institute, the electric utilities' trade association. These sizes, however, are conservative and if you want to be assured of hot water at all times when needed, I suggest you choose the next higher size than that recommended here.

SIZING AN ELECTRIC WATER HEATER

Family size	Electric water heater size
1 to 3	50-gallon
4 to 7	80-gallon
7 or more	100-gallon

FAST RECOVERY RATE

In addition to tank size, and no matter which kind of water heater (gas, oil, or electric) you may get, check on its recovery rate. This indicates how fast a heater can bounce back and provide more hot water when you're drawing a lot at once. It depends on the size of the burner. In other words, during a period of great hot-water demand you may soon exhaust all the hot water in the storage tank and your unit has to work hard to keep up with the hot water being drawn off. It may lack enough heating capacity to do that, and it runs out of hot water. This depends on its recovery rate.

Water heaters are also made, therefore, with high recovery rates, which means higher than the usual hot-water replenishing ability of a standard unit. Ask about the recovery rate when you shop. The recovery rate should be given in terms of being able to heat x gallons of water an hour by 100 degrees—i.e., heating 60-degree water to 160 degrees in an hour. Look for this on the nameplate. A 40-gallon unit with a high recovery rate can be better than a 50-gallon unit with a low recovery rate. The total amount of hot water it can give you within a prescribed time is the key fact to know.

THE TANKLESS WATER HEATER

This is the kind, mentioned earlier, that works inside a hot-water or steam boiler that heats the house. It is integral with the heating boiler, a pipe coil inserted inside the boiler. The same burner that heats the water for your radiators also heats the hot water supplied to kitchen, bathroom, and other water spigots.

Its main advantages are that it saves the space otherwise required for a separate tank water heater, and it costs less to buy than a separate tank heater. But it is less efficient, it costs more to operate, and it has limited hot-water capacity. The tankless kind is thus not recommended, especially for a family with large daily hot-water requirements.

It is also not recommended if you have very hard, mineral-laden water, or a hardness rating of about 7 grains or higher. Hard water tends to clog up domestic water coils with scale, thus reducing efficiency and requiring frequent cleaning. The hardness rating of your water can be determined by having a sample tested by a nearby water-conditioner dealer.

If, nonetheless, you get a tankless model, specify a brand and model that comes with an IWH seal. This is the seal of an approved Indirect Water Heater, a good-quality unit matched to the boiler. It should be noted on the water heater coil itself, which can be seen sticking out of the main heating boiler. Insist on an IWH seal.

In addition, adequate capacity is plainly essential so you won't be chronically short of hot water. Minimum rating for a one-bathroom house today is 2.75 gallons per minute (gpm) of water-heating capacity; at least 3.25 gpm with two baths. If you have more than two baths or a big family or use hot water liberally, get a 3.75 gpm coil or larger. A tankless water heater can be augmented with a supplementary water tank to hold hot water in reserve. If one of these is used, less heating capacity is required than the minimum rating given above.

SOLAR WATER HEATERS

A new solar water heater can cut your water heater bills by 15 percent and pay for itself in ten years, according to the Solar Energy Association, a trade group of solar heat manufacturers. But that's putting a very rosy light on solar heat, and it may pay off only if you now spend at least $1,000 a year to keep yourself in hot water; that usually means the use now of high-cost electric water heating. Solar heat is still too expensive to compete with gas or oil heating. Even if you now have an electric water heater, a solar water heater will not necessarily make sense, no matter how much we wish to promote solar heat.

For one thing, solar heat still requires a backup conventional water heater next to it to provide hot water when the sun isn't shining and you have exhausted all the reserve solar-heated hot water in storage. In the sunniest climates, a solar heater can provide hot water only 50 to 70 percent of the time. One reason for that, of course, is that no matter where you live, the sun doesn't shine at night when hot water is also needed.

Here's an actual example of the economics of buying a solar water heater, which, by the way, is said to be the most advanced kind of solar heat yet available for houses. A friend consulted me about buying one for his house for $2,100, which was close to the average price for solar water heaters for houses in 1978. He was enthusiastic because he would earn a $400 rebate from the federal government and another $300 from New York State for being patriotic and installing solar heat. Thus, his net cost would have dropped to $1,400.

The solar heater, it was claimed, would save him 15 percent of the operating cost of his present water heater. He had a gas water heater which cost him $200 a year, so a solar water heater would save him $30 a year (15 percent of $200). At that rate it would take him forty-seven years to get back the $1,400 spent for the solar water heater ($1,400 divided by 30). This assumes that it operated flawlessly and would require no service or repairs. (He should live so long.)

To earn back the $1,400 net cost of his solar water heater in ten years, he must save $140 a year. Saving 15 percent a year requires that he spend at least $933 a year to heat his household hot water. In other words, 15 percent of $933 is $140 saved a year. That's how to figure if a solar water heater will make sense for you, assuming that it will cut your total water heater bill by at least 15 percent.

Moreover, two other good reasons are cited for not plunging into buying a solar water heater or any other solar heat for a house at the present state of the art. First, buying any new product is not wise until it has been on the market long enough to prove itself. Bugs are inevitable in most products, and it takes time to iron them out. That applies to new cars and almost anything else. And solar heat is particularly complicated because of the pipes, controls, and sensitive heat collector that are all comparatively new.

The second reason for caution with solar heat is that like other radically new home improvement products introduced in the past, the proper installation, maintenance, and service for it require brains, knowledge, and experience. To start with, these three qualifications are not in long supply in the home improvement field and especially so for home solar-heating systems. Perhaps it's better to let other people serve as guinea pigs before one pioneers in solar heating.

Naturally, all of us much hope that solar heat has a bright future in U.S. houses, but it is still neither sufficiently economical nor practical for houses. Besides, if, in its early state, it is pushed too hard, unresolved problems with it could boomerang and cause a major setback.

CHAPTER 24
HOW TO SAVE ON
HOME AIR-CONDITIONING BILLS

Compared with home heating, cutting home air-conditioning bills involves doing things 180 degrees in reverse in summer. In summer, you want to keep hot outdoor heat out of your house. Certain indoor sources of heat and moisture should also be minimized or eliminated.

Here are eleven ways to cut home air-conditioning bills. Not only can they help you save money on central air conditioning and room coolers, but knowing them can also be a help when you buy new air conditioning for a room, the whole house, or a new addition being built on your house.

1. *Don't let hot sun pour into your house through windows.* Shade the glass, pull blinds down on the inside, or put up blinds on the outside. An enormous quantity of heat is unleashed into a house by direct sun shining through windows. That's why greenhouse temperatures climb to ovenlike levels.

What's more, the sun pours exactly the same amount of heat per hour per square foot of glass exposure into a house from the east in the morning as it does from the west in the afternoon. The sun may not seem as hot in the morning because the *air* temperature is not as hot as in the afternoon. Nonetheless, morning sun will dump considerable extra heat into the house, and will also drain overnight coolness from a house and start your interior heat load building up early. That makes the house tougher to keep cool later when the daytime heat level reaches its peak.

Shading windows with shades, awnings, or whatever else on the *outside* is much better than with inside shades. Outside shading keeps out about twice as much heat as inside shades. Once the hot sun's rays get through the glass, heat is halfway to its destination.

The best way of all to keep out the hot sun is by proper window design when new rooms are built, such as deep roof overhangs built over south-facing windows. Shade trees are, of course, also excellent, if not unbeatable.

2. *Stop hot roof heat from reaching into the house.* Sun pouring down on the roof is the single biggest source of summer heat in most houses. The sun beats down on the roof virtually all day long, but only on a single wall or window exposure at any one time during the day. Attics get as hot as 150 degrees F, and this heat can seep down into the house long into the evening. That's why upstairs rooms are so hot on a summer night.

The best protection from attic heat in an air-conditioned house is a thick layer of at least R-30 insulation (see Chapter 18) on the attic floor. The attic should also be well ventilated. This calls for screened air vents in the attic to let outside air blow in and wash out the hot air.

An attic heat-leveling fan can be particularly effective in a house where the air conditioning has difficulty keeping you cool during hot summer weather. It is used with borderline air-conditioning systems—it reduces the total heat load so that the air conditioner has an easier time cooling the house.

The darker the roof color, the more heat it will absorb and the hotter the attic. A light-colored or white roof reflects sun heat. Painting a roof white just to cut heat entry and air-conditioning costs, however, is not worth the expense; it will not reduce attic heat by that much. If, however, you are getting a new roof or building a new house or an addition to your present house, you could consider a light-colored roof.

3. *Keep doors and windows shut.* This should be obvious, but servicemen find that a surprising number of people have high cooling bills because windows and doors are blithely left open while the equipment is running. Hot outdoor air blows in, and high-cost cool air flows out.

A window or two can be left open a little bit and not make much difference in cooling operation. This is perfectly all right and understandable in, say, a bedroom where one desires "fresh" air at night. If a child leaves a door open occasionally, this, too, should not be a cause of alarm and no need to scream at the child. If children chronically leave a door open, an automatic door closer will reduce the loss of cool air (or screaming might be justified).

4. *Be sure your walls are insulated.* The walls of most houses built initially with central air conditioning were insulated during construction; but if air conditioning was installed later, particularly in older houses, the walls may have lacked insulation. That can cost you dearly. In fact, the cost of insulating the walls of a house with air conditioning that is also in a cold winter climate will come back very fast in energy savings summer and winter.

5. *Leave storm windows on in summer.* Don't take them all down and put on your screens, since windows are infrequently opened in a room or house with air conditioning. A few storm windows may be replaced with screens to allow you to enjoy the breeze on mild summer days. Storm windows left on in summer give a double-glass shield that cuts down on outside air-heat entry into a house through your window glass (though they do not reduce direct sun-heat entry through glass).

6. *Vent the clothes dryer.* A clothes dryer spews out a huge exhaust of hot, wet air, and this can overload the air conditioner even when the dryer is located in the basement. The hot vapor infiltrates the living quarters and soon gets to the air conditioner. Vent your dryer outdoors!

7. *Don't let moisture build up inside the house.* Water vapor from cooking, washing, and even a wet basement can, like the vapor from a clothes dryer, sharply increase the humidity in a house and make an air conditioner work harder. Remember that in addition to cooling, an air conditioner wrings moisture from the house air; it dehumidifies.

Steaming cooking vapors and fumes are best eliminated by a kitchen exhaust fan, used during cooking. Replacement air from outdoors should be drawn in by opening a kitchen window an inch or two rather than by drawing cool air from the rest of the house.

House chores that create moisture, such as washing floors and windows and ironing (especially with a steam iron), can be done early in the day. And don't hang wet clothes to dry inside the house. The moisture released into the house air requires extra work by the air conditioner.

A wet cellar should be dried out, since much of the vapor downstairs will inexorably rise upstairs. A slightly damp cellar that cannot be totally dried can, on the other hand, be kept dry by spilling a little air-conditioned air into the basement. This may require a cooling outlet installed in the basement. Among other things, this will prevent cellar mildew and wood rot.

Use plastic shower curtains in bathrooms. Canvas and cloth ones absorb shower water which later evaporates into the house air and loads down the air conditioner. A small bathroom exhaust fan, though not always essential, can also help rid your house of the cloud of bathroom vapor after a shower or bath. It can be worthwhile with a large family that takes frequent showers.

8. *Don't turn the air conditioner on and off all the time.* Don't keep it off in the morning, say, when it seems cool or when you leave the house for an hour or two and then switch it back on later when you return. Don't turn it off at night and fling open your windows before going to bed unless it's a cool night.

You'll get better results and lower bills if you let the thermostat control operate at all times or nearly so. Set it at 75 degrees F, more or less, and let the cooler go on and off as needed. If you turn it off and later turn it on when things are getting hot, the equipment has to work overtime to get rid of all the house heat and humidity that built up when it was off. Turning off the equipment when things may *seem* cool will ordinarily gain you little.

Of course, if the weather turns beautifully cool and comfortable for a few days or a week or so, it's perfectly all right to fling open a few windows and enjoy the breeze. Then turn off the equipment for a while, or set the thermostat up to about 80 degrees. The system will not go on unless there is a pronounced rise in the house temperature. Opening windows is not recommended, of course, if it is important to keep your house free of pollen to protect an allergic person in your family.

9. *Take advantage of storage effect.* During a heat wave, lower the thermostat setting 3 or 4 degrees below normal before going to bed at night. This is the other exception to the no-fiddling-with-the-thermostat rule. Turn the thermostat down to at least 72 degrees F. Your house is cooled more than usual while you sleep. Everything in the house—furniture and furnishings, as well as 10 to 20 tons of structure—will be gradually cooled down at a time when the equipment need not work hard. In effect, extra cooling is stored up to fight off the scorching heat of the next day. When the temperature soars the next day, you will be inexpensively cool because of storage effect. The cooled-down house and all its cooled-down contents help the air conditioner fight off the big heat of the day.

Storing up cooling can also help before a party or at any other time when a lot of people are expected. People make heat, particularly when they smoke. The additional ''people load'' from a gathering can make things uncomfortably warm even in an air-conditioned home. You prevent it by cooling down the house ahead of time and letting the storage effect help keep things comfortable.

10. *Let the cooling blower run all the time.* This utilizes the same principle, continuous air circulation (CAC), recommended for warm-air heating in winter. The air blower runs all the time, circulating air continuously through the house when the cooling compressor is off as well as when it's on. The small extra cost to keep the blower running is offset by the money saved as a result of greater air-conditioning efficiency. It also means greater comfort and more uniform temperature control.

The air-conditioning blower, often the same blower used for heating, can generally be turned to continuous operation with the summer-winter switch usually located on the equipment. You may also have to set your thermostat at continuous operation. If necessary, ask your air-conditioning dealer how to do it.

11. *Turn on the main electric switch for central air-conditioning equipment before the beginning of summer and at least a day or two before the first need for air conditioning is anticipated.* This is to warm up the internal cockles of the equipment in advance of operation. It's done by a small electric coil inside the equipment (some brands don't have this—check yours). The air conditioner will loosen up and be ready to run efficiently when it is first turned on. You avoid excessive wear that might otherwise occur when starting up from scratch.

ROOM AIR CONDITIONERS

Most of the suggestions just given for central air conditioning also apply to room coolers with a few obvious exceptions. A bedroom cooler, for example, need not run all day long when the room is unoccupied. It can help, though, if the thermostat is left no higher than 85 degrees F during the day so that the room does not get furnace-hot. During torrid weather the unit probably will have to be turned on at least an hour or two before bedtime if you want to be cool on retiring.

Air-conditioned rooms should be isolated from non-air-conditioned portions of the house by closed doors. If you have warm-air heat and a room cooler or two, close off the heating outlets in the air-conditioned areas during the summer, particularly the return-air outlets (usually in the floor). This prevents cool air from the room escaping down the ducts.

COMMON AIR-CONDITIONING PROBLEMS IN HOUSES

Here are the most common problems encountered with central air-conditioning systems in houses and what to do about them. Various points mentioned earlier will be repeated, to emphasize their importance, as well as to make this section complete by itself.

Not enough cooling, especially on the hottest days. The system is either undersized, not working the way it should, or not being operated properly. Is the air filter clean? Are the cool-air supply registers open? Are large windows exposed to direct sunshine? If so, draw blinds or shades over them when the sun hits. Are you letting the thermostat run the equipment? If not, set the thermostat at 75 degrees or whatever you need, and let it run day and night. Don't turn it off at night and open the windows. During a heat wave, turn the thermostat down at night—to 72 degrees or lower—and store up cooling in the house for the next day's onslaught of heat.

If none of that helps, direct your attention to the attic. Adding insulation up to a total of 10 inches at the attic floor might help, or install a thermostatic-operated exhaust fan in the attic to ventilate it. Remember, this kind of fan ventilates only the attic, not the rest of the house.

Uneven cooling. Some parts of the house are too cool, whereas others are too warm. Switch your air-conditioning blower to continuous circulation so the air will circulate all the time.

Too much house humidity. The air temperature is low enough, but you still feel sweaty and uncomfortable. It's usually because the equipment is cooling the air but not removing enough water vapor from it; i.e., the relative humidity in the house is not low enough. Too much water vapor may be present. It may be from an unvented clothes dryer, a wet basement, a fabric shower curtain, and sometimes indoor plants that are watered often (the water evaporates into the air through the leaves). Or, of all things, your equipment may be too big for your house, as follows:

Too large a unit. An oversized unit will quickly cool down a house and then stop working. It runs less frequently than a properly sized unit. As a result, the humidity builds up in a house faster than the heat does during those long off cycles. The tip-off to this problem is that the air conditioning keeps you cool and most comfortable on the hottest summer days. It runs the most then and maintains better control over your house humidity. Things are less comfortable and more sweaty for you during ordinary warm weather, when, say, the outside temperature is between 80 and 90 degrees.

Unfortunately, there may be no easy solution for this problem because it's due to an installation mistake. Your air-conditioning dealer might perhaps trade you a smaller compressor for your oversized one. Or try keeping your house at a lower thermostat temperature to keep the equipment cooling longer. Lower it enough, and your problem will be solved, though your house may begin to feel like an icebox, unfortunately. You could take some of the chill off by opening a window or two to let a little outside heat in. Extra operating cost is the price you pay in this case to achieve good dehumidification.

High cooling bills. Your house may have a very high heat load, and the unit must work overtime to keep you cool. Reduce the heat load, and the cooler can slow down. Shade those windows from the sun, add insulation to the attic, or install a fan to cool the attic. You want to get rid of excess moisture and other possible sources of excess heat in the house, as already noted.

Noisy operation. This irritating problem, alas, also stems from poor installation, poor system design, or just plain mediocre equipment. With poor installation the equipment often rattles and vibrates because it is not cushioned. Metal ducts bang and vibrate because they're screwed directly to the blower unit (instead of being connected with a canvas collar). Air whistles loudly through the ducts because the ducts are too small; this can be lessened if the ducts are lined with acoustical padding to sop up the noise. The first two problems require quieting the equipment with a vibration-free mounting or separating metal ducts from direct connection to the metal blower unit. You will probably need a serviceman for both of these.

If your outside compressor section is too noisy for neighbors, put a fence up between the equipment and the neighbors who complain. Make it a decorative fence of solid wood or, even better, concrete blocks. Put it close to the compressor to ward off the noise waves.

POOR ROOM-COOLER PERFORMANCE

The most common troubles with room coolers are caused by dirt-clogged air filters or coolers too small for the space. The first is remedied simply by periodically cleaning or replacing the filter. The second may or may not be correctable. Try reducing the heat load in the room by the methods suggested above; i.e., keep doors closed, shade windows, insulate the exterior walls of the room, and if there's an attic above, insulate the ceiling or ventilate the attic. If nothing helps, you need a larger unit.

CHAPTER 25

HOW TO BUY
CENTRAL AIR CONDITIONING

Air conditioning is not cheap, but it can be less expensive than many people think. It can be installed in old houses with excellent results. Operating costs are also less than you might expect; they are less per summer than central heat in the North and roughly twice as much in the hot South.

But first, is air conditioning worth having? My family found out, to its delight, that it is decidedly worthwhile in the North not only for welcome coolness during hot weather but also for relief from sweltering humidity. There are other compelling advantages, too. If you can afford the cost, it should be considered in any hot summer climate.

AIR-CONDITIONING BENEFITS

Sheer relief from hot summer heat is the principal advantage, but this is only part of the story. By lowering the indoor humidity in summer, air conditioning banishes mildew and sogginess, permitting salt shakers to flow freely, among other things.

Tests show that it filters out much of the pollen in the air, making the house a haven for hay fever, asthma, and other allergy sufferers. It is a boon for people with weak hearts and other ailments made worse by summer heat and humidity. Doctors prescribe it for such patients, and then its cost is tax-deductible. It means no more heat rash, particularly among infants, and, contrary to popular belief, fewer head colds in summer.

A common objection to air conditioning is the assumption that it makes the air cold and clammy. This stems from bad experiences in overchilled restaurants and movies and from walking into an air-conditioned store and being hit with a shock wave of cold air.

Things are different in houses. For one thing, most movies, restaurants, and stores are deliberately overchilled. For another, air conditioning in a house is set to the exact temperature and humidity a family desires; no need to set it at a very low temperature to be sure that all the numerous occupants will be sufficiently cool.

What about thermal shock, the strain on the body experienced when you go from 95-degree heat into an air-conditioned house or out again? This is not damaging to people in good health, according to exhaustive research at the University of Illinois College of Medicine. It is no more damaging than stepping out of a 70-degree house in winter into the cold 30-degree outdoors—a 40-degree drop.

A sudden, sharp change in temperature and humidity may be distressing to people with weak hearts. Such people should avoid abrupt temperature changes. In an air-conditioned house they could have the entrance foyer set at a temperature about halfway between indoors and out as a sort of decompression chamber. Better still, they should avoid excessive heat and humidity and during heat waves stay indoors with air conditioning, not expose themselves to the harsh effects of the hot, humid outdoors.

ROOM COOLERS VERSUS CENTRAL AIR CONDITIONING

Choosing between the two is often the first decision to resolve when you air-condition. I could have had four or five individual room coolers installed for my first house when we decided to get air conditioning. I did not chiefly because they shut out window light, are less efficient than one large unit, and cost more to operate than a central unit for the same house.

If I had installed them in the walls under windows, the cost of the entire job, including new wiring for each, would have brought the total cost almost up to the cost of central air conditioning. And regardless of where they are installed, they detract from the inside and outside appearance of a house.

On the other hand, one or two room coolers can be perfectly satisfactory for partial air conditioning or for a new addition. A through-the-wall installation is obviously neater than in a window, and it does not obstruct window light. Most models can be installed either flush with the interior wall surface or flush with the outside, but check this according to your requirements. (More on room air conditioners later.)

INSTALLING NEW CENTRAL AIR CONDITIONING

You are a big step ahead if your house has forced warm-air central heating and the air ducts, already in place, can be used for central air conditioning, too. The cost of installing a whole new duct system is saved; this means a lower price for new air conditioning. The new air-conditioning unit is hooked up so that the cool air is supplied in summer through the same ducts used for winter heating.

If you have hot-water heat, electric heat, or no central heat, a separate central air conditioner is the solution. It operates independently of the heating system. Air ducts will be needed, but they are simpler and less expensive to install than when needed for both heating and cooling. In a one-story house, for example, they can be installed between the basement ceiling beams with discharge outlets in the floor to each room. In a house without a basement they can be built in under the ceiling of a central hall with short stub ducts connecting to the rooms around. This latter is better than having cool-air ducts in the attic (which require expensive insulation).

There is also *chilled-water air conditioning,* long used in big-building air conditioning. Cooling is combined with hot-water heating. The same pipes used to distribute hot water in winter are used to distribute chilled water for summer cooling. The water is supplied to special heating-cooling coils encased in small cabinets, instead of radiators, in each room.

Each cabinet contains a filter and small blower. Air from the room is drawn into the cabinet, filtered, cooled, and dehumidified, then discharged back into the room. In summer the water pumped to the coils is chilled by a refrigerating mechanism (water chiller) located next to the boiler. In winter hot water from the boiler is pumped through the system to each room cabinet, and the room air drawn into each cabinet is filtered and heated.

A chilled-water system is more costly than comparable air conditioning with ducts—its main drawback. In addition, it does not lend itself easily to air-conditioning an existing house simply because all the supply pipes inside walls would have to be insulated first (to avoid sweating in summer).

Chilled water is chiefly for new houses and new additions to existing houses when new heating and cooling are required. Its biggest advantages are that it eliminates ducts, using pipes instead, and that the individual room units permit individual control of the temperature and humidity in each room, but such control must be specified.

ATTIC AIR CONDITIONERS

These are sold largely for existing houses because they require a minimum of installation work and therefore come with temptingly low price tags. By installing the equipment and the ducts in the attic, the dealer avoids the trouble of breaking into walls. Air is discharged down into each room through outlets in the ceiling.

There are two kinds of attic systems. In one only the air-blower section of the equipment is in the attic. The ducts are supplied cool air from this section, and tired, used air from the house is returned here to be cooled, dehumidified, and filtered and then recirculated, a continuous process. The other part of the equipment, the compressor-motor or refrigeration section, is located elsewhere, which usually is on the ground outside the house. It is connected to its attic mate by refrigeration pipes. The other kind of attic unit involves locating the whole shebang, compressor and air-blower sections, in one combined package in the attic.

This second attic system (compressor in the attic) should be avoided because of its noise and vibration. A compressor is a mass of fast-moving machinery. Located in an attic, it requires an exceedingly careful and properly made installation to prevent noise and vibration overhead, and even then it will not necessarily be quiet. Servicing the equipment may also be difficult. Installing only half the air-conditioning system (the blower or fan-coil unit) in the attic is considerably less noisy and therefore far more tolerable.

No matter how much equipment is located in the attic, remember that ducts will be installed there; these could make your attic hardly usable for storage or any other purpose. The attic is largely sacrificed to air conditioning. Check this with the contractor *before* he starts work. If necessary, insist that the ducts be installed so that maximum attic space is left usable for other purposes.

To sum up, an attic unit is recommended only if the attic is too low for other uses and only if the blower-cooling section of the equipment is located in the attic and the noisier compressor section is located outdoors. Because of attic heat, the equipment and ducts should be very well insulated. The equipment should be lined with insulation in the factory—look for this. If omitted, the dealer should provide it.

AIR- VERSUS WATER-COOLED UNITS

Most air conditioning for houses is air-cooled. The heat extracted from the house is dissipated into the outdoor air; that is why room air conditioners are located in windows. Access to outdoor air is essential, just as people need it to breathe. Outdoor air is pulled through a cooling coil to carry off the heat removed from the house air.

The other way to dissipate heat is via water cooling. A stream of water is continually run over the hot refrigerant coil to drain and carry off its heat. But considerable quantities of water are usually required, and this makes cooling with ordinary city water expensive. Air-cooled equipment costs more to install, but it reduces operating costs substantially, compared with water cooling. An exception is having a large quantity of water available at a low price. It could be a freshwater stream going by your house or a good water well with access to plenty of underground water.

Conclusion: If you have a good and ample source of low-cost water, use it for air conditioning. An air-conditioning dealer can tell you how much water you need and if it makes sense for your house. If it does, your air conditioning will cost less than with air-cooled equipment.

Water-cooled operation, by the way, should not be confused with chilled-water air conditioning. A water-cooled unit simply uses water for removing the heat accumulated inside the mechanism. The unit itself may supply its cooling to the house via cool-air ducts or chilled-water pipes.

BUYING AIR CONDITIONING

Buy only from a really good dealer or contractor, again the old stock advice but even more important than usually. When you buy an appliance or even a new car, the dealer passes on to you only what a manufacturer made. With air conditioning, like heating and building a house, the people you buy from must also install the thing and must make it work properly. Before you buy, reduce the house heat load to a minimum. Even more than home heating, good insulation, sun control, and other measures to reduce the summer heat load will save you money via a smaller, lower-priced, cheaper-to-run air conditioner.

Buy from a dealer who handles a well-known national brand like Carrier, Lennox, York (a division of Borg-Warner), and sometimes General Electric and Westinghouse. By and large, such dealers have the most experience with home cooling. Get bids from two or three different dealers. Ask each dealer for the names of people whose houses he has air-conditioned. Call some of these people to find out how the jobs turned out. Don't necessarily choose the lowest-price job; that can be folly.

A doctor I know got three bids for air-conditioning his house. Checking, he found that the low man had omitted two important items that the others had included. He would have been stuck later. He took the middle bid chiefly because it was made by the most experienced dealer around. Among other things, this dealer gave him a list of more than 150 homeowners whose houses he had air-conditioned. There's a postscript to that story. Two months later the doctor learned that both the dealer who made the low bid and the manufacturer who made his equipment had gone out of business.

HIGH-EFFICIENCY AIR CONDITIONING

Whether you buy a room cooler or central system for your house, get a brand and model with an energy efficiency ratio (EER) of at least 7.5, the lowest acceptable, and preferably about 10. The higher the ratio, the lower your operating cost will be for a given amount of cooling.

A high ratio means that a unit produces more cooling capacity for your house from a given quantity of electricity. A unit's EER is computed from its cooling capacity in BTU's per hour and the electric power in watts required for operation. Both are listed on the nameplate. Divide the BTU cooling capacity by the watt rating to get a model's EER. For example, a unit with a cooling capacity of 12,000 BTU's an hour and an electric input rating of 1,500 watts has an EER of 8. That's 12,000 divided by 1,500. The EER should be noted in the equipment's literature.

The equipment you buy should also carry the certification seal of the Air Conditioning and Refrigeration Institute (ARI). Equipment without this certification should be turned down.

HOW MUCH COOLING CAPACITY?

In other words, what size unit for your house? A 2- to 3-ton-air-conditioning system is ordinarily needed to cool a house of from 1,000 to 2,000 square feet of living area. An insulated house ordinarily requires about 1 ton of air conditioning for every 500 to 600 square feet of floor area. A very well-insulated house with its large windows shaded from the sun can be cooled by about 1 ton for every 600 to

700 square feet. Conversely, the hotter the climate, the greater the cooling capacity needed per 100 square feet of house floor area.

One ton of air conditioning, by the way, is not a pile of equipment 2,000 pounds in weight. It's a quantity of cooling capacity equal to the cooling effect you would get from a 1-ton block of ice. Scientifically, it's the removal of 12,000 Btu's of heat from the air every hour. Thus, a 2-ton unit will remove 24,000 Btu's of heat an hour.

HOW COOL INSIDE?

The cooling system should be guaranteed to maintain the house interior at 75 degrees and 50 percent relative humidity during the hottest summer weather where you live. Thus, the equipment should be capable of lowering the house temperature by 20 degrees in cities like New York and Chicago, where the highest summer temperature (called outside design temperature) is generally 95 degrees, and 30 degrees if you live in Phoenix, Arizona, say, where outside temperatures hit 105 degrees.

An air-conditioning dealer may casually say that 80 degrees inside is all you need and that is all he guarantees. Or that an air-conditioning system should be designed to reduce the indoor temperature by 10 to 15 degrees below outdoors and that's all. This is nonsense, even though it is mistakenly believed by some air-conditioning people (and some doctors).

Nearly all humans require 75 degrees and 50 percent relative humidity indoors for comfort in summer, give or take a degree or two. This is the temperature and humidity people require for human comfort in summer in offices, factories, and homes. It is borne out by research sponsored by the American Society of Heating, Refrigeration and Air-Conditioning Engineers (ASHRAE). It is the condition required indoors almost regardless of what the outdoor temperature may be. The body has no built-in radar telling it what is going on outdoors when it is indoors.

Surveys show that most families set their cooling thermostats at from 73 to 77 degrees in summer. A few people are unusual and like their houses as cool as 70 degrees; others, as warm as 80 degrees. They set the thermostat up or down until the temperature and humidity are comfortable, and these are the settings that result.

If your system is designed to maintain 75 degrees indoors, rather than 80, it is assurance that there always will be capacity to keep you comfortable in the hottest weather. If you like it really cool, plan for extra capacity; this may call for a larger unit.

On the other hand, the President of the United States and others have recommended that to save energy, home air-conditioning systems be set at 78 to 80 degrees F. That's fine, though there's a catch. Most people are simply not comfortable in summer at these temperatures, as mentioned above. We begin to feel discomfort when the temperature rises above 77 degrees. If you can tolerate a higher air-conditioning temperature, fine. You'll conserve energy and also cut your cooling bill by 4 to 7 percent for each degree you raise the thermostat setting. You save most of all, however, by properly insulating and shading your house and following through on other energy-conserving measures mentioned for reducing the heat load.

Don't buy an oversized system. I mentioned earlier that some dealers will, for example, try to sell a 4-ton air-conditioning system when a 3-ton job would do the job. This happens because—so the dealers say—many homeowners want enough air conditioning to cool their houses quickly during a heat wave. The dealers claim that many people tend to use their air conditioning only during very hot weather and turn off the system at other times. Extra cooling capacity is therefore needed to cool their houses at such times. If that extra capacity isn't there, the people call the dealer and howl.

To forestall such howls, the dealer then begins to sell everybody oversized equipment. If, however, your air conditioning is sized to run all the time during a heat wave, it will do the best job of keeping you cool and dehumidified. But heat waves don't last all summer. Much of the time the air-conditioning system will be coasting and operating less than twenty-four hours a day. It beats having an oversized unit in more ways than one.

WHAT ABOUT THE HEAT PUMP?

The heat pump is an electric air-conditioning unit that not only cools a house in summer but also heats (by electricity) in winter at roughly half the cost of regular electric resistance heating. Electric resistance heating works like an electric range burner.

The heat pump is different. In summer it extracts heat from inside a house, cooling the house air, the heat extracted being ejected outside. But in winter its operation is reversed, and it extracts "free" heat from the outside air and pulls this heat inside.

The heat pump is growing in popularity because it can mean reduced costs for home heating, compared with regular electric heat, especially if central air conditioning is also desired. It could be a good way to heat and cool a new addition or replace an old house heating unit with a device that heats and cools. Its initial cost is several hundred dollars more than central air conditioning.

But a heat pump isn't necessarily all peaches and cream. In winter it is still electric heat, though at lower cost than regular resistance electric heat. But your operating cost for heating with a heat pump will still be considerably more than gas heat and approximately on a par with oil heat at a cost of about 50 cents a gallon for oil. Its exact competitive relationship with oil heat depends on the particular heat pump brand bought and the severity of your climate, as noted below.

The trouble with heat pumps so far is that their efficiency falls when the outdoor temperature drops to 30 degrees F or lower. When the outdoor air gets colder, many heat pumps no longer can extract its residual heat efficiently, and they automatically switch over to regular backup electric resistance heating. For this reason, using a heat pump is still not dependable in any climate colder than Washington, D.C. (4,333 winter degree days), according to heat pump engineers at the U.S. National Bureau of Standards. Some manufacturers claim that their heat pumps will perform well in colder climates, or down to 20 degrees F outdoor temperature, before having to switch over to the more expensive resistance heaters which heat pumps come with.

Buying a heat pump

Get a good one, which means one with an energy efficiency ratio (EER) of at least 7.5. That measures its summer operating efficiency; the higher it is, the lower your operating bills for summer cooling. It can also mean greater heating efficiency in winter, though a unit's coefficient of performance (COP) gives a direct indication of winter heating efficiency. The COP should range from about 2.0 at 15 to 20 degrees F outdoor temperature to about 2.8 at 45 to 50 degrees.

A particular heat pump's EER is obtained by dividing the unit's Btu's per hour of summer cooling capacity by the electrical consumption in watts. The COP is determined by dividing the Btu's of heat produced by the electrical input in watts. Both the EER and the COP should be noted on a unit's nameplate or in its description sheet.

You can also get such facts, plus other information about heat pumps, from an industry Directory of Certified Heat Pumps, available for $1 from the Director of Engineering, Air-Conditioning and Refrigeration Institute, 1815 North Fort Myer Drive, Arlington, Virginia 22209.

Only a heat pump that has been tested and certified by the ARI should be bought; that means one listed in the ARI Directory. The National Bureau of Standards also emphasizes the importance of buying from a reputable local dealer who knows how to install and service heat pumps—i.e., one who has installed a number of them in your area.

If you're still in doubt about the feasibility of a heat pump for your climate, talk to people who have them. Ask how the units work, particularly during very cold winter weather. And what about operating costs? In short, can you count on the one you buy to be really dependable?

CHAPTER 26

HOW TO AIR-CONDITION A TOUGH OLD HOUSE

My family and I learned about central air conditioning from firsthand experience. Some of what happened was unpredictable, and that, plus certain lessons learned, could help readers.

We lived in the old Victorian house mentioned at the beginning of this book. It's an example of one of the toughest kinds of houses to air-condition. Like many people, my wife had mixed feelings about cooling the place. But she later became a big booster of air conditioning because of unanticipated benefits, including the highly salutary effects it had on our small children.

We decided on central air conditioning because we needed a new heating furnace. The ancient furnace was in the last stage of old age, and its fuel appetite was astronomical. This was the time to get air conditioning, too, a combination heating-cooling system rather than just a new furnace. The extra cost for installing the air-conditioning part would be considerably less than the later cost of installing a central air conditioner by itself.

Another element that tipped the scale in favor of air conditioning was that we needed new window screens for our twenty-eight windows. They would not be needed if we put in air conditioning. This represented a big saving which could be applied against the air-conditioning cost. A few screens were left on windows so we may enjoy the breeze on nice days.

BIGGEST INSTALLATION PROBLEM
In most houses the installation of ductwork from the basement to the second floor is the hardest part of the job. We could use the existing

heating ducts, but there weren't enough of them. Ductwork accounts for one of the biggest expenses of home air-conditioning cost, and its design is crucial for good heating and cooling.

I made a room-by-room inspection with the air-conditioning contractor, looking for the best places to run new ducts up from the basement inside existing interior walls. For one room upstairs, an interior duct was impossible. The alternative was a vertical 4-×-12-inch duct tucked into an open corner of the living room and boxed in. It is hardly noticed today.

SPECIAL CONTROLS

We got a two-zone temperature-control system, a thermostat upstairs and another one downstairs. This cost $150 over the cost of a single thermostat, but it enabled us to keep each level of the house as warm or cool as we want, independent of the other level. It's a blessing. We found, for example, that the second floor requires more cooling in the summer than the first floor (because of the attic above).

On mildly warm summer days, in fact, we found that cooling is often needed only for the second floor. Enough cool air floats down the stairwell to keep the first-floor rooms comfortable. In winter the reverse is true. Thus, the zone controls help reduce operating cost, as well as provide balanced air temperatures throughout the house.

HOW WE SAVED ON EQUIPMENT SIZE

The house required a 2.6-ton air conditioner, equivalent to the cooling effect given off by 2.6 tons of ice. At first the contractor specified a larger, 3-ton size. We discussed reducing the summer heat load in the house by adding special insulation to the attic (noted later) and leaving most of the storm windows in place all summer long (thus reducing the outside air-heat flow into the house through the glass).

All this meant that we could use the next-size-smaller, lower-cost air conditioner. It has proved more than ample on the hottest, most humid days. It cools and dehumidifies 1,750 square feet of floor area on two levels—eight rooms and one and a half bathrooms. This works out to 1 ton of air conditioning per 673 square feet of floor area, about par for the course for a well-insulated two-story old house in a northern climate.

An air-cooled unit was chosen since it does not require a steady supply of water to carry away the heat removed from the house. It works like a large window air conditioner. Air is drawn in over the hot refrigerator coils (called the condenser), cools them like the air breeze through a car radiator, and is then ejected back outdoors.

The air conditioner is split into two sections. The part containing the refrigeration mechanism is located outside under a porch, where it has free access to outside air. It is connected by copper refrigeration pipes to the cooling coil section located on top of the furnace in the basement. This is where the house air is actually cooled and dried.

This kind of air-cooled split system is the most popular kind of central air conditioning. It is the easiest and usually the most economical to install in old houses. That's if you have warm-air heat and can utilize your present ducts.

Additional savings result because the cooling coil could be matched to the furnace and installed at the same time as the new furnace. Only one blower and blower motor and one filter and one set of ducts are needed for year-round heating and cooling.

TWO UNEXPECTED TROUBLES

Noisy operation plagued us at first. Even the best equipment generates some noise. The noise, however, comes almost entirely from the refrigeration mechanism (compressor) outside. We did not hear it inside. But our closest neighbors did, since the unit is not far from their bedroom windows. This threat to peaceful coexistence was licked by putting up a 4-foot-high wood noise fence, plus a few shrubs, in front of the compressor between it and their house.

The second trouble confronted me when I entered the basement a week after the system had been started up for the first time. It was during a wave of hot and muggy weather. I saw, to my distress, a wide pool of water spreading over the basement floor. This represented the many dozens of gallons of moisture (humidity) removed from the house air at the cooling unit. It was not draining away properly.

The drainpipe discharged into a drain in the basement floor. I did not know that the floor drain was simply a small hole under the floor capable of absorbing only a small quantity of water at a time. Both the air-conditioning contractor and I had thought it connected to a pipe drain under the house. Because it did not, a new drain system had to be installed. This is mentioned because even with an air-cooled system a drain must be installed to carry off the humidity moisture removed from the house air.

OVERCOMING COMMON PITFALLS

Two of the most widespread obstacles to air-conditioning old houses are overloaded wiring and no thermal insulation. Without adequate wiring, air conditioning is impossible; without proper insulation, it is unwise. Our house had been previously rewired with a 100-ampere, 220-volt main electric board, the minimum size recommended today. This handles the central air conditioner without flinching.

After buying the house, I had insulation blown into the exterior walls for heating comfort and lower fuel bills. The attic floor had been previously insulated with 3½-inch mineral wool batts. Because of air conditioning, I increased it to 6 inches. (Later, when the energy crisis hit, the same insulation was increased to 9 inches.)

I went a step further in the attic, since roof heat seeping down into a house is one of the biggest single entry routes of summer heat. I had sheets of aluminum foil stapled under the roof beams at the attic ceiling. This sharply reduces the amount of roof heat that is normally reradiated from the underside of the hot roof down to the attic ceiling and then into the bedrooms. The foil bounces the radiant heat back, or is supposed to.

At the same time large aluminum vents were installed at the gable peak at each end of the attic. These are imperative not only to let outside air wash in and blow away attic heat, but also to prevent condensation in winter.

Because of the foil cover over the attic interior and the new vents, I found that the attic is much cooler in summer than it formerly was. Without these heat controls and without insulation the house would have required a larger, more expensive air conditioner, and operating costs would be considerably higher.

COSTS

Here is the cost breakdown for the new air-conditioning system and new furnace, showing the actual dollar costs in 1959, when the work was done, and the estimated cost for the same work if it were done in 1978 by the same contractor. The original contractor (Henry Weiner, Inc., Spring Valley, New York) prepared the estimates for the new edition of this book.

I emphasize, however, that the cost of home air conditioning can vary from house to house even with the same equipment put in different houses. That's because the cost of installation, particularly for the ductwork, can vary greatly from house to house.

	1959 cost	*1978 estimated cost*
2.6-ton air conditioner	$ 824	$1,050
New furnace	272	375
Total installation of equipment, new ducts, labor, zone temperature controls, and their installation	1,096	1,430
Carpentry (for installing new ducts)	75	100
Wiring equipment and controls	105	175
Optional air purifier and winter humidifier	300	400
Total	$2,672	$3,530

A similar air-conditioning system *without new heating* in a two-story house like mine normally will cost about one-third less than the above figures for a similar house. The increased cost in 1978 over the 1959 cost for the same home air-conditioning system may not seem as much as you would think over nineteen years, but the figures are accurate. Like the prices for major appliances such as refrigerators, prices for home air-conditioning equipment did not climb all that much in this period. Labor costs were also kept from going sky-high by, among other things, the introduction of new low-cost techniques for installing air conditioning.

The cost of operation averages $72 a month, or $216 for three full months of central air conditioning each summer, based on a comparatively high local electric rate of 7 cents a kilowatt-hour for cooling electricity in 1978. Because the air conditioner is sized for the full capacity needed on the hottest days, it runs virtually twenty-four hours a day during a heat wave, less on milder summer days. The climate is hot and humid—typical suburban New York City climate. The temperature hits a high of 95 degrees a few times most summers, and every few years there are a few days when it breaks 100 degrees.

CHAPTER 27

ROOM AIR CONDITIONERS

How do you buy a room air conditioner? To work well, there are three basic requirements (which also apply to central air conditioners): It should meet industry certification standards, it should be properly sized, and it should have a high energy efficiency ratio (EER).

The Association of Home Appliance Manufacturers (AHAM) certifies room coolers, and a certified model will carry an AHAM certification seal. It certifies that the unit's cooling capacity (in BTU's per hour) is up to par, on the basis of industry standards. If you do not see this seal, don't buy. Most room coolers made are certified.

But a certification seal assures you only that the unit will deliver its rated cooling capacity. You also want a unit with the right capacity for the room to be cooled, one that runs quietly, and one for which service is available when necessary.

The unit size required can be determined accurately only by computing the heat gain of the room it will cool. It's easy to do with a "Cooling Load Estimate Form," available free from a room cooler dealer; or send a stamped, return-addressed envelope for one to AHAM, 20 North Wacker Drive, Chicago, Illinois 60606. The computation will tell you how much cooling capacity is needed. Choose a room cooler with a capacity equal to or slightly less than required. Yes, slightly *less* so you will have good dehumidification all the time.

Like central air conditioners, a room cooler with a high energy efficiency ratio will cool at the lowest operating cost. Buy one with an EER of at least 7.5 and preferably 10 or more.

OTHER BUYING TIPS

Be sure to get one that is not noisy unless you don't mind a little boiler factory humming away in your house. Some brands are noisier than others, which is putting it lightly. What's more, the noise characteristic of a particular brand may vary from good to bad or back again with annual changes in manufacturers' models. A neighbor's 1978 model of Brand A may be nice and quiet, but a later model of the same brand may have turned noisy. You have to listen to models in a showroom, compare one against the other, and listen hard for the quietest ones. Be sure that the unit is set at cooling, not at the fan setting only.

Check *Consumer Reports* and *Consumer Research* for their latest ratings. Each publishes test data and recommendations on room air conditioners every year or two.

Complaints about poor service are most common with units bought from discount houses or ordinary appliance dealers who have no facilities for service. You can save money, to be sure, when you buy from a discount house, but find out first what kind of service guarantee you get. It may be wiser to buy from an air-conditioning dealer who has his own service department. The extra price you pay is good insurance for service.

WILL YOU NEED NEW WIRING?

As a rule, a unit with a capacity of less than 8,500 BTU's can be plugged into an ordinary 115-volt outlet. Exactly how much current does the unit require? It may draw only 7 amperes, which is low, or as much as 15 amperes, which will probably blow fuses, depending on your wiring strength. If in doubt, choose one of the special 7-ampere models that run off an ordinary electric outlet. This assumes that it is a 115-volt model.

The 7-ampere model, however, is not exactly robust and has limited cooling capacity. It can handle a small room or large closet, and that's it. Therefore, be sure that one will be strong enough for your space; i.e., its rated capacity should clearly be able to deal with the calculated heat load of the space.

There are also 240-volt models which are more efficient but require a new 240-volt electric line for the air conditioner. Some dealers have special plug-in devices that tell whether or not your wiring will take a room cooler. Ask about this. If you need a new wiring line, it can cost as much as several hundred dollars.

INSTALLATION

There are models that are placed in windows, through-the-wall types, and portable units. The usual window model may be objectionable because of unsightliness and because it obstructs light entry. It usually requires a window at least 27 inches wide. Special models are available for casement windows. Measure your window to be sure the unit will fit.

The through-the-wall installation costs more because the wall must be opened up. But it is neater and better-looking, especially in a new room or new addition.

The portable unit is designated to be lifted in and out of windows and switched from one room to another as desired. But once it is in place, most people don't bother moving it. Because it has small capacity and can't match the cooling power of a permanent model, it is not recommended, unless you take it with you in summer to a vacation place.

SPECIAL FEATURES TO GET

1. *Thermostatic control.* Is there a control to turn the cooling on and off automatically, according to your present temperature requirement? Some units lack this control. You must turn the unit on and off by hand, a big nuisance, particularly at night. Some have limited control; others have a broad range of settings.

2. *Good air distribution.* Look for adjustable louvers that can aim the air in various directions over the heads of people nearby. Some units have louvers that can be adjusted up or down (for vertical loft) or side-to-side control, some one or the other, and some neither. Try for both or at least adjustable louvers that aim the air up or down.

3. *Convenient controls.* They should be clearly marked, easy to work, and easy to reach (not so far back that they are blocked by window shades or so hidden you have to search for them). Some are so complicated they are a nightmare. Try them out before buying.

4. *Ventilation.* A good unit can ventilate a room while it is also cooling and also without cooling (for winter use). This is done by a special control which pulls in fresh outdoor air. Other units have an exhaust feature which pumps out stale or smoky room air (but not always possible at the same time the unit is cooling). Look for one or the other, a feature that will be highly appreciated.

5. *Accessible filter.* Is the filter easy to remove, clean, and replace? Filters are either replaceable glass wool or permanent metal mesh or plastic. All are roughly equal in filtering ability, but even the permanent kind has to be removed and cleaned periodically. If the replaceable kind is used, find out the cost of new ones.

6. *Rustproof construction.* Rust and corrosion are the biggest enemies of a room cooler. Whether a unit lasts only six or seven years or twice that time depends chiefly on its resistance to metal corrosion. Better units contain metal parts of aluminum or galvanized steel, usually protected by a baked-on enamel finish. Sometimes it is called bonderized paint. Run a fingernail over the cabinet; you should not be able to scratch the paint.

Consult the manufacturer's specifications, usually tagged to the unit, for mention of rustproof construction. Look inside the cabinet, especially the rear end, which will stick outside exposed to the weather, for the silvery glint of aluminum or galvanized steel.

CHAPTER 28
HOW TO TAKE ADVANTAGE OF FREE SOLAR HEAT

With all that free sunshine in the sky, why not let it pour directly into your house to keep you warm? An elaborate system of collector plates, pumps, and pipes is not needed. You will save all its expense, and you end up with surprisingly large heating savings.

The trick is proper location of the big windows of a house, and not just when you remodel or add new rooms to a house. Merely installing a few properly placed windows in an existing house can capture a considerable amount of solar heat for free extra warmth in winter.

There's another bonus. Sunshine pouring into a house can cheerfully brighten up one's life, as when it pours delightfully into a bedroom at morning wake-up time. Sun, flooding into a kitchen or dining room at breakfast or lunch, can make one's day. For that matter, relocating a window or two can transform a small gloomy part of your house into a "large," pleasant place.

The orientation of a house and the rooms within—their exposure—makes the difference.

Regardless of where you live in the United States or any other part of the Northern Hemisphere, the winter sun is in the south almost all day long. It rises in the southeast and sets in the southwest. But in summer the sun rises in the *northeast,* travels a much higher arc across the sky, being almost directly overhead at noon, and sets in the *northwest.* A few facts emphasize what this means:

1. Every room on the south side of a house receives five times as much sun heat in winter as in summer.

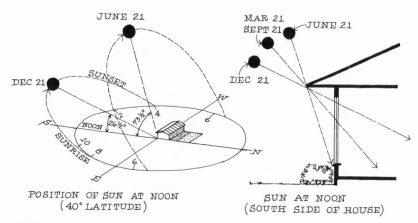

POSITION OF SUN AT NOON
(40° LATITUDE)

SUN AT NOON
(SOUTH SIDE OF HOUSE)

This diagram of the sun's travel in the Northern Hemisphere shows why a house (and its large windows) should face due south to receive the most free solar heat in winter. In summer, the same south-facing windows are easy to shade from hot sun heat. Roof overhangs keep out the high summer sun. The farther north the house, the deeper the overhangs required. Of course, trees or other shading devices can also be used.

2. East and west rooms, on the other hand, receive six times as much sun heat in summer as in winter.

3. Rooms and windows facing north receive no sunshine at all in winter and only a little in summer; the farther south you are, the more sun the north side of your house gets in summer.

As a rule, therefore, a house should face broadside to the south to receive the most sunshine in winter, the least in summer. Actually, the house itself can face any direction. The important thing to remember is that the big windows of your daytime living areas (kitchen, dining, and family rooms) should face south for sunshine, light, and heat to flood in. A southern exposure is less important for the living room, unless you use it a good deal during the day; many people use it mostly at night.

New bedrooms obviously have less need for sun and are best facing north or east. On the east, you may welcome the bright sun and free heat flooding in first thing in the morning. Bedrooms on the west can get awfully hot in summer by the time you are ready for bed. Put a new carport or garage on the west as a sun shield in summer or on the north as a wind shield in winter.

To let the most free solar heat pour into a house, large new windows should be installed on the walls facing south. Conversely, to keep heat loss down to a minimum, don't add new window glass on the vulnerable, wind-lashed north side of your house. That includes a wall exposure ranging from northeast around to west, depending on the prevailing winter wind where you live.

Additional winter protection can be had with a windbreak of evergreen trees on the north, as is frequently seen near farmhouses in the wind-scourged Great Plains. (The evergreen windbreaks planted throughout the Great Plains—one of Franklin D. Roosevelt's little-publicized New Deal conservation projects—turned out far more successfully than its most ardent advocates had expected.) If you live in the South, a southward orientation may be less desirable. You will have more shade if a house faces north with the patio on the north or northeast. Try to avoid a southwestern or western orientation.

According to the Smithsonian Institution, putting major windows on the south side of a house for maximum winter sunshine intake can cut home heating bills as much as 35 percent. Go a step farther, and reduce northern window exposures or protect vulnerable north-facing glass from cold winds in winter, and total heating energy costs can be reduced by about 40 percent or more.

SUMMER HEAT CONTROL

The beauty of facing windows to the sunny south is that they are comparatively easy to shade from hot summer sun, and summer cooling bills are lower. Roof overhangs extended over the windows when new rooms are added can most easily keep out the summer sun. That's because the summer sun shines down from a much higher angle in the sky.

As shown in the accompanying sun diagram, in winter the sun orbits lower in the sky and easily shines in under the same roof overhangs. The farther north a house is located, the deeper the overhang necessary to keep out the sun in summer. Summer shade can be provided for new windows being added to existing rooms merely by a new roof overhang directly above, by awnings or other outside shades, or by shade trees.

The exposure given to a new patio or porch obviously will also affect how cool and comfortable it will be in summer. If it faces west, it probably will get much too hot for comfort on a summer afternoon and evening. It would be better located on the south, east, or north sides, provided, of course, that it will be conveniently near your main living area. A southern or southwestern exposure can be excellent for a terrace or patio, but only if it is protected from the western sun in summer. A few strategically placed trees or a simple fence can do this. Then you may have a marvelous sun trap in late fall and early spring, ideal for sunning yourself at times when it would otherwise be idiotic to be outdoors.

The prevailing breeze also bears on the best location for patio or porch. A call to the nearest airport will get its usual direction in summer and winter. If the requirements for catching the summer breeze clash with the need for good sun protection, a compromise is in order. By and large, the sun is your bigger foe, and protection from it ranks first.

MECHANICAL SOLAR HEAT

As for spending money to install a mechanical solar heating system, the cost (as this is written in 1978) is, alas, much too high to make it practical. As mentioned in the previous chapter, solar heat is most favorable when compared with the high cost of electricity for water heating. But even then it may be questionable.

In addition, a standby regular heating system is usually needed for those long periods when the sun doesn't shine. Solar heating systems are still mechanically complicated. A number of the first ones so far installed are reportedly not working well and are subject to mechanical breakdowns. That's understandable because they are so new and have inevitable bugs. There is also a widespread lack of capable installation and service people. No matter how much we need solar heating, the plain, unvarnished fact is that it still has a long way to go to be perfected.

Other past innovations for houses, such as television and central air conditioning, required an introductory period of—brace yourself—ten years or more before they were developed to the point of being relatively trouble-free, not to mention their cost. Similarly, we must expect solar heat to take years of development before it can be considered a truly practical method. There is a chance of it taking less time, however, because of the large sacks of government research money being spent to speed up its development.

PART SIX
Coping with common problems in houses

Nearly everyone knows that high service bills constitute one of the most widespread problems in houses. But there are other equally widespread and sometimes more troublesome ones.

In this section is what these problems are and how to cope with them, starting with the widespread problem of dark and cold interiors. One of the most satisfying solutions is to install a good new window or skylight, as reported in the next chapter. Other common problems and their solutions are presented, winding up with a checklist on how to avoid home repair bills.

CHAPTER 29

HOW NEW WINDOWS AND SKYLIGHTS CAN LIGHT UP AND WARM UP DARK, COLD AREAS OF YOUR HOUSE

Probably no other single change can transform a house at such low cost as a new window or skylight can. Not only can one let sunshine and its warmth pour into dark, cold areas, but it can also exploit a good view or enhance a room like magic, as shown in the photos with this chapter.

Indeed, don't think of a window as merely a sheet of glass. Consider it a medium for letting sunshine, light, and brightness flood into a room and turn a dark room into a bright, cheerful space. The transformation makes a small room feel much bigger than it is. In addition to conventional windows, the same results can be had by means of a handsome new skylight installed in the ceiling.

The danger with windows is that they may be a source of chills, drafts, and cold in winter and of excessive sun-heat entry in summer. The trick is knowing how to plan a window so that the room will get plenty of warm sunshine in *winter* but not in summer and at the same time avoid cold chills in winter.

WINDOW LOCATION IS THE KEY

We have seen in the last chapter why a window's location determines, right from the start, how much—or how little—warm solar heat it will let into your house in winter. The underlying principles

Opening up the walls of this house turned an upholstered cave into part of the out-doors. *Libbey-Owens-Ford Glass Co.*

that apply were also given. They are amplified here in terms of how new windows and skylights should be installed.

First, a brief review of the facts. All other things being equal, the best location for a new window (if you live in the Northern Hemisphere) is usually facing south, because there it receives more sun in winter than in summer and is comparatively easy to shade against summer heat entry. A window on the north will get much daylight, but little sunshine. North is less desirable than south because of the cold winter winds from that direction. This, of course, is less important if you live in a warm climate. A window on the west is the least desirable because of exposure to searing afternoon sun during the periods of hottest outdoor air temperatures. A window on the east works only half the time, in effect getting warm sunshine only in the morning in winter and in summer getting a lot of hot sun in the morning but none the rest of the day.

Excess cold can be controlled with double-glass or storm windows and by means of heating outlets under the window. Double-glass or storm windows, however, sometimes may be omitted on a south-facing window even in the temperate North. Wide horizontal windows located well above the floor are best for reducing heat and cold, especially in air-conditioned houses. They are effectively shaded by roof overhangs and create the fewest floor drafts.

Because a large window can let an enormous load of sun heat blast into a house in summer, plans for shading should be made when the window is designed. This is of special importance if you have air conditioning, obviously, unless you don't mind swollen electric bills. A window with any exposure can be shaded to keep out hot summer sun but let the sun enter in winter.

I also mentioned that shading a window on the outside is better than on the inside because outside blinds are twice as effective for keeping out sun heat. Once the sun gets through the glass, even the best inside blinds deflect only part of it. Deciduous trees (those that lose their leaves in winter) are best because they let sunshine through when you want it.

A roof trellis can give good shade over south windows. Better still are wide roof overhangs, particularly over south windows. They keep out much summer sun but let it in in winter, because it is at a lower angle from the sky. Overhangs are less effective above windows facing east and west because the morning and afternoon sun shines in at such a low angle the year round that only the very widest overhangs can keep it out. Sometimes a sun fence 8 to 10 feet high can effectively shade first-floor windows facing the east or west; the higher the fence and the closer to the window, the better the shading.

SEVEN WINDOW TYPES

In addition to supplying light and air, windows should be chosen to establish the basic character of a house. There are seven basic types. Choose the right kind.

Double-hung windows slide up or down and are popular for traditional houses. Old-fashioned sash cords have been replaced with special metal holders and spring counterbalances. Air entry is easily controlled by adjusting the amount of opening. The best ones can be removed from their frames for easy cleaning.

Casement windows swing out on a vertical axis by means of a crank or lever. The entire window can be opened fully to the breeze. Precise control of air entry, however, is difficult. Screens must be placed inside the windows. Some casements open *into* the room; yes, they interfere with curtains and shades.

Multipane windows contain three or more individual panes of glass. Small panes are less expensive to replace if broken. Some of the panes swing out for ventilation, while the others are of fixed glass, or all the panes can be fixed glass. Sizes and shapes vary from tall and narrow (for floor and ceiling glass) to very broad units.

Awning windows swing out on a horizontal axis. They usually contain two or more separate panes with one crank control. In one kind, called a hopper window, the top pane swings out while the bottom pane swings in to open up the entire area for ventilation. Hopper windows provide good protection against rain.

Jalousie windows resemble venetian blinds. They consist of a series of small, horizontal glass panes which swing out and up like an awning window when a crank which swings them all together is turned. They are best in warm climates. Screens are placed inside the window. Except possibly for summer porches, they are ill-advised for the North because they are often leaky. Get a top-quality brand with a sturdy and smoothly operating crank mechanism, or they will be troublesome in operation.

Horizontal sliding windows may be thought of as double-hung windows turned horizontally. Instead of the sash cords moving up and down as in double-hung windows, they slide right or left. These windows are trim and neat-looking and are easily fitted with screens and

Handsome glass doors in this Illinois house give the dining area a lovely private view outdoors. *Hedrich-Blessing, for Andersen Corp.*

storm windows. Get the kind that can be easily removed from their frames for cleaning, and taken completely out in summer, for that matter, leaving only the screens for ventilation.

Glass block windows are decorative and best when you want light and a special effect more than a view. They come in a variety of patterns and textures and can be used to build an entire wall or a skylight. Special blocks for venting are installed if air is desired. Blocks may be clear enough to see through or just enough to let light in.

CUTTING WINDOW COSTS

A fixed-glass, custom-made window costs the least of all because it doesn't have any moving sections. Every window doesn't have to open. Many may be closed all the time, so they might as well be built and installed that way, without expensive provisions for being opened. I described how I saved money by using fixed window glass in a new attic room in Chapter 12. Still another example is given later in this chapter.

Low-cost fixed windows can be installed almost anywhere. Each one requires only a frame, usually wood, and glass to fit the frame. The window size and frame are generally chosen to fit a standard glass size. Details on how that's done are also given later in this chapter.

CHOOSING GOOD-QUALITY WINDOWS

The market is flooded with a huge variety of window brands, many of which are cheap and shoddy. It pays, therefore, to get brand-name windows, such as Andersen, Curtis, Malta, and Pella.

The three most common kinds of window frames are aluminum, wood, and steel.

Aluminum requires less maintenance than wood or steel and little or no painting. But aluminum can get cold in winter and cause troublesome moisture condensation. The panes fog, and water may even drip from the frames. But this can be avoided with good-quality aluminum windows. They are made so that the inside movable section containing the glass does not touch the cold outside frame. This is done with the use of nonmetallic fittings, such as nylon, and an insulating layer such as vinyl or neoprene between the glass and the frame, which separates the two. The windows do not get as cold. Look for this feature.

Steel windows require periodic painting and are susceptible to rust and corrosion.

Many people prefer wood windows for their appearance. Condensation is less of a problem with them than with the ordinary aluminum and steel kinds because wood is a better insulator. It doesn't get as cold as metal.

All windows should come with integral weatherstripping. Look for a flexible metal or plastic seal between the movable part of the window and the adjacent frame. They should be tight to prevent air leaks and easy to wash from the inside.

Before.   *After.*
Three 2 x 4-foot sections of fixed double glass make the new window.

SPECIAL CHARACTERISTICS OF WINDOWS

New windows clearly should harmonize with older ones already there and with the style of your house. Look at different kinds in houses while you're out walking. Which would go well with your house? Notice large windows especially, and how they are located and placed in the wall. Can you look in easily (which is not desirable)? You will want privacy when indoors.

When you visit friends, take notice of the windows of their homes from the inside. Do they add to the feeling and character of a room? How high are they from the floor? Would you like them higher or lower? Do they add light and cheer to the room, or are they always covered by curtains for privacy? Can they be conveniently opened and closed and washed when necessary? You may think a large, bow (curved) window with many little sections of glass is nice to have, but will you mind the chore of cleaning all those panes, one by one?

Looking at a lot of windows will give you ideas that you would never learn otherwise. It's an excellent way to determine the kind of window you will like for your house.

CASE STUDY OF A NEW WINDOW

Here is how I replaced a small porthole with a large new window with dramatic results. It transformed the room, as shown in the accompanying photographs. It was done for $187 in the low-cost days before the Vietnam War. I estimate that its cost in 1978 would have been about $350. The window was put in a small 8-x-10-foot second-floor study, though it could have been any other kind of room. It replaced a small conventional window that hardly did justice to a sweeping view of the Hudson River.

I hired a carpenter to rip out the old window and replace it with a new wide one, measuring 4 x 6½ feet. The room was opened up, as if by magic, as a result of what architects call borrowing space from outdoors. The large, new window makes the room feel twice as big and cheerful as before, as well as lets us drink in a ten-mile view up and down the river and across to Westchester County.

How it was designed

To cut costs, the window was made of fixed glass; it cannot be opened. This reduced the cost by about half. Ventilation was not important because the room is air-conditioned, and there is another window in the room that can be opened in case the cooling unit breaks down.

Sealed, double glass (Thermopane in this case) was used to prevent condensation and reduce cold-air drafts in winter. This increased the cost but was worth it because the window is exposed to bitterly cold northeast winds in winter. A double-glass fixed window is also neater and nicer-looking than a movable window plus storm sash.

A local millwork shop made the window frame from a sketch I drew. The frame was designed to take three sections of 24-x-48-inch glass. I used three vertical units of glass set next to each other because they look better than one broad sheet of glass.

One error I made, however, was not ordering the double glass in advance. It was not one of the manufacturer's stock sizes (normally stocked by local distributors), so I had to wait three months for delivery. This meant extra expense. The carpenter had to install single glass temporarily and then return later to replace it when the double glass arrived.

The two largest cost items were for the carpenter's labor (two days) and the cost of three sheets of 2-x-4-foot sealed double glass. Besides the cost of the frame, painting the window was also required, but I did this myself. I recommend redwood for window frames because it is naturally rotproof and termite-resistant, as well as very handsome.

How did the window work out? Because it faces east, it receives a large amount of morning sunshine the year around. On a typical summer morning the sun strikes it before 7:00 A.M. and does not pass

Modern skylights in the roof above light up the interior corridor. *Wasco Products, Inc.*

A skylight can be located almost anywhere in a roof and should open for natural ventilation.

overhead until 11. The room gets a little warm despite the air conditioning, and a shading device is needed outside over the window. This was proof that a window facing east will receive as much sun heat in the morning as a west window in the afternoon.

NEW SKYLIGHTS FOR OVERHEAD WINDOWS

It used to be that a skylight was a flat wire-glass affair that looked as though it belonged in a factory. It was a chronic dirt catcher and transmitted little light to a room.

Handsome new skylights are now available designed especially for houses. Most notable are the plastic domes or bubbles made of the same tough plastic as the blisters on the old B-17 bomber. They include new window skylights designed especially to replace expensive window dormers in attic rooms. They can work wonders!

The principal purpose of a skylight is to shed light and air into the interior of a house. A good example is in the ceiling of an inside bathroom that would otherwise lack natural light. Skylights can permit the use of a low-cost square or nearly square addition to a house rather than a more expensive rectangular shape. Living space in the middle of the addition is enhanced by providing overhead air and light through the skylight. This also reduces the amount of exterior window area needed.

A utility room, laundry area, and even part of the kitchen can be relegated to an interior location, without loss of light and air, and allow more valuable space to face outdoors. Better zoning between living and bedroom areas can also result. A center hall, often a dark pocket, can be made a pleasant space in new additions and old houses.

PLASTIC DOMES

The new dome skylights are factory-made and delivered ready for installation. They are leakproof and made with shatterproof plastic, such as Plexiglas. Round, square, or oblong shapes are available in sizes less than 12 inches square up to about 8- x 9-foot rectangular units. They can be had in clear, opaque, or tinted shades and with single- or double-glass (or plastic) construction. The double cuts heat loss and prevents condensation in a cold climate like regular double-glass windows.

Skylights can be installed in almost any kind of roof overhead; this means you can punch a hole in the ceiling and look up at the stars at night. If there's an attic above between ceiling and roof, a skylight can still be enjoyed in many cases by having it in the roof above and installing a tunnellike light shaft from it down to the ceiling.

Besides the popular plastic-dome kind, skylights can be made with flat or curved panels of glass or structural plastic and with glass block. Some manufacturers offer finished skylights made of such materials, or, of course, you can have your own custom-made to fit special requirements.

LIMITATIONS

Like regular windows, two big hazards to guard against with skylights are excessive sun heat and glare. Ignore these hazards when you install a new skylight and you risk being roasted out of your house or blinded as a result of furnacelike solar heat and/or glare pouring in through the skylight.

Heat entry is controlled by careful location and limiting skylight size. A skylight on the northern slope of a roof obviously lets in much less sun heat than one on the south. Heat can also be controlled by specifying a colored or tinted plastic or glass, which cuts solar entry; by inside shade accessories, which are offered by some manufacturers or which you can design and rig up yourself; and by using the smallest practical size. In addition, Paul Bechtold, president of the Ventarama Skylight Corporation, says that nearly every skylight should be openable for ventilation—i.e., to let trapped heat out.

The glare problem is directly related to the total amount of light entering a room (the same problem encountered with poor electric lighting). The greater the concentration of light from a single source and one direction, the greater the glare problem. Thus, much glare can be expected from a skylight that is the main source of light in a room. It is particularly hard on the eyes. A tinted skylight or one with a shade should be considered. Less glare results when there is another good light source in the room.

Conversely, a skylight can help reduce an existing glare problem, as in a deep living room with a large area of window glass in one wall but little or none in the other walls. Your eyes hurt because of the concentration of light at one end, with no offsetting light balance from the rest of the room. You will notice that curtains usually are kept drawn over such windows to reduce the glare.

One good remedy for a condition of this kind is a ceiling skylight as deep inside the room as possible. The resulting daylight shed inside provides a balance to the high concentration of light from the window. This is possible, of course, only in rooms directly under the roof.

AVOIDING CONDENSATION

Heavy moisture condensation may form on skylights in cold weather, as on regular window glass. It is worse with skylights because it drips on your head. Prevention is therefore essential. In the North this calls for a double-dome skylight. It has two sheets of plastic glass, using the same principle as a double-glass window. Some skylights with only single-skin plastic contain a small gutter around the underside of their frames to catch the moisture before it can fall.

Experts say that condensation is not a problem in a moderate or warm climate with single-skin skylights if the unit is installed close to the ceiling line. This exposes the skylight to inside air circulation that will carry off water vapor before it can condense.

BUYING SKYLIGHTS

Some brands are sold by home-product stores and lumber-supply houses. To get a good picture of what's available, write to manufacturers for literature and the names of their nearest suppliers. (A list of names follows.) Because of the variety of product design and product changes every year, I cannot say that all the skylights made by these firms are of the best quality. You must check the specifications against the tips given here. Also look for waterproof seals at the frame and leakproof construction.

In general, it is best to buy one made by a manufacturer located in your climate zone. The products of a northern manufacturer are more likely to be designed for cold climate exposure than those of a southern manufacturer, and vice versa. Also ask if his skylights are accepted by the FHA.

Here are some manufacturers' names and addresses:

Bohem Manufacturing Company
Portland Road
Conshohocken, Pennsylvania 19428

Rollamatic Roofs, Inc.
1400 Yosemite Avenue
San Francisco, California 94124

Bristol Fiberlite Industries
3200 South Halladay Street
Santa Ana, California 92705

Ventarama Skylight Corp.
75 Channel Drive
Port Washington, New York 11050

Naturalite, Inc.
3233 West Kingsley Road
Garland, Texas 75040

Wasco Products, Inc.
P. O. Box 351
Sanford, Maine 04073

CHAPTER 30

WHAT TO DO ABOUT A NOISY HOUSE

The usual remedy recommended for a noisy house is acoustical tile on the ceilings, but this is a halfway measure. Acoustical tile subdues noise less than many people think chiefly because it reduces only one of the two kinds of house noise.

If you are plagued by noise, sort out the particular kind that most bothers you. The problems and solutions are not the same in every household. If the noise assailing your ears is really bad, you could, of course, flee to an isolated island, but even there civilization and jet planes will ultimately seek you out.

The biggest noisemakers are children, radio and television sets, kitchen and laundry appliances (especially dishwashers, mixers, and clothes washers), mechanical equipment (especially fans and heating units), plus kids outside, the blaring of car horns, and the roar of trucks, chain saws, and overhead jets.

Not only is life noisier than ever before, but the evil is further compounded because houses today are smaller and more compact than before—8-foot ceilings instead of 9 or 10 feet, for example. Every noise is amplified. The trend toward contemporary design and informal contemporary living also makes matters worse. With less heavy upholstery and fewer rugs and drapes, the inevitable noise in every house has less chance to be absorbed and toned down. We have more hard surfaces and more glass which bounce noise waves back to our ears.

Indeed, the best noise deadeners in houses are thick rugs, upholstered furniture, and window drapes whose very softness absorbs a portion of the noise waves flying around a house. Furnish your house with thick rugs, curtains, and drapes, and you take the first definitive steps toward reducing noise. Wall-to-wall carpeting, the thicker the better, works well, assuming, of course, that you desire it for other reasons, too. Full carpeting over stairs and in hallways is especially good for reducing the spread of noise from the living to the bedroom areas of a house. Rugs and carpeting by themselves can reduce noise levels remarkably.

ACOUSTICAL TILE

Acoustical tile works on the same principle. It is a soft fibrous material, somewhat spongy in texture, which will absorb from 50 to 75 percent of the sound waves that strike it. By contrast, the usual smooth, hard wall and ceiling surfaces in a room bounce back nearly 100 percent of the sound waves present.

Acoustical tile can help most on the ceilings of the kitchen, playroom, living room, and hallways. It is recommended especially for kitchens, where the normal clatter of pots, pans, and whirling appliances is made worse by the presence of hard-surfaced appliances and cabinets and an uncarpeted floor, all of which bounce the sound waves around like Ping-Pong balls. An acoustical ceiling, however, will trap and absorb many of the sound waves, thus reducing the pounding on your ears.

An acoustical ceiling can in the same way—though not always— reduce the chatter of children's voices in a playroom, produce quiet conducive for conversation in a living room, and enhance the natural quiet of a bedroom.

Special mention should be made of acoustical tile for hallways, which often serve as noise tunnels, allowing noise to reverberate from one end of the house to the other. If acoustical tile is put at the upper wall levels in a hall, as well as at the ceiling, it works much like heavy carpeting in halls. Because the material is soft and fibrous, it should not be installed lower than shoulder height, as bodily contact will bruise it and reduce its effectiveness. Acoustical tile, however, should not be used in a music room or stereo corner because it will mute the tone and quality of music.

What kind of acoustical tile?

A large variety of acoustical materials for houses is now on the market. This is a welcome change from a few years back when practically all tiles were 12 inches square, had the same perforated design, and could hardly be told from one another. Today there are such varied types as fissured tile which looks like stained marble, finely textured tile with neither perforations nor deep fissures, tile with striated ridges and different colors, and a variety of more expensive types with embossed designs. The new products that are available range in size from small squares up to large panels.

Acoustical tile is made of fibrous material such as wood fiber, mineral wood fiber (rock wool), glass fiber (Fiberglas), and polystyrene plastic. The wood-fiber kind was first on the market, is generally the cheapest (by a few pennies per square foot), and comes in a large variety of designs. Its biggest drawback is susceptibility to high humidity and wetness. Excessive moisture will destroy its cement bond, warp the material, and make the individual tiles look bad, if not cause them to fall off. Don't use wood-fiber acoustical tile where moisture is prevalent, such as in a bathroom or kitchen. The others—mineral wool, glass fiber, and polystyrene—are proportionately better in moisture resistance, with the polystyrene being the best for areas where moisture is present.

Each of the various kinds has tongue-and-groove edges and extended flanges for covering the nail and staple heads with which they are held up. They can be cemented directly to an existing ceiling if the ceiling is fairly smooth. In another installation method, they can also be stapled to wood furring strips applied over an old ceiling, or for a new ceiling in new rooms. To enable you to figure how much tile will be needed, make a scale plan of the ceiling before the job is started. The work should start at the exact center of the ceiling so the tile comes out even on all sides.

If the installation is done properly and if nonmoisture-resistant tiles are kept free of moisture, they should last as long as the walls. Dust may accumulate from time to time but is removed easily with a vacuum-cleaner extension or simply by wiping the tiles with soap and water. Try to avoid having to paint an acoustical ceiling. Coats of paint will gradually reduce the effectiveness of the tiles. One coat of washable paint, roller-applied, is enough.

Limitations of tile

Acoustical tile is not a cure-all for house noise. It is best at reducing noise that originates within the room itself. This is important to know. It does not help much against noise that originates *outside* that room or outside the house. Thus, lining a study with acoustical tile will do little to insulate you from the sounds of children nearby, or from any other noise originating outside the study.

THE TWO KINDS OF NOISE
Either noises are airborne and get into a house through open windows and doors, or they arrive by impact and travel through the walls and frame of a house like little shock waves.

The only way to stop airborne noise is by shutting off all unobstructed openings between you and the noise source. Doors and windows should be kept closed. Weatherstripping around doors is also helpful, particularly around bathroom doors. Leaving a window open can undo all the effectiveness of the most thoroughly sound-conditioned house. Closing windows in summer will also, of course, shut out welcome breezes. This is why many homeowners turn to air conditioning for quiet, as well as coolness.

Noise waves that arrive by impact are a major problem because they are the hardest to stop. Impact noise can be reduced only by sheer mass—thick, heavy walls between you and the noise source; the thicker and heavier, the better. This is another reason why things are noisier today, since the typically light construction of modern houses is less resistant to noise penetration than the thicker, heavier houses of yesteryear. It is also why the appallingly skinny walls in new apartment houses have led to many complaints about interapartment noise.

To be realistic, even the thickest solid brick walls can go only so far in reducing really powerful impact noises, such as the heavy rumble of traffic over a nearby highway. You would need a solid wall at least 10 feet thick between you and a nearby highway to bar the entry of traffic noise into your house. Unfortunately, therefore, if you are particularly bothered by loud traffic, trains, or overhead planes, your only recourse is to move.

SOUNDPROOF CONSTRUCTION
Much can be done to put a damper on ordinary everyday noises by soundproofing the existing structure or a new addition you build. I mentioned above that the heavier and weightier the wall, the more it will stop noise travel from room to room, as well as keep out noise impinging on the house from outdoors. The ideal noise barrier would be walls of thick lead. More down to earth is the use of heavy ma-

sonry walls, especially for exterior walls. If you are concerned for your quiet when you build a new addition, masonry walls of concrete block are best for interior partitions.

Conventional wood-frame walls can be beefed up to reduce noise transmission. They can be filled with special acoustical insulation, which looks like pads of thermal insulation. Another possibility is to ask for what is called staggered-stud wall construction. The wall is made with two sets of 2 x 2 studs, 2 inches apart, one set for each side of the wall. Overlapping sheets of fiberboard or fibrous noise insulation are hung in the air space in between. That's the super-duper way of insulating a new wall, according to engineers, but it's expensive. Merely installing a blanket of mineral wool or fiberglass insulation inside a standard interior wall will cost less and provide reasonably good, if not equal, noise suppression. It's the same material used for thermal insulation, though it doesn't need a vapor-barrier cover.

Other good ideas are locating new closets or bookcases between a noisy room and one you want to keep quiet. The weight (mass) of many books is an excellent noise stop and a reason why libraries are so quiet.

What about soundproof floors and ceiling to reduce vertical noise travel from one floor of a house to another? Like walls, they can be beefed up with built-in insulation (as well as heavy rugs), as I did in my new attic room (Chapter 12). Sometimes the problem is due to squeaky floors as a result of flimsy construction. The remedy is to cross-brace the floors (easiest to do the first floor since you can brace it at the basement ceiling). Little can be done to an upstairs floor other than carpeting it.

APPLIANCES AND EQUIPMENT
Strike at the source of the noise, the machine involved. Mount appliances and equipment (a new furnace or air conditioner) on resilient cork or rubber pads to isolate vibration from the house structure. Keep equipment oiled, and check it occasionally for quiet operation.

Excessive noise from heating pipes and ducts is usually due to careless installation. For example, heating pipes bang against floor beams because the opening in the beam is not large enough to allow for the inevitable pipe movements when water surges through. This puts emphasis on a good installation when new heating is installed (see Chapter 21).

If you are bothered by television used by other people in the family, have a set of earphones hooked up to the set for the viewer. This can be done for a very few dollars' cost, including the earphones. Door slamming can be eliminated with automatic door closers, a big step in the right direction.

When you shop for appliances and equipment, take the time to check one brand against another for such things as quiet operation. It is particularly important for such chronic noisemakers as kitchen exhaust fans and room air conditioners.

This should be easy in the future since the consumer is finally getting a break. Appliance makers are beginning to rate their equipment in sones, an indication of operating noise. Fan manufacturers are among the first to do this. A number of fans, including the kitchen exhaust type, are tagged with their sone ratings.

A sone is an international unit of loudness, somewhat like a decibel. One sone is approximately equivalent to the sound of a modern refrigerator operating in a reasonably quiet kitchen. A 6-sone fan is twice as noisy as a 3-sone fan. The Home Ventilating Institute has set a limit of 8 sones for kitchen fans, and 6.5 as the maximum allowable for bathroom fans. The lower the sone rating, the quieter it is.

In 1977 the Federal Environmental Protection Agency (EPA) won a bureaucratic civil war with the Consumer Product Safety Commission to take jurisdiction over household appliance noise, and the EPA began plans to have noisemaking appliances conform to standards. Sone ratings will be given for other appliances and equipment used in houses, and noisy ones can be spotted and avoided before they are bought.

THE PSYCHOLOGY OF NOISE

The rest of this chapter has to do with a few fundamental facts about noise, its effect on people and perhaps how you can come to terms with it. Scientists define noise as "unwanted sound"—sound that bothers you but not necessarily another person.

A power mower next door may drive you insane, but it is accepted by the neighbor using it because he gets a direct service from the noise. The hum of a refrigerator is taken in stride by most of us because we are used to it and because subconsciously we are benefiting from the cause of the noise (it preserves our food). The roar of an overhead jet may be one of the absolutely loudest noises yet inflicted on humans, but it can be music to the pilot's and passengers' ears, since it means safety; the sudden ceasing of the jet's engines would understandably alarm its pilot and passengers.

The fact is that sheer loudness per se is not the only measure of the noise. What's more, loudness by itself is not necessarily harmful to our health, despite popular belief to the contrary. The human body has great capacity for tolerating noises up to the limit where the noise can cause deafness.

The limit is in the neighborhood of 110 to 120 decibels, the decibel being the usual measure of sound intensity. This level is comparable to the intensity of a jet engine when you are standing about 50 to 100 feet away. The farther away you are, the less the decibel intensity on your ears. In addition, the longer your exposure to intense sounds, the greater the potential harm to your eardrums. The classic example here is workers in boiler factories who become deaf.

Sustained exposure to loud noises can cause ear damage, though some experts say that short, very loud blasts of noise sometimes can be literally deafening. All experts simply don't agree. For example, Consumers' Union, publisher of *Consumer Reports,* says that noise made by the household appliances and equipment is more of an annoyance than a hazard to health. Even the noisiest of the bunch is not operated long enough at a time to cause injury, CU has said.

One ear specialist, Dr. Maurice H. Miller of New York City, claims that excessive noise can damage a person's ears. According to the *New York Times,* Dr. Miller gives three warning signals for household appliance noise that can hurt you. If, after you use a noisy one, like an ice crusher, food blender, or noisy electric shaver, you have ringing in the ears; if, while such a noisemaker is on, it interferes with normal conversation, and if the voice of someone speaking sounds muffled to you, Dr. Miller says one should "seek professional advice," which presumably means see an ear doctor.

Most experts believe, though, that the usual noises in houses may cause mental anguish but are practically never harmful to health. The noises that bother us most fall into five main categories.

First is what's called interference with voice communication. We can dine in a noisy restaurant and not be bothered by the noise around until it prevents us from hearing our dining partner. At home a housewife will tolerate children playing in another room until the children's noise prevents her from talking on the phone or from chatting with a guest. The surrounding noise level may approach deafening intensity, as in a plane, but it is remarkable how much we can tolerate it until it interferes with our conversation—i.e., voice communication.

Second is unexpected noise, which takes us by surprise almost without regard to its intensity. Examples are the creaking of a door at night, which can unhinge a person, or the barely audible click of an electric blanket thermostat, which Consumers' Union once likened to the "stomping of a robin on the lawn."

Third are intermittent sounds such as a furnace going on and off. You are taken by surprise because there is no rhythmic pattern to the noise. The more regular the sound (the less intermittent), the more tolerant we become of it. People who live near noisy airports or subway trains learn to take them in stride. More complaints about such noise are made by people living farther away who hear the same sounds more intermittently, are less used to them, and are therefore more annoyed.

Fourth are sounds that threaten an invasion of privacy. If you are having a confidential talk, nearby voices will upset you because they create a subconscious reaction: "If we can hear them, they can hear us."

Fifth are what are termed intelligible sounds. A college professor cannot concentrate in his study because of the barely audible voices of others downstairs, yet college students can concentrate amazingly well in dormitories despite radios blaring all around them. If we can make out as few as six or seven words out of every hundred spoken nearby, they begin to make sense. We are psychologically disturbed because they distract us, largely out of curiosity. This is what disturbs the college professor. It is particularly disturbing when we are reading a book or engaged in any other solitary activity.

The usual and sometimes accidental remedy for such disturbing noises is to raise the background level of sound so you no longer hear intelligible sounds. Thus, more than one college professor in a household full of kids has found that he can concentrate again simply by turning on a radio to a low volume of music that serves to cancel out the intruding voices from downstairs. He is using the masking technique, a widely used noise-control technique in office buildings. There the background level of sound is raised by the introduction of artificial sounds through the air-conditioning system, which in turn masks the sounds of voices in other offices. The voices of people nearby are no longer intelligible.

In other words, you may be bothered by noise in a house chiefly because your house is super-quiet to begin with. Every little sound that is heard, indoors or out, seems loud and annoying in relation to the low sound level of your house. If this is your problem, then consider the introduction of masking sounds via a radio, records, or—a neat trick if you can swing it—the installation of a water fountain whose constant trickle is soothing because it is masking, for much the same reason that the sound of an idyllic little brook is satisfying.

NOISE-SENSITIVE PEOPLE

Scientists also say that a certain number of people are noise-sensitive or just plain fussy about sound. Little or nothing can be done to relieve them of noise irritation, short of seeing a psychiatrist. One reason such people suffer is that they were brought up amid quiet surroundings and are not conditioned to a loud environment confronting them later in life. Being unconditioned to sound is also a painful experience for people with a hearing loss that has been restored by surgery. They suddenly find the world so noisy with sounds other people take for granted that it takes long readjustment before they become conditioned to ordinary everyday sounds.

Still another reason is that certain sounds may subconsciously remind us of unhappy memories of long ago. The reasons, which we need not explore here, have nevertheless been substantiated. Some of us seem to be particularly bothered by sounds that leave other people cold—e.g., the ring of a telephone which one time brought shocking news; an old popular song we associate with an unhappy love affair. Finally, there are also people who are neurotic for any of a variety of reasons. Certain disturbances such as noise will shake them up violently.

The foregoing discussion is given to broaden your understanding and help you solve household noise problems which may or may not be solved merely by expensive soundproofing of your house. Before you spend the money, consider whether it will really produce the relief you desire in light of the above facts.

CHAPTER 31
WHAT TO DO ABOUT DRY AIR IN HOUSES

People who suffer from dry air in winter belong to a large club. It's a common problem and a big pain that can cause great distress.

Dry air makes your nose and throat hurt and may cause excessively dry skin. Joints of furniture loosen up and crack, book bindings suffer, and moisture is drained out of practically everything in the house.

It occurs because the outside air is naturally dry in winter. Its humidity is low. The same air in a house is warmed up by the heating system, becoming even drier in the process. The relative humidity indoors is thinned out to as little as 5 or 10 percent, which is quite low.

Relative humidity is the amount of moisture present in the air, compared with the amount it could hold if it were 100 percent saturated. Air described as having a relative humidity of 20 percent contains 20 percent of the total moisture it could hold if it were saturated. When the air cannot hold any more moisture, it rains. Sometimes the relative humidity can be less than 100 percent, and for technical reasons it will still rain.

As a rule, most people will be comfortable at an indoor relative humidity of 20 percent in winter, according to Frank Powell of the National Bureau of Standards, a leading authority on the subject. Some people, including some doctors, erroneously say that the relative humidity should be as high as 35 to 40 percent. But that's much higher than shown by scientific studies, including the definitive research on the subject at the Institute for Environmental Research at Kansas State University. Besides, relative humidity that high is virtually impossible to maintain inside a house in winter.

Things get too dry for comfort when the relative humidity falls below 20 percent, particularly if your nose and throat are sensitive. If you think you are suffering from dryness, find out for sure by checking with an instrument called a hygrometer. Obtain a good one; there are many cheap units on the market that are notoriously inaccurate. The best kind has a human hair element and should cost about $15 to $25. Cheaper ones (with no hair element) are often a waste of money.

There is also some good news from the dry-air front. Low humidity is becoming less of a problem as a by-product of the better insulation and general tightening houses are getting these days to preserve energy. This confirms the opinion long held by some experts that enough moisture is created inside many houses by cooking and other moisture-generating activities to maintain the humidity high enough for comfort. The catch is that many houses are so loosely built that the moisture and vapor created indoors quickly leaks outdoors. Insulation, storm windows, and vapor barriers were not installed when they were built. In winter, when moisture in the air is strongly drawn to the outdoors, it easily escapes through loose windows and the walls.

In addition, the temperature maintained inside a well-insulated house (68 to 72 degrees F) is usually lower than before it was insulated (75 to 80 degrees). Less moisture is therefore required to maintain comfortable relative humidity, as I discussed earlier. Maintaining the relative humidity at 20 percent in a house at 70 degrees F requires about 25 percent less total vapor than if the temperature was 78 degrees.

HUMIDIFIERS

You probably need a humidifier if you live in an old house. Excessively dry air is less likely to be a problem in newer, tightly built houses. The water vapor created by cooking, bathing, and moisture-generating appliances is less likely to escape to the outdoors and is usually sufficient to keep the humidity level high enough for comfort.

If your house is a borderline case, can the house be made tighter with storm windows, weatherstripping around windows and doors, and insulation? Before buying a humidifier, determine how low your relative humidity is with a good hygrometer. If it falls to only about 15 percent, you may get it up to a comfortable 20 percent by closing up leaks. Then the moisture ordinarily generated in the house may be enough to prevent dry air. If, however, the hygrometer indicates a low level of 5 to 10 percent, you probably need a humidifier.

CHOOSING A HUMIDIFIER

One kind of humidifier, the whole-house type, is designed to add moisture to the whole house. Others are smaller and are for single rooms.

You may already have a humidifier on your furnace and still suffer from dry air. This is because the humidifier that ordinarily comes attached to the furnace is not very good. Its capacity is too small for it to provide more than minimal moisture. It is also unreliable, because it clogs quickly with impurities found in water. Then it stops functioning. It must be cleaned regularly to keep it working.

WHAT SIZE HUMIDIFIER?

First consider one for the whole house. A rule of thumb calls for 1 gallon of moisture a day for each room of your house. Thus, a 7-room house would require a 7-gallon-a-day humidifier; a 9-room house, 9 gallons a day. But that's for an average house, and many houses require more or less than average.

The Humidifier Institute, an association of manufacturers, offers this chart for choosing a whole-house humidifier. The main variable is the tightness of house construction. The tighter the house, the smaller the humidifier required.

HUMIDIFIER CAPACITY REQUIRED
(IN GALLONS OF WATER PER DAY)

Type of construction	Size of house in square feet of living area					
	500	1000	1500	2000	2500	3000
Tight	2.1	4.2	6.4	8.5	10.6	12.7
Average	3.3	6.5	9.8	13.1	16.3	19.6
Loose	4.6	9.2	13.8	18.4	23.0	27.6

House size is based on 8 feet ceiling height.
Deduct 2 gallons per day to take credit for other sources of humidity, based on a family of four.

Here is how to determine your house construction, according to the American Society of Heating, Refrigeration and Air-Conditioning Engineers (ASHRAE). It defines a tight house as one "assumed to be well insulated, have vapor barriers, tight storm doors and windows with weatherstripping, and its fireplace will be dampered. An average house will be insulated, have vapor barriers, loose storm doors and windows, and a dampered fireplace. A loose house will probably be one constructed before 1930, have little or no insulation, no storm doors or windows, no weatherstripping, no vapor barriers and quite often will have a fireplace without an effective damper.''

If your house is classified as "loose" construction, it clearly should be tightened with insulation, storm windows, weatherstripping, and whatever else is needed to reduce leakage of heat, as well as moisture. At most, I would install a humidifier with no more capacity than required for an "average" house. In most cases I recommend the smallest one given in the table, in other words, that for a "tight" house, even if your house may not be tight. The above table from the Humidifier Institute is based on providing an indoor relative humidity of 30 to 35 percent and 20 percent should be adequate.

KINDS OF HUMIDIFIERS

The two main kinds are: atomizing, which uses a spray nozzle to inject water into the air; and vaporizing, which uses an electric heating element to turn water into steam, which is then ejected into the air. Its chief drawback is the need for an electric heater, thus extra operating cost for electricity. There is also a third kind in which water is evaporated from the surface of a small tank. It is not very efficient.

Here is a list of manufacturers of home humidifiers that are "certified" by the Humidifier Institute. These brands are therefore likely to be among the better ones on the market. I would not buy one that does not meet the industry standards and does not bear a certification.

AutoFlo Company
12085 Dixie
Detroit, Michigan 48239

General Filters, Inc.
43800 Grand River
Novi, Michigan 48050

Herrmidifier Company
1810 Hempstead Road
Lancaster, Pennsylvania 17604

Humid-Aire Corporation
3757 West Touhy Avenue
Chicago, Illinois 60645

Lewbill Industries, Inc.
P.O. Box 221
Scottdale, Pennsylvania 15683

Lobb Humidifier Company
3080 Oakley Park Road
Walled Lake, Michigan 48088

Shuttle Manufacturing Company
Route 1
Marietta, Ohio 45750

Walton Laboratories, Inc.
1 Carol Place
Moonachie, New Jersey 07074

LOCATION AND INSTALLATION

A whole-house humidifier can be located nearly anywhere in a house, but it will work best from a central location. Its moisture is discharged freely into a main part of the house, preferably a living room, dining room, or central hall. Neither ducts nor pipes are needed to distribute the moisture to your rooms. Unlike heat, the water vapor automatically spreads throughout the house. Its travel may be impeded to rooms with tightly shut doors. They should be left ajar where moisture is desired.

The installation is simple. The unit can be located at the basement ceiling, in a utility room, or even a closet, with a short duct from the unit to the nearest room. Moisture is supplied to the room through a discharge register in the wall or floor, then to the rest of the house. Depending on the brand, operating noise may bother you, so check this in advance. But this may be more easily said than done, since humidifiers so far do not come with noise ratings. If you're sensitive to noise, a good way to check noise level before you buy is visit someone with the same unit in operation and hear it yourself. Get the names of present users from a dealer or two.

AUTOMATIC OPERATION

An automatic humidistat control is essential. Like a thermostat, it turns the unit on when humidity is needed, turns it off when it is satisfied. You set it for the relative humidity you desire. Without one, you must turn the unit on and off by hand. An automatic humidistat control can also save you grief by turning off the unit before the house is flooded with too much moisture. This can be severely harmful to the structure, furnishings, and clothing, as noted later in this chapter.

The installation requires a wiring connection to supply operating power and a simple pipe connection to a water line. You could omit the water hookup, but then you would be saddled with the chore of refilling the humidifier all the time.

If your house has warm-air heat, a humidifier could be operated in conjunction with the furnace. Its moisture is fed to the warm air that is supplied to the house. The chief advantage is that moisture is distributed directly through your heating ducts to all rooms. This hookup is recommended for large houses, particularly if bedroom doors are kept shut. It will assure you of uniform moisture distribution. All things being equal, I would choose an independent humidifier. Moisture distribution to all rooms may not be quite as uniform as in a duct system, but independently operated humidifiers work satisfactorily.

COSTS

A humidifier large enough for a whole house will cost from about $125 to $300, depending on the size and the amount of installation work required. Anything cheaper generally indicates a compromise in quality or moisture capacity or both. Operating costs generally run from about $6 to $12 a month.

ONE-ROOM HUMIDIFIERS

One of these may be right for you if you are bothered by a dry nose or throat chiefly at night when you sleep (when the air is driest). Sometimes called vaporizers, they are portable units that are set on the floor and plugged into an electric outlet. They do not require a water supply connection. Instead, you replenish their water tank by hand two to three times a week.

Prices range from about $35 to $75, depending on size, brand, and mode of operation. Choose an atomizing kind, if possible. It is also best to have an automatic humidistat control (optional feature for about $10 to $25 more), to turn the unit on and off automatically while you sleep.

BEWARE OF TOO MUCH MOISTURE

Don't let a humidifier flood your house with moisture, or there will be serious side effects, like a medical drug that kills not only the disease but the patient, too. In Washington, D.C., for example, a pianist was plagued with air so dry her piano would not stay tuned in winter. She installed a powerful humidifier to overcome the trouble. It helped the piano, but so much moisture poured into the house that serious exterior paint damage resulted. The paint blistered and peeled so quickly that an expensive new paint job was required every two years.

This is by no means unusual. Humidifiers running amok in houses are one of the two biggest reasons for blistering and peeling paint and other structural damage. (The other is leaks in the roof and outside walls that let pernicious water in.) The possibility of damage from a humidifier cannot be ignored. Caution is essential. Use a humidistat control to set a limit on the moisture generated. A little experimenting will tell you the lowest setting that will provide adequate moisture.

Does your house have vapor barriers? Since these prevent vapor from infiltrating the structure, they are particularly important when a humidifier is used. As also noted in Chapter 18, they can be included when insulation is installed at the attic floor. Or a sheet of vapor-barrier plastic should be put down before the insulation is put over the ceiling.

A vapor barrier can be applied on walls with two coats of alkyd semigloss enamel wall paint. In many houses, however, built-up coats of existing paint installed over the years already provide a vapor barrier, especially if it is oil-base paint. It takes at least five or six layers of latex paint to provide the same resistance to vapor travel, as latex is much less resistant to vapor travel than oil-base paint.

CHAPTER 32
NEW IDEAS FOR REWIRING YOUR HOUSE

In the years following World War II a new ailment developed in millions of American houses—inadequate wiring. It was because most of them had been built with only enough wiring capacity for the house lights and a few small appliances, a comparatively small load.

After the war all kinds of new appliances were bought in carload numbers. There were new washers, dryers, television sets, and dishwashers—in all, dozens of different kinds. People bought them and plugged them into their electric outlets.

But a funny thing happened. As more and more appliances were plugged in, it became almost like England during the war. The lights began to dim in growing numbers of houses each time a big new appliance was plugged in. The television set flickered as if hit by a body blow, and other appliances, already present, groaned and slowed down. The old house wiring was sending a message. It could not handle any more demand. Wiring standards had to be sharply increased, and rewiring old houses became big business.

Today many families have wholesale quantities of electrical devices, usually thirty to forty per house (count your own, including radios, electric clocks, shavers, and so on). Some of them, like an electric dryer or range, require more electricity than many houses had before World War II. In all, there are more than seventy-five different electrical devices in use today, and the number is growing. It is no longer possible to exist without up-to-date house wiring. If your house has vintage wiring, rewiring is virtually inescapable.

When you modernize or add new rooms to any house, providing

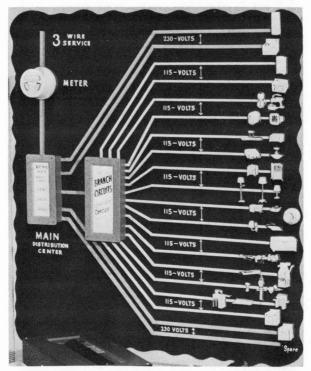

The main electric board (distribution center) is the heart of the house wiring system. It feeds electricity to a series of branch circuits for lights, outlets, appliances, and everything else.

adequate new wiring is essential. Even if you already have ample wiring capacity, there are new wiring and lighting ideas that could brighten up your life. But first you should know a few of the basics.

THE THREE MAIN PARTS OF YOUR WIRING SYSTEM

Every house wiring system is made up of three main components:

1. The main electric board, the heart of the electric system. It is sometimes called the electric service entrance. It is to your wiring system what the size of the pipe that supplies water from street to house is to your plumbing needs. If it is not large enough for the house, you'll not have adequate electrical capacity.

The minimum-size service for most houses today is three-wire, 100-ampere, 120/240-volt service. This is the minimum required by most electric codes. However, a larger 150- to 200-ampere service, also 240 volts, may be needed if you have an electric range, electric heat, or central air conditioning or a large house of more than 3,000 square feet. If the present capacity is only 30 or 60 amperes, you will probably need a larger box. The capacity is noted on the main electric box (where fuses or circuit breakers are located), and the ampere rating should appear on the board or on the inside of the cover.

The term *three-wire service* means you can usually see three separate wires, not just two, running overhead from the street to the house. Sometimes the wires are contained in a single cable, but you can count the number emerging from the cable at the point where it is attached to the house. Don't confuse them, however, with your telephone lines.

The connections from these wires to the main electric board should be thick No. 2 wires in size, not smaller No. 3 or 4, which carry less electricity; the lower the number, the heavier the wire. Then you will almost always have enough electrical capacity to meet any contingency.

Many people prefer an electric board with circuit breakers rather than fuses. When an overload or short circuit occurs and lights go out, a circuit breaker automatically snaps open, cutting off the electricity to the problem area. When the cause is found and corrected, you merely push the circuit breaker back to "on" and electricity flows again. You do away with the fuss and bother of changing fuses. If you prefer circuit breakers, tell your electrician.

2. The number of branch electric circuits (wires) from the main switch box to the house. Most houses need at least ten separate circuits, but many have only six. If you have much electrical equipment, many appliances, or a large house, you need twelve to fifteen circuits, perhaps more. Each individual 120-volt circuit is represented by a separate fuse or circuit breaker. Each 240-volt circuit is protected by two fuses or a double circuit breaker.

A typical house requires three to four individual circuits just for lights and outlets, plus two to three heavier circuits for kitchen appliances and one circuit each for such things as electric range, furnace, washer and dryer, water heater, dishwasher, freezer, and attic fan. In addition, it pays to order two or three spare circuits, available for future equipment or other use. An electric board with twelve to twenty circuits costs only a few dollars more than one with only six, if installed when a house is rewired. Increasing its size later can cost considerably more.

3. Electric outlets and switches. A good rule for outlets is one for every 12 feet of wall because lamps and appliances have 6-foot cords; closer than 12 feet when a door comes between two outlets. This is also required by many codes. Without it you end up spreading extension cords all around. The kitchen should also have a series of outlets above the countertop to handle appliances safely.

You may also want special appliance outlets in the dining room and for an outside patio to plug in a toaster, waffle iron, or coffeemaker. These should be fed by heavier No. 12 wire, not the usual No. 14 wire for ordinary outlets. Light switches should be located at the entrance to every room, at the tops and bottoms of stairs for safety, and at garage and basement doors. Adding switches and outlets costs a minimal sum when new rooms are being built, twice as much afterward.

To get good-quality wiring, ask for "intermediate" grade outlets and wiring quality. There are also "competitive" grades, the cheapest in quality, though only pennies less in cost, and "specification" grades, best of all but generally recommended only for heavy-duty commercial or marine use. Also, ask for wiring no smaller than No. 12. Lights flicker and appliances work sluggishly because so much wiring today is the smaller No. 14 size.

MAKING A WIRING PLAN

You don't have to be an engineer to draw up a usable wiring plan. It can save you misunderstandings and money. I forced myself to do it for my present house, as much as I abhor such detailing on paper. Surprisingly it was fun.

You start with a room-by-room sketch of the house and then mark exactly where you want new outlets, switches, and lights installed. This forces you to go from one end of the house to another and determine in advance where and what you need. Don't worry about which circuits they will go on. Leave this to the electrician.

I made carbon copies, one for each electrician called in to bid on the job. The electricians were surprised. The sketch enabled them to bid exactly on my work. Later, when the electrician who did the work thought he was finished, I mentioned that a couple of outlets and switches had been omitted. The seeds for an argument were there. We pulled out the wiring plan, which showed the missing items. He acknowledged his mistake and installed them with no fuss and obviously at no extra charge.

Doing your own wiring, however, is not recommended unless you know what you're doing. Such work is loaded with booby traps, it's easy to violate local codes, and you risk loss of fire insurance coverage in case of fire.

But don't be scared off if you want to do your own wiring, *provided* you take the time to learn to do it. Then it's not all that hard and complicated. Doing it right is important if you don't want your house to go up in flames as a result of poor wiring. In some places, to be sure, the law requires a licensed electrician for all wiring.

GET A GOOD WIRING GUIDE

It's easy to draw a wiring diagram with a good guide at your side. Look in the Sears or Montgomery Ward catalogue for them. Sears has had very good free ones in the past, but this changes from year to year. You must look it up when it's needed, or shop in a bookstore for one.

Once you have drawn a good plan and handed it to the electrician to follow, you can't let it go at that. You must also mark the location desired for each switch, outlet, and light with a pencil or chalk in each room on the wall where desired. I did not do this, and as a result, the electrician simply installed certain switches where it was more convenient for him.

A good example is a light switch at the entrance of a room. It should be just inside the door so you need not grope for it in the dark. In my house two switches are so far inside the room that they require a 10-foot pole to reach. I curse my own carelessness every time I grope for those switches.

WIRING COSTS

Rule-of-thumb cost figures are generally available from electricians, such as $10 to $15 for each new switch or outlet installed in a house, between $20 and $35 for each new wiring circuit, and more for extra-long or heavy-duty circuits. Some electricians figure that a new electric service to a house will run, say, $350 to $600, depending on the size required. Add up all the new switches, outlets, and new circuits needed, plus a new electric board and service, if required, and you'll have an idea of the total cost.

Obviously, the prevailing costs in your area must be used for each kind of work; get these from a contractor or electrician. An accurate cost, however, will require an estimate from an electrician done on the basis of your plan.

NEW WIRING FEATURES

Here are special wiring features you may want. Although electricians may not mention them, some are good, but inexpensive. Others are decidedly luxury features; not everyone will want them. Decide for yourself.

Silent, no-click light switches. These are a delight, particularly if noise irritates you. There are quiet mechanical switches, silent mercury-action switches, which are better, and flat-plate switches set flush against the wall (light finger pressure on the top pressure plate turns the light on, on the bottom turns it off). Cost is little more than ordinary click switches. They can be obtained to replace existing conventional switches, as well as when rewiring.

No-shock switches, a safety feature in a family with small children. They are designed so a child cannot jab a hairpin into the outlet and get a shock. About $1 each.

Ivory or white outlets and switches, rather than the usual brown, which may clash with your decor. The white kind may cost slightly more and take extra time for delivery.

Grounded outlets, particularly in the kitchen, bath, basement, workshop, and outdoors. This is added protection against shocks and is also required by many electric codes. The cost is small, but you'll also need three-prong plugs for the appliances plugged in.

Multiple switch control, which allows you to turn a light on or off from two places—the entrance and exit of a room and from the top and bottom of stairs. From about $15 to $25 per switch.

Automatic closet lights, which turn on the closet light when the closet door is opened and turn it off when the door is closed, the way a refrigerator light works. From $10 to $20.

Dimmer control, which is actually a dial for adjusting light brightness up or down according to your needs. Illumination in a room can be dimmed to candlelight glow for a dinner party or turned up brightly for reading. Special bulbs are not needed. Dimmers are chiefly for living and dining rooms. A dimmer switch usually costs between $5 and $10, and installing it is an easy do-it-yourself job.

Remote-control lighting, which permits you to turn indoor and outdoor lights on or off from a central location such as the kitchen or master bedroom. A remote kitchen switch can control front-door or garage lights, for example, saving steps. A control panel next to your bed will eliminate that final tour of your house and grounds every night to make sure all lights are out. Cost: $50 and up, depending on the number of lights to be controlled.

Automatic garage-door opener, which enables you to open the garage door from within your car. About $100 to $150.

Electric snow-melting panels for the front walk, driveway, or both. They are turned on when snow begins to fall. From $400 to $650 for a 40- to 50-foot drive if installed when new paving is put down; more if the paving has to be torn up.

Continuous strip outlets, which consist of a metal or plastic strip of outlets that is installed along a wall baseboard or at the back of a kitchen counter or workbench. Outlets are spaced at 6 inches to several feet apart. They do away with the need for breaking into walls for new wiring and provide an abundance of outlets where several appliances are used at once. From a few dollars for a 6-foot-long strip up to $50 for longer ones or others requiring special installation.

CHAPTER 33

HOW TO AVOID TERMITES, OTHER PESTS, AND WOOD ROT

These two problems are often related. Both are usually caused by damp timber in a house structure or wood that is in contact with the damp ground.

Consider termites first. What is the first thing to do if you discover termites in your house? How do you make a new addition or a whole house termiteproof?

If termites are discovered, the first rule is: Don't panic. They work slowly and may take months, if not years, to do real damage. Even if they have bored deeply into the structure, there is almost always time to assess the damage and discuss it with experts. Don't be hasty and don't be frightened into signing up with the first exterminator that arrives. First learn a little about how termites work and what they can and cannot do.

HOW TERMITES WORK
They usually nest in the ground with as many as 250,000 in a typical colony. Their basic needs are food and water. They build a network of tunnels from the ground into a house for food (wood) and make regular round trips back to the ground for water. This is important to know because cutting off their routes to the house will keep them out and will also do away with any inside the house by depriving them of moisture.

If, however, they can obtain moisture inside the structure—from a

The subterranean worker termite causes the major damage in houses. Less than ¼ inch long, it has a large head, no wings, and a stubby body. *U.S. Dept. of Agriculture, Forest Service.*

water leak or other source of dampness—they can remain indoors, thriving on the house structure. In one case on record a termite colony was found flourishing on the tenth floor of a hotel, obtaining water from a toilet-tank leak and food, of course, from the structure. For the same reason, they have been known to infest house attics, subsisting on dampness caused by condensation, though this is rare.

Their first target is wood closest to the ground: the wood under porches and outside stairs, exterior wood walls close to the earth, trellises, wood fences, and the wood framing of basement windows. They also enter through cracks as small as 1/64 inch in foundation walls, piers, and concrete slab floors of houses without basements. A concrete slab house, in fact, is quite vulnerable, despite what many owners think and sellers say. Slab floor houses are damaged by termites as much as other houses.

About 95 percent of all termite damage in the United States is done by the subterranean species of termites. They shun light and air and work in dark places. They are seldom seen except in late winter or early spring, their mating season, when swarms of them take to the air. Seeing them swarm or spotting their discarded wings on the ground is often the first sign of their presence. This may occur as early as January in a warm climate to as late as May in a cold climate.

It should not be mistaken for the flying ant (a different bug), which has a narrow waist. The swarming subterranean termite is identified by its black body and glassy, translucent wings. The subter-

Termites build mud termite tunnels to travel up the walls into a house without exposure to hated light or air. Tunnels may be built and seen on the inside or outside walls of a house. *American Wood Preservers Institute.*

ranean worker termite does the damage inside houses. It has a large head, grayish white color, no wings, and a stubby, oblong body which does not pinch in at the waist like an hourglass. You will rarely see them unless you dig into infested wood or break open one of their mud tunnels.

Another telltale sign is their flattened mud tubes, about ¾ to 1 inch wide, leading from the ground up the inside or outside of foundation walls or running up a pipe or metal beam into a house. They may be spread over the masonry walls of a house like the veins in your hand, but a good many people see only a dirt-streaked wall and don't give it another thought.

You are not safe from subterranean termites even in most of the coldest northern states, except perhaps Alaska. They are troublesome in nearly every part of the North except North Dakota and the Rocky Mountain states, where they are rare, and in Alaska, where they are virtually unknown. Other species of termites that invade houses include dry-wood termites, found mainly in the southern United States, including Southern California, and dampwood termites found mainly in Florida and Southern California. These breeds generally do less damage than the subterranean termite, the scourge of the species.

TERMITE SAFEGUARDS

The best safeguard is a periodical inspection of the house, especially in an area with a high termite incidence. You can learn to do it yourself, but it's better to have a service contract with a good pest-control expert. A service contract is cheap if bought before damage occurs. Then, if termites are discovered, getting rid of them is done at little or no additional expense. A service contract generally includes an annual inspection and spot treatment if termites are found. It may or may not include a guarantee against future invasions. The better firms in the business are usually members of the National Pest Control Association, 8150 Leesburg Pike, Vienna, Virginia 22810. When you talk to a termite control firm, ask if it's a member.

A proper inspection involves a visual check of all the interior and exterior wall surfaces, the basement, crawl space, or concrete floor slab and a probe of the vulnerable underpinnings with a knife or ice pick. In a concrete-floor house, the inspector looks for cracks in the concrete, especially at floor openings through which plumbing pipes and wires run into the house. The plumbing supply-pipe box, usually in the bathroom, is a favorite entry route for termites, so opening it and looking in is something that should be done regularly.

Other precautions include maintaining good drainage away from the house on all sides. All wooden parts of the house should be at least 4 inches above soil level. Dead tree stumps nearby should be pulled and removed because they attract termites and provide a jumping-off point into the house. The underside of porches, outdoor stairs, and inside crawl spaces are especially vulnerable and must be kept dry and well ventilated. Fireplace wood should not be stacked in or near a house. It behooves us to carry out these precautions. By letting them slide, we may leave the door open for damage later.

WHAT TO DO WHEN TERMITES ARE DISCOVERED

Unfortunately, there are no hard-and-fast rules to follow. It depends on where you live and the kind and extent of the damage. The termites must be eliminated. Any good pest-control firm will be able to exterminate them. Not all termite firms, however, make structural repairs; if any are necessary, you might also have to hire a construction contractor. Like all other work on houses, get bids from at least two or three.

Listening to different termite people can be confusing. They are likely to assess the damage in different ways, and their prices will vary accordingly. You must determine exactly what each intends to do—the exact kind of repairs and how much preventive work. Before signing up, ask your local Better Business Bureau about the company.

If the damage is severe, wood beams and other parts of the structure may have to be replaced. If there is less damage, termite-killing chemicals can be pumped into infected beams.

In some cases even the best treatment cannot be guaranteed. The trouble is that once termites infect an existing house, a running battle may be required before they are eventually eliminated. You may win one skirmish, only to have them regroup under the house and find other weak spots to enter. It pays, therefore, to obtain a service contract with some arrangement, if possible, to cover the cost of repairs that might have to be done. But again, not all termite firms do structural repairs, another kind of business. The termite treatment is for the entire house to prevent termites from entering at any point. There is usually a one-year guarantee, but this guarantee should be read carefully.

EXAMPLES OF DAMAGE

A friend of mine paid $400 for a termite treatment job after he discovered them in his house. He had the foresight to buy a service contract even though the termites were supposedly routed. New termites have shown up nearly every year since, and the termite people come back to get rid of them every time at no additional charge, under the terms of the service contract. The house is located near the South Shore of Long Island, which has become a notoriously bad termite area. Practically no house there is safe from them.

Another man I know has had termites in his last three houses, including the one he currently occupies. He has learned to accept them, knowing that his area (Westport, Connecticut) is infested with them. He is taking steps to eliminate them in his present house (by soil poisoning, described below), but he also knows he must maintain constant vigilance to prevent a future breakthrough.

These two examples are in the North. Things are considerably more hazardous for people in the South, Southwest, and California. Ignore termites for too long and the necessary repairs can cost several thousand dollars. It is therefore important to understand what can happen and act ahead of time to prevent it. An exterminator can be called in at any time to make an inspection that is well worth its small cost.

TERMITE PREVENTION TACTICS

One or more of the following safeguards are recommended when a new addition to a house is to be built. These are given in order of importance. The first one, soil poisoning, can also be done for an existing house.

1. Soil poisoning is the injection of a special chemical into the ground under and around a house. It is anathema to termites for at least twenty-five years but harmless to tree roots and plants. After that time the treatment may have to be repeated.

There is only one commercially available soil chemical for homeowners, chlordane (distributed by the Velsicol Corporation, 330 East Grant Avenue, Chicago, Illinois 60611). But this chemical may be "restricted" in the future by the government's Environmental Protection Agency. If that occurs, it will mean that chlordane may be applied around a house only by a dealer; the chemical cannot be sold to homeowners for do-it-yourself use.

A chemical to use to get rid of dry-wood termites is the nonpoisonous fluoridated silica aerogel. It's a fine white dust that absorbs the wax coating on the termite's shell, causing the body fluids to evaporate and doing in the termite. The dust is blown into the walls of a house, on the house underpinning, or in the attic.

2. The use of chemically treated lumber for the main underpinning of a house, preferably all wood around the base of the walls and under the floor. Pressure-treated lumber, which can be ordered from most lumberyards, should be used. In this special process, a chemical preservative is forced deep into the lumber.

Do not confuse pressure treatment for lumber with paint-on preservatives or wood simply dipped into a chemical bath; both of these cost less, but are not accepted by FHA and are not worth the money. Special pressure-treated lumber (Wolmanized, for example) is also available from factories. Information on treated wood can be had from the American Wood Preservers Institute, 111 West Washington, Chicago, Illinois 60602.

The cost of pressure-treated wood may amount to a few hundred dollars, to more than $500, for all the wood used in the most vulnerable parts of a new addition. It may be expensive but is good protection against termites and decay, the scientists' term for wood rot. It's not the perfect defense, unfortunately. Though termites won't attack these treated timbers, they can and will tunnel over such wood to more tempting targets.

Three species of wood are both toxic to termites and have natural resistance to rot. They are foundation-grade California redwood, tidewater red cypress, and pitchy southern pine lightwood. The 100 percent heartwood grade of each, not the sapwood grade, must be used. Even then these woods are not absolutely immune or as resistant as pressure-treated wood, according to the U.S. Department of Agriculture. For that matter, each of them may be difficult to obtain in some parts of the country or more expensive than pressure-treated wood. If you do use one of these woods, you can expect fairly good termite protection, but don't believe you have complete protection over the years.

3. The use of reinforced-concrete foundation walls, rather than walls of concrete block or cinder block unless capped, as noted below. The concrete must be free of cracks and porous areas.

4. A 4-inch-thick capping of concrete laid over the top of concrete-block or cinder-block foundation walls. The hollow spaces inside blocks are an open invitation to termite entry straight up into walls without any exterior signs of them. Capping the top layer of blocks can stop them. In addition to a 4-inch cap, filling the top layer of blocks with concrete is also a good idea.

5. Metal termite shields, placed all around the top of the foundation walls to prevent termite entry into the house. Shields, however, are not the perfect defense. They are, in fact, "in disrepute," according to the man who invented them some fifty years ago, Dr. Thomas E. Snyder of the Smithsonian Institution. They crack, break at the joints, or simply do not extend far enough from the foundation walls. If you have shields on your present house, every inch of them should be inspected off and on for termite breakthrough.

OTHER PESTS

Damage is also caused to houses by other pests such as carpenter ants and the old house borer.

The carpenter ant

Carpenter ants are widespread in the northern half of the country and extend south to mountainous areas, particularly in the Southeast. They may attack homes and wood much like termites, especially when the wood is wet. But unlike the white termite workers, carpenter ant workers (the troublemakers) are black and do not shun light and air as termites do. You can often see the black workers wandering around in search of food. Their presence is often indicated by otherwise-unexplained sawdust piles beside the timber they are nesting in.

Much the same preventive measures used for termites apply to carpenter ants: Keep your house dry, don't let wood be in direct contact with the ground, provide plenty of ventilation for parts of the house that tend to be damp, and inspect periodically.

The old house borer

Despite the name, the old house borer most often damages new houses and buildings. (The name has come down to us because it was a major pest in old buildings in Europe.) It causes severe damage chiefly in the eastern part of the country, from Massachusetts down the Atlantic coastline to Florida, and as far south and west as Louisiana and Texas, but except for Texas, it has not been encountered west of the Mississippi River.

It is a brownish black beetle about ½ to ¾ inch long, slightly flattened in shape, with gray hairs spouting from its head and forward part of the body. Each of its hard-shelled wings has two patches of gray. But it is rarely seen and usually not discovered until it has begun to cause damage.

Signs of its presence include: a rasping or ticking sound made while it is boring or feeding; powdery borings in its tunnels, seen by breaking the wood surface where tunneling exists; wood blistering when its larvae are close to the surface; boring dust below infected lumber; or an actual sighting of the beetles in the house.

If they are discovered, the speediest remedy is fumigation of the entire house. This takes special care and training. It should be done only by a first-rate, pest-control operator who will take all necessary precautions. Nobody should reenter the house until after it has been thoroughly aired. If these pests are found in a few isolated beams, they can be killed by the local applications of special chemicals. These applications, too, must be done with care by an expert since the chemicals are highly poisonous to people and animals. Don't try them yourself.

Excellent sources of information about house pests are: "Subterranean Termites, Their Prevention and Control in Buildings," USDA Bulletin 64, 45 cents; and "The Old House Borer," Leaflet No. 501, 35 cents; both available from the U.S. Government Printing Office, Washington, D.C. 20402. Order these from your congressman and sometimes you'll get them at no charge.

WOOD ROT

This causes even more destruction than termites virtually throughout the country, particular in wet and humid climates. The overriding principle to remember is that a dry house will not rot because dry wood does not rot. There is no such thing as "dry rot," a misnomer which came about because rotted wood in the final stage of decay looks dry.

Sometimes rotted wood is mistaken for termite-infested wood, and vice versa, even by experts. I have seen a construction engineer find "termites" in a house's underpinning when the trouble actually turned out to be an advanced case of wood rot. The difference can be hard to determine at first glance. Wood rot is caused by a minute fungus which eats away at damp wood. The wood becomes mottled as if it had a case of grayish white measles. The wood can be saved if the fungus is caught in time and the source of the moisture eliminated. Otherwise, the infected wood will literally rot away and require expensive replacement.

Here you should learn to differentiate, however, between rotting wood and new white-pocket Douglas fir lumber which has little white pockets that look like rot but is nevertheless sound. This lumber is perfectly good, provided it is dry. But if wood feels damp and soft to the touch, it is rotting.

Like termites, wood rot spreads first to damp parts of a house near the ground, under unventilated porches and steps, to wood walls touching the ground, and in damp basements (spreading to the basement ceiling beams, even though the dampness originates at the floor or wall). It also occurs in unventilated attics, in the floor and walls of a bathroom (owing to cracks around the bathtub and shower), and around the kitchen sink.

Rot can also attack wood quite distant from the original source of the moisture because of the insidious ways of water vapor. Water from the basement, for example, is absorbed into the air as vapor and then can spread up through the inside of your walls to the attic, causing damage there. This is not uncommon.

The way to prevent wood rot is to keep your house dry. Good drainage that takes moisture away from the house is important. So is keeping the exterior wall wood out of touch with damp earth; installing ample vents for crawl spaces, under porches, under stairs, and in the attic; and spotting water leaks from roof gutters and drains before they damage the house.

When you build an addition to the house, the appropriate controls should be incorporated in the plan—e.g., built-in vents, vapor barriers, and waterproofing, all discussed elsewhere in this book.

CHAPTER 34

HOW TO GET A GOOD NEW ROOF

The business of putting new roofs on old houses began booming in the United States in the 1970s because of the great home-building boom of the 1950s. It happened much the way selling new mufflers for automobiles started booming in the 1960s.

The Midas Muffler people realized that the mufflers that came with new cars were not made to last very long, so if you set up a few stands selling new mufflers for old cars, you should pretty soon be selling a lot of mufflers, like hotcakes in a breakfast bazaar. The Midas people figured it right, and their business boomed throughout the country.

The roofing put on American houses lasts longer than car mufflers, but after fifteen to twenty years it starts to wear out and spring leaks, and new roofing is needed. Many of the 10 million new houses built in the 1950s began needing new roofing in the 1970s; thus, the boom in reroofing houses. In addition, most of the older houses built before then need a new roof every twenty years, more or less.

A leak is the first sign that a roof has seen its best days and that it's time to do something about it. Most leaks result from normal weathering over the years. Once the roof is worn through at one spot, starting the first leak, other worn-out spots show up in rapid progression. Patching only delays the inevitable, but the signals are clear: Time is running out for the old roof.

There are a few exceptions. Roof leaks sometimes occur in new houses because of sloppy roofing work. They occasionally happen in a roof that is basically in good shape. Most such leaks are around chimneys and dormers, usually because of defective flashing (the metal seal at roof joints). Occasionally they are caused by a defective shingle. Repairing the flashing or replacing the shingle may be all you need. But in most cases the first leak unfortunately is a clear sign that you need a new roof and you had better get out your checkbook, painful as it may seem.

There are two kinds of roof cover—standard, which has to be renewed or replaced periodically; and permanent, which can last at least a lifetime and perhaps for centuries. The copper roof of Philadelphia's famed Christ Church is over 200 years old and still going strong. Here are facts about each, starting with the renewable kind.

ASPHALT SHINGLES

Asphalt shingles, the most common roof cover, are found on the great majority of new houses and for reroofing some 90 percent of existing houses, according to the Asphalt Roofing Manufacturers Association. They are what most people have on their houses today and the kind most likely to be put on when a new roof is needed.

The various types of asphalt shingle differ mainly in thickness and weight. The minimum weight accepted by the FHA today is a 235-pound asphalt shingle, weighing that much per 100 square feet of roof.

The 235-pound asphalt shingles can be installed over most old roofs, as well as on a new addition. They should last about fifteen to twenty years, more or less, depending on your climate. The hotter the sun and the farther south you live, the shorter their life. There are also thinner and cheaper grades down to 150-pound-per-square asphalt shingles. These are questionable materials and should be turned down.

Determining the weight of asphalt shingles you may buy has, however, become difficult because they are no longer marked with this information. New government regulations and red tape have forced manufacturers to omit these data from their roofing. Some makers, though not all, list the weight of their roofing in their literature.

After you decide on a reroofing job, a problem can arise when you get bids from different roofers. The bids may be for different weight roofing; in other words, different quality roofing shingles. A roofer should specify at least the approximate weight of the roofing he will

One of the new textures and patterns available with asphalt roofing shingles is shown here. The idea is to give asphalt roofing the same varied eye appeal that wood shingles and shakes have long had. *Asphalt Roofing Association.*

provide. One who offers heavier shingles than others will understandably charge more.

A drawback of some asphalt shingles is that they may flap in a high wind or be blown off your roof, especially if you live in a hurricane area. To be sure of getting shingles that will withstand high winds, specify that they come with a UL (for Underwriters Laboratory) wind-resistant label. This means the shingles must withstand test winds of at least 60 miles an hour for two hours without any tab's being lifted. Wind-resistant shingles are often made that way with a factory-applied thermoplastic seal that cements down each shingle.

Another kind of wind-resistant asphalt shingle is called the interlocking kind. It comes with tabs and slots that hook each shingle into the next shingle on each side; each one helps the other stay put. Interlocking shingles, however, give a sawtooth appearance to a roof which not everyone likes. Check the appearance before buying interlock roofing.

Different "three-dimensional" patterns available with asphalt roofing. *Asphalt Roofing Association.*

HEAVIER, BETTER ROOFING

You can step up in quality and durability of asphalt shingles by specifying 250- to 285-pound-per-square asphalt roofing, an intermediate grade, or shingles with a weight of 300-pound-per-square or heavier, the premium grade. The greater the weight and thickness, the better and longer-lasting the roofing. But again, determining the weight of a particular type and brand requires checking the manufacturer's literature. Naturally, the heavier and better the roofing, the higher the price. But the extra cost can pay off in reduced maintenance and no need to reroof the house for at least twenty-five to thirty years.

1	2	3			4		5	6
		Per Square			Size			
PRODUCT	Configuration	Approximate Shipping Weight	Shingles	Bundles	Width	Length	Exposure	Underwriters' Listing
Wood Appearance Strip Shingle More Than One Thickness Per Strip Laminated or Job Applied	Various Edge, Surface Texture & Application Treatments	285# to 390#	67 to 90	4 or 5	11-1/2" to 15"	36" or 40"	4" to 6"	A or C - Many Wind Resistant
Wood Appearance Strip Shingle Single Thickness Per Strip	Various Edge, Surface Texture & Application Treatments	Various 250# to 350#	78 to 90	3 or 4	12" or 12-1/4"	36" or 40"	4" to 5-1/8"	A or C - Many Wind Resistant
Self-Sealing Strip Shingle	Conventional 3 Tab	205#- 240#	78 or 80	3	12" or 12-1/4"	36"	5" or 5-1/8"	A or C - All Wind Resistant
	2 or 4 Tab	Various 215# to 325#	78 or 80	3 or 4	12" or 12-1/4"	36"	5" or 5-1/8"	
Self-Sealing Strip Shingle No Cut Out	Various Edge and Texture Treatments	Various 215# to 290#	78 to 81	3 or 4	12" or 12-1/4"	36" or 36-1/4"	5"	A or C - All Wind Resistant
Individual Lock Down Basic Design	Several Design Variations	180# to 250#	72 to 120	3 or 4	18" to 22-1/4"	20" to 22-1/2"	-	C - Many Wind Resistant

Different Kinds of Asphalt Roofing Shingles
Source: Asphalt Roofing Manufacturers Association

NEW FIBERGLASS ROOFING

Weight, however, does not enter the picture as much with new fiberglass-based asphalt shingles, which weigh less than standard shingles. Proponents of fiberglass roofing say it provides greater durability, especially from hot sun in the South, than standard asphalt roofing. Fiberglass has demonstrated its durability in other products and it could well become the top-grade roofing material of the future.

FIRE-RESISTANT ROOFING

Fire safety is obviously important since a roof is vulnerable to air-blown sparks and burning debris. Asphalt shingles come with three UL fire ratings, from C to A in order of increasing fire resistance. Shingles with a UL Class C rating are good for "light fire exposure." They will not easily ignite, not readily support the spread of fire over the roof area, and will not add to the fire hazard by emitting burning brands which can cause new fires. Roofing with a Class B or Class A label has been tested for protection against even more severe fire exposure.

Roofing for nearly all houses should meet at least the UL Class C standard. Most asphalt roofing is made to meet that standard or better. If you live in a hazardous fire area, such as much of California, specify roofing with a UL Class A fire rating. Some roofing materials, such as slate and clay tile, are naturally fireproof. On the other hand, wood shingles and shakes do not meet any UL fire-resistance standard unless they've been chemically treated. To be sure of fire resistance with asphalt roofing or wood shingles or shakes, look for the UL rating on the bundles. Avoid roofing with no fire rating.

AVOIDING WARM-CLIMATE ROOF STAINS

People in the warm South know that their roofing is subject to unsightly staining and discoloration caused by fungi and algae. These growths are particularly noticeable and therefore most objectionable on white roofs. Fungi and algae can be removed with a chemical solution which is at best a temporary remedy.

In the South, particularly along the Gulf and South Atlantic coasts, you can now get asphalt shingles with fungus- and algae-resistant white granules designed to help white roofs stay white longer. Since a white roof can make a house cooler in summer, the new treatment can be a good thing.

LOW-SLOPE AND FLAT ROOFS

If your roof has a very low slope or is flat, asphalt shingles are not recommended. Ordinarily they should be put on a roof with a pitch of no less than 3 in 12; some brands can be used on a low 2-in-12 slope, depending on the brand and the manufacturer's recommendation. A 2-in-12 roof slope means a roof rise of 2 feet for every 12 feet of horizontal level.

A roof that is flat or low in slope is generally covered with built-up roofing, alternate layers of roofing felt and asphalt covered with a top surface of gravel or white marble chips. It may last five years or ten to twenty years, sometimes more, depending on the number of layers, or plies.

Five plies are best; fewer mean shorter life and expensive upkeep. Cheap-quality two- and three-ply roofing is too often used; that is why flat and low-slope roofs frequently deteriorate and leak in a maddeningly short time. Ask how many plies or if it is a ten-, fifteen-, or twenty-year roof. That's a key question.

There is also what is called roll roofing, a second-grade material. It comes in rolls of asphalt sheet material, cemented down and overlapped on the roof, one layer after the other up to the top of the roof. It is generally not recommended for houses because it doesn't last long.

WOOD ROOFING

Wood shingles and shakes were long considered the next step up in quality from asphalt roofing. In recent years, however, they have been made thinner and thinner, with consequent erosion of durability and quality. But they still cost from 25 to 100 percent more than asphalt shingles, even in the West near the great lumber forests, where their price is lowest. Shipping costs make them more expensive elsewhere.

Because quality depends on shingle thickness, the thicker the wood, the better. The cheapest are wood shingles approximately ⅜ inch thick, which will last fifteen to twenty-five years, more or less. Then come wood shakes, which vary from ⅜ inch to 1¼ inch thick. The best shakes are the heaviest and thickest ones, usually ¾ inch to 1¼ inch thick, which can last fifty years or more. But unfortunately, authentic shakes that thick are becoming increasingly rare, even in California, where they have long been highly popular. Check on the thickness you want, and don't accept skinny ones.

The handsome and varied texture of wood shingles has long been admired. But because of their flammability, wood shingles should be chemically treated for fire resistance and have a good fire rating.

Wood shingles and shakes have a handsome rough texture that is considered the height of fashion in many circles. But remember that they can be a distinct fire hazard. Sparks and flames from a house fire, from brush fires, and from almost any other kind of building conflagration have landed on wood roofs and ignited them miles away from the originating fire. Wood roofs are therefore outlawed by many municipalities. Even if they are permitted where you live, you should nevertheless consider this hazard before buying.

OTHER ROOFING

There are also asbestos-cement shingles, tile, slate, copper, and terne. Asbestos-cement shingles are made of hard-wearing asbestos fiber and portland cement. They are somewhat higher in cost than asphalt shingles, but are the cheapest of the so-called permanent roof covers. Fewer have been made in recent years and thus they are becoming less available for house roofing. Nevertheless, you might have them on your present house or one you may buy. If so, re-member that they are brittle and may crack if walked on. This is their biggest shortcoming. Use sneakers or soft shoes, and insist that the TV repairman do the same, or lay down walk boards if he goes on the roof.

Ceramic tile, slate, and terne (tin-lead alloy) are the Cadillacs of roofing in quality and price. Most people associate tile with the oval-shaped orange tiles seen on Spanish and California mission houses. Thick, flat tiles are more common today. They give a rich, substantial appearance. Both kinds will last for generations. But insist on a hard-burned tile. When tapped with a coin, it will ring with a clear tone. The cheaper, soft-burned kind is of uncertain quality. Hit with a coin, it gives off a flat sound.

Like tile, a slate roof is also handsome and durable. But because of cost and heavy weight, it is usually practical only within convenient shipping distances of slate quarries in Virginia, Pennsylvania, and Vermont. Like asbestos, both tile and slate are brittle. A misplaced step or stray home-run ball can crack them. Freezing rain and snow in winter can also mean occasional cracked shingles to be replaced.

Terne is a tin and lead alloy popular at the end of the nineteenth century but was not used for a long while afterward. But it still can be a good choice for a durable, long-lasting roof if it is available where you live and a good roofer experienced with it can install it for you.

ROOF COLOR

Light-colored roofs were highly popular during the 1960s largely because they reflect sun heat and help make a house cooler in summer. In the 1970s, though, white went out of fashion about the time the miniskirt began losing its appeal and hems became longer. Asphalt shingles in darker "earth-tone" or "environmental" colors—browns, buffs, olives, and slates—became fashionable. Some asphalt shingles are also made to have a three-dimensional look, much like the texture of wood shake-shingle roofs.

Roof color is important. It should, of course, fit the color and style of your house, yet should contrast nicely to avoid a wishy-washy appearance. In general, a white or light-colored roof emphasizes the vertical lines of a house, giving a taller and slimmer look. It is, therefore, good for long, low ranch houses, where you want to de-emphasize the width and low height.

On the other hand, a medium or dark roof is generally best for smaller houses of one or two stories. In each case, it makes the house look broader and bigger. But don't be tied down by rules. Consider the design, color, and proportions of your house as a whole; choose the roof color that you will like, as well as one that will enhance the overall style and looks of your house.

ROOF TIPS

Regardless of the roofing material used, the details of its installation—the spacing of the shingles and even the number of nails per shingle—are important for a good job. Determine exactly how much roofing you are getting in total squares of material to be provided. This is an essential fact to determine before you buy.

Ask about shingle coverage. This has to do with what roofers call shingle exposure and lap. The exposure simply means the amount of each shingle that is exposed to the weather (the rest of it being covered by adjacent shingles). It varies according to the size, shape, and kind of shingles used. It is usually a 5-inch exposure with conventional asphalt shingles, sometimes 4 inches. Lap or head lap is the distance that a shingle extends (laps) over the next shingle below it. It is usually 7 inches for asphalt shingles. The smaller the exposure and the greater the lap, the greater the number of shingles required and the greater the protection (roof coverage).

Good tips on choosing roofing and particularly asphalt roofing and how it is installed are available in "A Homeowner's Guide to the Selection of Quality Roofing." An excellent guide on how to install an asphalt roof is "Good Application Makes a Good Roof Better." Both can be had for 50¢ each from the Asphalt Roofing Manufacturers Association, DY, Box 3248, Grand Central Station, New York, New York 10017. Installing your own roof, however, is probably the most hazardous of all do-it-yourself jobs. The next most dangerous is painting the exterior of your own house, particularly if it is two stories. Both cause many injuries because of falls. Before roofing or painting your house, be sure you have good ladders and use them properly—and then be sure you have the proper insurance coverage.

CHAPTER 35

HOW TO AVOID HOME REPAIR BILLS

A veteran home repair expert who has dealt with house problems for years says, "More than fifty percent of all the service calls and troubles I have seen could have been avoided by preventive maintenance."

Like an automobile, the parts of a house tend to loosen up, fall out of adjustment, use up their lubrication, or get tired and worn merely as a natural consequence of continual use. That's why, like a car, they need a little attention and loving care from time to time.

Do it before a small crack left unattended grows into a gaping hole and before moving parts break down completely and require replacement. That's how to avoid the most common home repair bills. The few periodic checks and repairs required take little time, and on the stitch-in-time principle, they can pay off in great dividends.

Here is a summary of common causes of damage and repair bills in houses and what to do about each before it causes trouble. Many are simple tasks which almost anyone can do with a screwdriver, pliers, or swab of paint. Others may require an expert, but by being familiar with them, you will know what to request and know if it is done properly. These include recommendations made in other chapters on the particular subject discussed, but they are repeated here to make this a self-sufficient checklist.

1. *Warm-air heating.* Inspect the air filter at least once a month, since dirt-clogged filters are a big cause of constricted heat supply and service calls. If the filter looks dirty, remove it from the furnace, and shake it outdoors or vacuum it. It is clean when you hold it up to bright light and can see through it. Some filters should be hosed with water, depending on the type. Follow the instructions in the furnace manufacturer's service booklet.

Oil the blower motor and pulley once a year, but don't overdo it. Too much oil is as bad as none. Not all motors require oil. Some have sealed bearings, lubricated for life, however. This should be noted either on the blower or in the manufacturer's instruction manual. Obtain a copy, if necessary, and refer to it for other service that may be required.

The blower pulley belt (like an automobile fan belt) should be checked for proper tension. It normally should have about an inch of slack. If it is badly worn, have it replaced.

Remove the air-outlet registers and return-air grilles, located in your rooms, about once a month and clean out the dust and dirt inside the duct throats, preferably with a vacuum cleaner nozzle. This is dirt and dust from the house air.

2. *Hot-water and steam heat.* Bleed the radiators every fall, especially balky ones that do not heat up. You do this by opening the water valve at the end of the radiator and draining off a bucket or two of water. Use a bucket, of course, to catch the water. This releases trapped air which prevents hot water or steam from circulating inside the radiator. If the radiator still does not heat properly, drain off more water. Don't be afraid to release too much since it is easily made up by a supply valve at the boiler.

There are three kinds of bleed vents for radiators: the manual, disk, and automatic float types. Most common is the manual kind, which sticks out near the top of one end of the radiator. It is circular in shape and about ½ inch long. It has a slot which you open with a radiator key (sold in hardware stores) or merely with a dime. Turn it open until the water comes out; then close it.

The disk kind looks like the manual kind except it contains a series of fiber disks. It is semiautomatic in operation in that it automatically lets air out when necessary. The disks swell up when wet, when there is water in the radiator as it should be, and not air. If air gets in, the disks contract, which opens the vent that lets out the air. Sometimes the disks get worn or dirty and won't close properly, so water may drip on the floor. Replacement disks are sold, in hardware stores and by heating dealers. The disk vent costs a little more than the manual vent.

The automatic float vent is highest in price and uses a small tank-

and-float device much like a toilet tank float but smaller. Water in the radiator keeps the float up and the vent closed. Air in the radiator instead of water lets the float come lower, opening the vent, which lets the air escape. The automatic vent seldom needs attention and does away with the periodic need to bleed radiators. Of course, it can go bad after a number of years and then must be replaced.

Drain and flush all the water in a hot-water or steam system, particularly if you have hard water, every year or two. This will prevent rust and corrosion from building up in pipes and heating unit. A can of rust inhibitor poured into the water system will also help.

The water circulating pump may require a drop of oil occasionally, unless it is a sealed, permanently lubricated pump. Refer to the manufacturer's manual for this.

With oil heat, the oil burner should be checked, cleaned, and adjusted every fall before cold weather sets in. The small service charge you may have to pay will come back with interest. While the serviceman is at it, have him drop an anticorrosion capsule into your oil tank. Oil-heat men report they are encountering more and more cases of tank leaks caused by corrosion. With gas heat, cleaning and adjustment are recommended every three or four years.

3. *Semiannual or at least annual termite inspection,* It's best to use an expert, though any moderately conscientious person can learn how. A step-by-step check is made around the interior and exterior walls of the house, including the foundation. Look for suspicious veins of dirt and termite mud tunnels, which may be anywhere from ¼ inch to as much as 1 foot wide in places. Wood at or near ground level should be jabbed with a knife to detect infested sections under the surface. Wood window frames near the ground and floor beams and posts, particularly near the exterior walls, should also get the knife test.

Don't leave wood piled up near the house since dead wood is a magnet for termites. Fireplace logs should not be stored in the basement or near the house. Keep at least 4 inches of clearance between the ground level and the lowest exposed wood of the house.

Cracks and crevices in foundation walls should be plastered with cement. If your house has a concrete floor directly on the ground, inspect the plumbing access hole regularly. This is the floor opening for pipes, usually located behind a panel in the bathroom, a common point of entry for termites from the ground.

4. *Wood rot.* Infected wood can be searched out during a termite inspection. Rotted wood is soft and decayed and breaks easily when knifed. If wood rot is caught in time, replacement may not be necessary, provided the cause—moisture—is eliminated.

Some moisture is usually inevitable in houses. It can be controlled by providing good ventilation where it occurs. This means plenty of natural air flow for crawl spaces, under porches and steps and in attics. If necessary, install large vents in such spaces for flow in and out. Inspect the spaces periodically to be sure they are not damp.

Two of the biggest causes of wood rot, as well as wet basements, are clogged roof drains and poor water drainage away from the house. Eight times out of ten one of these is the cause of the trouble.

The vertical downspout pipes from the roof should be inspected to make sure they are not leaking and that instead they are dumping their water away from the house or into a dry well. If downspouts drain into ground pipes or a dry well, disconnect them periodically to be sure the ground drainpipe is not clogged. Squirt water from a hose into each one to be sure the water is carried away. If it backs up, the drainage system is clogged and must be freed. It further means that the water from the roof is backing up in the ground and very likely into the house substructure, thus producing a wet basement.

Keep your roof gutters free of leaves and other debris. Gutters require checking and cleaning quite frequently, especially with trees around. You can save yourself this periodic chore by putting screening across the top of the roof gutters. Special gutter screening, usually in 6-inch widths, can be bought at hardware stores or from Sears, Roebuck. It is easily attached to keep out leaves.

5. *Drainage away from the house.* Don't allow water to pool up next to the house. The earth around your walls should slope gently away and shed rainwater. Look for depressions, fill them in with dirt, and regrade where necessary. Incidentally, it is best not to put flower beds up against the house walls. When you water them, much of the water, sinking into the ground, can cause a wet basement.

6. *Plumbing.* Don't let faucets and water outlets drip for long. Repair them. A hidden cause of leakage and high water bills is the toilet flush tank. To test for a leak here, deposit a dye—obtainable in a food or hardware store—in the tank. If the dye appears in the toilet bowl without the water's being flushed, you have a leak. It usually can be corrected by a new ball.

Other periodic plumbing checks: Remove bathroom shower heads and flush them out in the sink; remove and clean kitchen sink drains, especially the pop-up kind; and every fall make sure that outside water faucets and pipes are drained and shut off from the inside to prevent freezing and broken pipes.

7. *Septic tanks.* A properly sized tank normally requires cleaning every two to three years. It may be a good idea to have the tank inspected every year to determine if it is filling up to the point where it should be cleaned out. Catch this in time, and you will avoid an annoying emergency; i.e., toilets stop working. The cleaning should be done by a professional septic-tank cleaner.

He checks the level of the three layers of waste in the tank—a top layer called scum on the surface, then several feet of liquid effluent, and the settled sludge on the bottom. In general, a tank should be cleaned when the distance between the sludge surface at the bottom and the scum on the top is one-half or less than the total depth of the tank. This is determined with a measuring stick.

It is better to have the tank cleaned in spring or summer. If done during cold weather, the essential decomposition action of the bacteria within the tank slows down and getting it to function properly again could be troublesome.

A variety of septic-tank cleaning chemicals are on the market. Most experts say that they may help a bit but decidedly do not take the place of regular cleaning and proper care. To keep your system as trouble-free as possible, don't drain foreign matter into it, such as paper towels, wrapping paper, old rags, coffee grounds, cooking oils and fats, the contents of ashtrays, or anything other than food waste.

To avoid damage to the septic tank and its tile-pipe network just under the ground, don't allow trucks or other heavy equipment in this area. Don't plant shrubs and trees here either, as their roots can damage or clog the pipes. Check the area now and then to see that it remains well drained of rain since storm water can flood the system and make it inoperative.

8. *Outside walls, windows, and doors.* Inspect the outside of your house every spring and fall and after every bad storm. Worn and damaged spots should be repaired or painted. Cracks around windows and doors should be calked. Exterior painting should not be put off too long, or it will cost twice as much because badly worn or peeled paint has to be burned off and a new prime coat applied, in addition to a finishing coat of paint. Most houses require a fresh paint job every three to five years.

Brick, stone, or masonry walls should be checked for cracks, breaks, or holes. If they are not repaired immediately, rain can get inside the house and cause damage to walls and ceilings. The hinges and other moving parts of metal casement windows should be oiled at least once a year. The channels of sliding windows and wood windows should be cleaned periodically with steel wool.

9. *Chimney.* Cleaning is needed every three or four years, particularly with oil heat. Once a chimney becomes clogged with soot, blow-back is a dangerous possibility. So much soot accumulates that the filth may suddenly be blown back into the house.

A chimney should also be checked for cracks and loose or broken masonry. Holes or breaks in the protective screen on top should be repaired. Otherwise, birds or small animals can get inside and into the house.

10. *Wiring.* Faulty wiring is a major cause of house fires; check all exposed wiring regularly, including appliance and lamp cords. Replace worn or frayed cords. Check the cables leading from your main electric switch box (usually located next to the meter). If they are hot to the touch, call an electrician. Be careful. Wear protective gloves, and don't touch exposed wires. No one but an electrician should touch anything inside the box.

11. *Roof and attic.* The roof should be inspected whenever the walls and windows are checked, and broken or loose shingles should be repaired. As already noted, roof gutters should be kept clean of leaves and dirt. Check the attic for good ventilation all year round. Attic vents should *not* be shut in the winter because year-round ventilation is needed to prevent condensation. If the attic floor is properly insulated, you need not worry about excessive heat leakage from the house. Holes in attic vent screens should be repaired to keep out birds, squirrels, and insects.

12. *Door locks.* Exterior door locks need to be lubricated every four or five years. The best lubricant, powdered graphite, is available at hardware stores. Squirt it into the lock opening. A little graphite is also good for balky inside locks—especially the bathroom door lock, which has a way of getting stuck behind children. (Graphite can also do wonders for sticky car locks.)

13. *The water heater (for spigot hot water).* Once every month open the valve at the bottom of the water heater tank, and drain a bucketful of hot water. This gets rid of accumulated scale and sediment.

14. *Air conditioning.* As with heating furnaces, dirt-clogged air-conditioner filters often cause inadequate cooling and unnecessary service calls. Filters should be cleaned at least once a month, more often if you live in a smoggy city. If you have a central air conditioner, inspection and adjustment are recommended, every year or two, but this is not necessary for window units.

15. *Appliances.* Run-down appliances are the most frequent cause of service calls. Since the maintenance required varies according to type and brand of appliance, you should consult the manufacturer's instruction booklet and carry out the checks recommended. If you have lost your copy, write for another.

A few specific tips: Neglecting to clean out the clothes dryer lint trap is a common cause of operating trouble and fires. It should be cleaned after each load. Washers and dryers should not be overloaded. And sometimes both hot- and cold-water pipe valves to the washer should be shut except when washing, depending on the kind of washer. The manufacturer's instructions will mention this.

PART SEVEN

Home improvement contractors and repair people:
HOW TO TELL THE GOOD GUYS FROM THE BAD GUYS

Know how to find good home improvement contractors and you can skip 90 percent of the pages of this (or any other) book on the subject that deals with getting good work done on your house. There's one exception: the portions of this book devoted to good design and planning, which, by and large, you cannot leave to contractors. They are craftsmen, not architects and artists.

Unfortunately, there are many undesirable home improvement contractors, which means hacks as well as outright gyps. That makes it especially important to do what you can to find and use a reputable person who is also a specialist in the work you need. A jack-of-all-trades may be perfectly good for odd jobs, but a master of none that you require. Here is how to go about it.

CHAPTER 36

HOW TO DEAL WITH CONTRACTORS AND REPAIRMEN

There are three main kinds of home improvement contractors and repairmen:

1. *The "one-stop" remodeler,* who is equipped to handle a complete remodeling project, expand a house, add a new room or garage, do over a complete kitchen or bathroom. You deal with one firm and get one price for the entire job. This is best when you do not want to be encumbered with any details whatever, especially when you know little about construction and you don't want to deal with various subcontractors. The one-stop firm generally has carpenters and other specialists on its payroll, but it generally subcontracts heating, wiring, plumbing, and painting.

Some one-stop firms specialize in kitchens and bathrooms; others, in adding new living space, including finishing off an attic or basement. Determine a firm's specialty, and deal with one that is well experienced in the kind of work you need.

2. *Specialists,* who include plumbers, electricians, painters, roofers, and carpenters, each of whom confines his work to his specialty. They seldom do anything else, though some plumbers have expanded into bathroom and kitchen remodelers, some carpenters have become "cabinetmakers" or "builders." They will work directly for you and may also work for builders or one-stop remodelers as subcontractors.

The key point to determine is whether the man or firm you hire will actually do the work or subcontract it to others. You'll save money by dealing with one who will do the work himself, and it's also more likely that the work will be done well.

3. *Home-builder remodelers,* who are a good choice for jobs that involve new construction or structural alterations. A good builder, in fact, can be unbeatable for remodeling because of his construction experience and because he usually has skilled men on his payroll. Many builders do remodeling work, especially during the slack seasons for new-house building, notably winter. Names of builders who also do remodeling can be had from a local builders' association.

CHOOSING A REPUTABLE CONTRACTOR

The old stock advice is to deal only with reputable firms and repairmen. But no one has a surefire rule on how to spot a reputable man. We are told to obtain the names of other people whom the contractor has worked for. But no contractor will give you names of his dissatisfied customers. Of course, if he will not give you any names at all, he should be shunned. If he is the rare man who will give you a list of all his customers, you can choose at random. Merely having such a list says much for him.

Check with friends and relatives for the names of firms that did well by them. When more than two or three mention the same name, you are probably on to a good one. Top priority should be given to the man's place of business, according to Pete Johnson, president of the Hackensack, New Jersey, remodeling firm Comfort Control Corporation and past president of the National Remodelers Association, a national group of home improvement contractors. "Does he operate from a businesslike office or from a telephone booth?"

For example, Johnson cites a New Jersey state investigation of one fast-buck operator accused of shoddy workmanship. This gyp was found to be operating under seven different company names with no more than a telephone answering service for each. His homeowner victims could have avoided much heartache if they had checked on his place of business beforehand. That means *visit* the firm's office. Anyone who does not follow up on this advice proceeds at his or her own peril.

Ask the man for bank references. Johnson says, "Not just his bank for deposits, but more important the banks or finance companies that handle his installment-loan paper. If he cannot give you a few bank names, watch out, since banks have too much at stake to accept business from unethical contractors.''

Call a few building product distributors and wholesale suppliers. Ask them for the names of good repairmen. If your man's firm is not mentioned, bring it up. If you get an immediate and unqualified endorsement, fine. If anything else, punctuated by hemming and hawing, it's probably a silent condemnation. We have already mentioned that calling local suppliers is also a good way to find contractors when you don't know any.

Do not deal with a contractor who does not carry insurance to protect you, as well as him. If one of his men falls from a ladder and breaks a leg, you could be sued. If a stranger passing by is injured by the contractor's truck backing into your driveway, you may be liable. This depends on the kind of insurance he has. A good contractor will have property damage and liability insurance and workman's compensation insurance. The first protects you against damage to your house and injuries to people and subsequent lawsuits while the work is being done. Contractors should carry cards showing that they have each kind of insurance; ask to see them. Or ask for the name and phone number of the contractor's insurance agent, whom you should call for information. Workman's compensation insurance is mandatory in most states except for one-man and partnership contractors.

Ask for the trade associations the contractor belongs to. Is he a member of a national group such as the National Remodelers Association or National Home Improvement Council? Go a step further, and determine if he is a member of the local Chamber of Commerce, Rotary Club, and so on. Being a member of such groups is a plus mark.

Call the local Better Business Bureau. This should be routine before you spend a substantial sum for almost anything. Its phone number will be in your telephone book. But a BBB office may give you inconclusive information; also, some BBB offices are decidedly better than others. It depends on where you live. There are some 120 BBB offices in the United States and Canada.

In a noncommittal way, the typical BBB person you get on the phone is likely to say that Firm A, the one you mention, has been in business for X years and there are no justifiable complaints in its file about it. In general, this is a good indication. The tip-off to a questionable firm is when you are told that there is a record of one or more unresolved complaints. Before buying an expensive camera advertised at a low price, I called the BBB to check on the store. I was told that it had recently been fined by the city's license bureau for selling secondhand cameras as new. This was enough for me. I bought elsewhere.

Some BBB officers, such as the one in Cleveland, will go a step further and check a firm for you if they have no information in their files. In addition to Cleveland, other cities that reportedly have very good BBB offices are Boston, Akron, Louisville, Cincinnati, Chicago, St. Louis, Los Angeles, and San Francisco.

OTHER WAYS TO CHECK CONTRACTORS

Find out how long a contractor has been in business locally, using the same company name. The longer, the better. A firm that has been at the same stand for ten or twenty years, if not more, is likely to be there in the future when you may need it for repairs. It also indicates that it must be doing something right. Operating with the same name should be verified because there are sharks new in the business who take the name of an old concern, now out of existence, and trade on it as though it were theirs all the time.

Pete Johnson offers two other practical tips. Ask the salesman or whomever you deal with for his home address and telephone number. Johnson says that many contractors hide behind a telephone answering service, and you can never get through to them. Or you may call one's office repeatedly to no avail. Yet it could be important to get through to him, for example, when something goes wrong.

If the salesman refuses to give his home number, think twice about dealing with him. True, many business people don't wish to be bothered at night, especially with pointless calls, with good reason. Nonetheless, if you cannot reach the person during regular business hours, you have good reason to call him at home later. You will need his phone number for this.

And be skeptical about guarantees. No matter how impressively worded, a guarantee is only as good as the firm behind it. Pressed to honor a guarantee, many a questionable firm is as slippery as an eel in avoiding its responsibility. The best guarantee, Johnson points out, is a reputable contractor who has been around for a long time and intends to be there just as long in the future.

GETTING BIDS

Get bids from at least two or three different firms. This is the only check on the price you pay. But don't buy solely according to low price. This can lead to grief. For one thing, the low bid may omit essential work or include low-quality materials. Make sure that each bid is based on the same specifications and the same grade of materials.

The bids you obtain may vary greatly in price, leaving you confused. An economist named Allen F. Jung, of the University of Chicago, had an architect draw up plans and specifications for adding a second story to a typical one-story house. To determine price variations he asked *forty* different contractors to bid on the job. The bids ranged from $6,500 to $10,600.

How in the world can there be such disparity? There are several possible reasons. For one thing, in spite of working from identical plans and specifications, some contractors figure on cutting corners and substitute cheaper materials to get their costs down. Others deliberately figure high because they may be loaded down with other work and not want new work unless it is highly profitable. Still others make estimating mistakes.

In most cases, the bids for a job tend to cluster together, with no more than a 10 to 20 percent spread from the lowest to the highest. Any bid that is sharply higher or lower than the rest should be viewed with suspicion. It will bear scrutiny and normally should not even be considered. If in doubt, ask each man why his bid may be different from others. Don't be timid.

Incidentally, when you get bids, let each man know that you are getting other bids. Sometimes a salesman assumes that he is the only bidder and will figure that he can charge all the traffic will bear. Knowing that he has competition will force him to sharpen his pencil and stay within bounds. Make it clear, though, that you are not going to buy the lowest-price job. You want a good job even if it costs a little more.

Also ask, frankly, how busy his firm is and if he is really interested in taking on your work. When can he start? How long should it take? How many jobs like yours has the firm done?

UNDERSTAND THE CONTRACTOR'S PROBLEMS
Home improvement work is a tough business. The typical contractor has to deal with a variety of suppliers, on the one hand, and with many a fickle customer, on the other. And finding good workers and holding onto them are hard.

It is also surprising, a good many remodelers have told me, how many homeowners are out to chisel the contractor. Some never pay their bills. Once a contractor gets stung by a chiseling homeowner, he automatically becomes wary of all the rest of us. If only one job in ten boomerangs, it may represent all his profit for the last three months going down the drain.

In brief, try to understand the contractor's problems. Have patience. Give the man leeway. Don't tell his workers how to do their jobs. If you have questions, take them up with the boss. Mistakes are inevitable. A good contractor not only expects them but can be relied on to return and make the necessary corrections.

A good contractor wants to get your work done as speedily as possible and be paid. Most operate on a small margin, and delays cost them money. Their overhead expenses continue every day, rain or shine, regardless of whether your work stays on schedule or not. The contractor may have half a dozen other jobs in progress at the same time and sometimes everything goes wrong all at once. By understanding his problems, you can go a long way toward getting a good job done as quickly as possible.

AVOIDING DAMAGE AND DELAYS

To prevent unnecessary damage, get your carpeting and furniture out of the way before workmen arrive. Remove your favorite shrubs and plants outside, so that they are well clear of new construction work. You cannot depend on even the best workman to watch out for such things (no more than a woman can depend on the average husband). Another problem is cleanup. Your contract should state that the workmen will clean up and remove all building debris before leaving.

Clear out the space where remodeling will be done. Remove anything that is portable, including curtains and pictures; cover up anything else, such as a piano. Lay down newspaper for workmen's routes in and out of the house. Put down shoe-wiping mats between the part of the house being remodeled and the rest of the house. Close the windows to keep wind from blowing dust and dirt around; there will be plenty.

As for delays, even the best men in the business cannot guarantee a job's being done by a given date. The best they can do is give you "an approximate completion date" because of the nature of work on houses. Union problems may arise, and everyone knows how disruptive they can be. A key worker may go fishing or disappear for a week when the hunting season opens. Or sudden trouble may arise when your house walls are opened up, requiring rerouting of wiring and pipes.

Allow at least one to three weeks before work starts on the average job. It takes that long at least to draw up plans, order materials, and arrange for myriad other details. Any salesman who promises that work will start tomorrow is out of his mind. Allow a few weeks to a month or two, depending on the size of the job, for completion, regardless of what you may be told.

On the other hand, some men will keep you waiting for weeks and months before they show up. After everything else had been completed on a new bathroom, a neighbor of mine waited for nearly six months for the tile man to return and complete a new shower stall—a maddening delay. The only way to avoid such delays is to check in advance on the man's dependability and have an escape-hatch clause in your contract that calls for the work to be completed by a specific date. If it's not completed in time, the contract is voided, and you should have the right to have the work finished by another firm. Its cost is taken from the sum that otherwise would have been due the original contractor. Of course, when you have an emergency that demands prompt repairs, you want immediate service.

A FINAL WORD

Unfortunately, the best advice on home remodeling and repairs can be wasted because many of us freeze up when a man sits down in the living room to sell us his services. It seems that he knows so much and we so little that we are intimidated. We nod silently and ask few questions because of natural human timidity about something we know little about (other than that it will cost us money).

This should not be. There are two essential things to know: what you can spend and what you want to accomplish. If you stick to your objectives, your chances of success are increased. In addition, arm yourself with information beforehand. Talk with friends, relatives, and contractors before you are ready to buy. Get a few books and magazines on the subject from your library. Visit showrooms.

You will be confused at first, because contractors and repairmen constantly offer conflicting advice in answer to the same questions. (But so do doctors and lawyers.) This is disconcerting, but after a while the pieces begin to fall into place, and you'll be surprised at how much you're learning. You also will begin to spot the four-flusher salesman who talks persuasively but doesn't know beans about his subject.

So speak up. Don't be cowed. Ask your questions and settle the sticky points before you sign up. That's the way to be sure of getting a successful job and satisfaction.

CONTRACT CHECKLIST

Here is a review of important points noted in this chapter to check before you sign a contract for a home improvement job. The contract should include:

• A precise description of the products and materials to be provided by the contractor and the work he will do; also, essential materials and work that he may not be providing—i.e., that which you are to provide.

• An agreement that the contractor will clean up afterward and remove all debris.

• A specified completion date, after which time the contract is voided if the contractor has not finished his work.

• A warranty, which states the contractor will repair or replace any product or work that is defective within a given period of time, usually six months to a year.

Payment terms will vary according to the type of work and the contractor's desire. Some contractors request a down payment when the contract is signed, though it's to your advantage to keep this percentage to a minimum, no more than 10 percent, if possible. Other payments are made as the work progresses, such as one-third of total payment made when the work is one-third completed, two-thirds when two-thirds done, and the balance paid on completion. It's a good idea, however, to withhold about 10 percent of the payment on completion until you are sure that the job is really complete and nothing is missing. In other words, when a contractor asks you for the final payment at the end of his last day, you may not be sure that he is utterly finished; this may take a little time for inspection. So withholding a small portion of the job payment until completion is assured is justified. This may also be your only way to make the contractor return and provide work or material that was inadvertently omitted.

CHAPTER 37

HOW TO AVOID THE TEN BIGGEST HOME IMPROVEMENT RACKETS

Not long ago a story on the family page of the *New York Times* reported a common tragedy that can befall us when work is done on our houses. A woman whose home was in the midst of remodeling was asked by her contractor to sign the completion slip. His bank was withholding money, he said, until he produced this signed certificate, and he needed the cash urgently to finish the job.

Eager to see the job finished and sympathetic with his plight, the woman signed, although she vaguely realized that she probably should not until the work was finished. The contractor got his money and disappeared, leaving the family with a half-finished remodeling job on its hands.

According to the Better Business Bureaus, this happens often. It is one of the worst home improvement rackets. It puts emphasis on an important rule: When you finance work through the contractor, *never* sign a completion certificate until the job is completed and completed satisfactorily. A completion slip is required when your work is financed. The bank requires it before it will pay off the contractor.

If you pay cash, don't let your payments get ahead of the work in progress. When the work is completed, it is a good idea to withhold about 10 percent of the total bill from the contractor for a few days. This gives you a breathing spell in which to determine for sure that everything is properly done. If corrective work is required, it is remarkable how quickly a man will return to remedy it (with *his* money at stake).

This is not meant to paint all contractors as scoundrels. Some are highly reliable, others just so-so, and still others are indeed downright gyps. In addition, there are the pathetic men who are not dishonest and in many cases quite conscientious but whose glaring shortcoming is stupidity or ignorance. They make mistakes because they don't know any better.

This chapter is to familiarize you with the most common gyp schemes and how they work. According to people who are supposed to know such things, the home improvement business accounts for one of the largest number of consumer frauds in the United States every year (including such other things as the used-car racket and gyp radio and television repair people).

YOU MAY ALREADY HAVE BEEN A VICTIM

You may think that you are smart enough not to fall for any of the blatant schemes perpetrated every day, but don't be so sure. You may already have been taken, for example, by point 7 on the following list.

Most gyps prey on housewives home alone during the day, on elderly couples, and on low-income and small-town homeowners who tend to be more trusting and less sophisticated in the ways of the smooth-talking gyp artist. But records show that a good many men, young and middle-income couples, and city people are also mulcted by slick home improvement con men. We are particular targets when we are honest ourselves. We assume other people are honest, too, and never suspect that the sincere young man with the clean-cut features could be out to cheat us.

HOW TO PROTECT YOURSELF

In addition to the number one racket, obtaining a signed completion slip in advance, leaving the homeowner with incomplete work, here are the nine other most common home improvement rackets and schemes, based on records of the Better Business Bureau and the FHA and on state investigations, with advice on avoiding them:

1. *The "model home" scheme.* A salesman tells you that he can give you a big break on the price of new aluminum siding—or a new roof or almost any other major home improvement—because your house would make an ideal "model" for his firm's product.

What's more, it won't cost you a cent because the firm will pay you $100 for every person who buys a similar job as a result of seeing your house. "Surely you know at least half a dozen people who need new siding. That's six hundred dollars right there. You'll have your money back in no time," he says. "All you do is sign up for this thirty-five-hundred-dollar job; normally, it's forty-five hundred dollars," he says, "and your money starts coming back as soon as we're finished."

The owner, of course, will seldom, if ever, get a nickel back. In fact, the sales price quoted may be as much as twice the cost of the same work by a legitimate dealer. The gyp salesman farms out the work to a cheap local contractor for half the price, pockets the difference, and is never seen again.

Moral: Be extremely wary of offers of a special deal that uses your house as a model. If a salesman mentions it, show him firmly to the door, regardless of how persuasive he may sound and regardless of how big a carrot it seems. Some other salesmen will offer you $25, say, for every lead you later send to him that he converts into a sale. This is another matter, but don't depend much on such bonus money.

2. *Furnace-dismantling racket.* The operator rings the doorbell and offers a free inspection of your furnace. Sometimes he poses as an official inspector for the city or fire department. He insists on seeing your furnace, perhaps because dangerous-looking smoke is pouring from the chimney. One woman let such men in, and on going down to the basement a half hour later, she found her furnace and oil burner completely dismantled, the parts broken up and strewn over the basement floor.

"We had to do it," the men said, "to safeguard your family. You'd be asphyxiated." She was forced to spend a lot of money for a new furnace even though the old one was perfectly good. Sometimes the operators offer a free furnace-cleaning job but then "discover" that the furnace is in such dangerous condition that they have to dismantle it and carry it off.

Moral: Do not allow "inspectors" into the house, regardless of how impressive their credentials may look at first. In the rare cases of a legitimate inspection, scrutinize the man's identification card and make sure he really works for an official agency. If he cannot produce identification or if in doubt, call the local police department for confirmation. Official inspections, by the way, do occur during and after remodeling work, not before you order such work ordinarily (unless you have applied for a building variance). And avoid special offers for furnace cleaning.

3. *Bait-and-switch advertisements.* The Federal Trade Commission (FTC) defines this racket as "an alluring [bargain price] but insincere offer to sell a product the advertiser does not intend to sell. Its purpose is to switch consumers from buying the advertised merchandise, in order to sell something else, at a higher price."

An example of a typical bait ad often in newspapers offers a complete new stone front for a 30-foot house for only $149—quite a bargain, it seems. The charming little house pictured in the papers is dressed up with one of the new stone fronts. What you actually get, however, for that price is cheap asphalt paper with a stone design that is nailed on. The genuine stone shown in the ad would cost considerably more. The idea is to hook you into answering the ad and then to switch you to a more expensive job.

The same scheme is used for selling a variety of other products, including "aluminum" patios and awnings (for a mere $99); a finished basement (for only $4.50 a week, but all you would really get is a 12 x 12 cubicle, far from finished); "complete" new kitchen for $895 (for a few cabinets only, as noted in Chapter 8); and low-cost combination storm window bargains.

Moral: Beware of tempting low-price bargains offered in ads. Better still, avoid wild bargains. The best bargain is a good job.

4. *Debt-consolidation schemes.* This scheme is used on families in debt who need repairs on their houses. You may owe $2,000, say, on loans you've taken out and also need $1,500 worth of work on your house. The operator says he will consolidate your $2,000 worth of debts and the $1,500 worth of new work in one new loan with attractively low monthly payments.

But you usually pay dearly for the privilege. There will be penalty fees of several hundred dollars just for paying off your existing loan, plus another $500 charge, more or less, for arranging the new loan, plus stiff new credit and interest charges for the new loan.

In one such case the homeowner found out too late that the new loan indeed came with low monthly payments (which added up steeply over the years), but it turned out that it cost him over $4,500, plus interest, to pay for $3,000 worth of loans consolidated. In a rash of such cases in Cleveland, the home improvement dealer was found to be pocketing all the money and not even paying off the old loans that he had promised to consolidate for his customers.

Moral: Don't consolidate existing loans unless it will truly benefit you. If you do, never do it through a home improvement contractor. Talk with several banks, and deal directly with the one with the best terms.

5. *Chimney-repair racket.* A particularly vicious example is what happened to a seventy-five-year-old Bowling Green, Kentucky, woman. She was told that her chimney would topple in the first strong wind unless it was repaired at once. She was pressured into buying a $3,600 repair job. A crew of four men, posing as experts, dabbed cement on a few cracks and vanished, she tearfully told police. She had been swindled by crooks.

Such swindlers will claim that they just happen to be working down the street and notice that your chimney may collapse any minute. It's going to topple. But they can fix it immediately at low cost because they are working nearby. Warmed up, they will paint dreadful pictures of the damage done to houses by toppled chimneys. The owner is frightened into signing up for an expensive repair job. It is completed in a few hours, and the men vanish.

Moral: Don't be frightened into buying immediate repairs for a chimney condition (or for any other kind of emergency repairs). Many chimneys indeed require repairs, but take your time and hire a reputable repairman with an established local business.

6. *Fake termites.* The quick-buck operator examines your house and emerges with a piece of wood crawling with termites. (They are from a small bottle carried in his pocket.) He warns that you face an immediate collapse of your house unless repairs are done at once. Pressure is exerted to sign you up so he can go to work without a moment wasted.

Moral: Don't be frightened by a termite scare, and don't let yourself be pressured into buying. Investigate the condition yourself, and before buying, call in other dealers for alternate bids.

7. *Two-for-one paint bargains.* Paint stores offer the "best-quality" paint for $8.98 a gallon, every second gallon free. It's done all over the country. Sometimes the second gallon costs a penny more. Actually, it's the old two-for-one gimmick, two gallons of cheap $4.50 paint masquerading as top-quality paint.

The low quality of an actual sample of such paint was determined by tests. The paint sold for $8.98, plus a second gallon free. A federal paint standard requires paint to withstand 500 cycles of a special brush test. The $8.98 paint began to disintegrate after only 250 brush cycles and was worn away at the end of 500 cycles. Two ordinary low-price paints tested at the same time showed no visible wear after 250 cycles.

Moral: Don't expect good paint free any more than you would expect a second car given free when you buy a new car.

8. *Low-balling.* A Chicago couple wanting to add a new room to their house signed up for a low $1,500 offer. Two legitimate contractors had bid $2,500 for the same work. *After* signing up, the couple were told certain extras were needed: finished flooring, wallboard, finished ceiling, painting, insulation, and the installation of each, none of which was included in the original $1,500 price. They had to pay another $1500, thus $3,000 in all, for the complete job they thought they were buying in the first place.

Called low-balling, in the trade, this practice has flourished for years as a way to elbow legitimate contractors out of the job. Once you sign up, you are hooked, and the dishonest contractor blithely says he never claimed he was furnishing all those "extras." ("Where did you ever get that idea? It's impossible at that price.")

Moral: Be wary of very low bids way under the competition. Determine exactly how much work will be done, what materials you get, and if the price also includes installation of all materials. Get an itemized list.

9. *Fraudulent fire-alarm salesmen.* A phony salesman gains entry to your house by claiming he is from the Fire Safety Council or some other equally impressively named but fictitious organization. He claims he is educating homeowners with fire-prevention demonstrations. Once inside, he displays a series of horror pictures and terrifying newspaper stories reporting the disasters and lost lives caused by house fires. His object is to scare you into buying an alarm system for a lot of money. After the order is signed, a couple of men string a few wires around the house and disappear.

Moral: Again, don't be pressured and frightened into buying. If you are concerned about fire, a complete alarm system can be had for as little as several hundred dollars. Individual smoke alarm devices are available for $25 to $50 apiece, depending on the type and brand.

Another common racket, the aluminum storm window racket, is described in Chapter 19.

In summary, it can be seen that certain common tactics are characteristic of fraudulent home improvement deals. Many appeal to our instinct for a bargain, offering items at a special price that seems so low you can't afford to pass it up. In fact, they are far from bargains. And many rely on high-pressure scare tactics. These are the hall-marks of the phony deal.

Index